Praise for *Exoneree Diaries*

"Having experienced the unending nightmare of being wrongfully convicted, and the mind-blowing trauma that hits like a tidal wave after release from prison, I can attest that Alison Flowers has nailed it—and then driven it home. This book will help anyone living with or experiencing profound trauma, and sometimes that's all we can ask for, to have a measure of understanding."

—**Damien Echols, former "West Memphis Three" death row inmate and author of *Life After Death***

"Alison Flowers's *Exoneree Diaries* is a must read, a welcome addition to the literature of wrongful convictions. With Ms. Flowers as our tour guide, we meet four exonerees—Jacques, Kristine, James, and Antione—and follow them as they begin to rebuild their lives after all the excitement and hoopla of their exonerations has faded. The world they encounter is an alien one, which often treats them with indifference and hostility. But we marvel at their courage as they 'get busy living' and move, sometimes forward and sometimes backward, in both baby steps and giant leaps. Ultimately, *Exoneree Diaries* is a testament to human resiliency and the power of the human spirit to not only survive but thrive against great odds."

—**Steven Drizin, lawyer for Brendan Dassey of *Making a Murderer* and clinical professor of law at Northwestern Pritzker School of Law***

"At least 2.3 percent of the millions imprisoned in America did not commit the crimes for which they were convicted. Alison Flowers is the rare journalist who does not allow the people treated as collateral damage in the era of mass incarceration to remain invisible."

—**Spencer Ackerman, US national security editor, the *Guardian***

"Why should we care about the exonerated? From Flint to Florida, the inequities and injustice in our criminal justice system have put America in crisis. The most under-covered and misunderstood aspect: the plight of the exonerated. Alison Flowers has tackled that deficit with keen analysis, investigative savvy, and good old-fashioned shoe leather. Her absorbing portrayals of the exonerated make a potent case for why we should care—and act—with compassionate and common-sense policy change."

—**Laura S. Washington, columnist for the *Chicago Sun-Times*, political analyst for ABC 7-Chicago***

"*Exoneree Diaries* exposes the deeply flawed system that puts so many inno-cent men and women behind bars, and also reveals the long-lasting trauma that these survivors of our 'justice system' have endured. In the wake of the tragic suicide of beloved exoneree Darryl Hunt, Flowers gives us crit-ical insight into the human beings whom we as a society have wrongfully caged, and leaves us grappling with the questions of how we can better em-brace and support them once their innocence has been proven, their release achieved, and their ordeal, in many ways, still just beginning."

—Jen Marlowe, author of *I Am Troy Davis* and *The Hour of Sunlight: One Palestinian's Journey from Prisoner to Peacemaker*

"*Exoneree Diaries* is an immersive and powerful journey through the depths of a violent system. These nuanced, vividly portrayed stories bring to life the heart-wrenching experience—and lingering effects—of having one's freedom stolen by the state. This is a beautifully written and urgent-ly necessary book."

—Maya Schenwar, author of *Locked Down, Locked Out: Why Prison Doesn't Work and How We Can Do Better*

"This book is an amazing account about the real experiences of exonerees like me. Alison Flowers captures the cruel absurdity that persists within the criminal justice system."

—Kirk Bloodsworth, first death row inmate exonerated by DNA

"Alison Flowers has written the definitive book on life after exoneration— beautifully rendered, achingly powerful stories capturing with nuance and depth the perilous leap of faith, hope, and despair that actual freedom requires of the actually innocent. A rare storyteller, indeed."

—Pamela Cytrynbaum, executive director of Chicago Innocence Center

"No author has covered the years after exoneration with the same depth as Flowers does in this disturbing book. She ably shows that even under the best of circumstances, exonerees struggle with family relationships, job searches, recovery from prison-related health problems, adjustments to new technologies, and more. *Exoneree Diaries* is a thoroughly re-searched, provocative book of justice gone wrong."

—*Kirkus Reviews*

"*Exoneree Diaries* is a page-turner about the triumph of courage over Kafkaesque injustices that befell a woman and three men who were imprisoned a total of more than seventy years for crimes they did not commit. The stories of how they survived behind bars and coped with the unrelenting challenges of life after exoneration are at once tragic and uplifting—and unforgettable."

—**Rob Warden, executive director emeritus of the Center on Wrongful Convictions at Northwestern Pritzker School of Law**

"Alison Flowers has written an important book—filled with vivid, unforgettable stories. Meticulously told through the perspectives of people who have been exonerated, you feel the stress of watching their tragedies unfold with an eye toward redemption. Their experiences will stay in your mind and heart long past when the last page is finished. There is no substitute for great reporting. These pages represent a measure of justice."

—**Amy Bach, executive director of Measures for Justice and author of *Ordinary Injustice: How America Holds Court***

"Alison Flowers deserves our kudos for penning this book. May her work signal a paradigm shift in our system of justice. Flowers challenges what most people do not realize: that we have such a tenuous grasp on our liberty. There is a certain disbelief when it comes to wrongful convictions—a belief that our justice system is too good for injustice to happen to anyone, let alone ourselves. Much like Kristine, Jacques, James, and Antione of *Exoneree Diaries*, I simply could not believe that I could be convicted for something I did not do. During my own trial, I kept thinking the purpose of it all was to find the truth and that the truth would set me free. Instead, when I shared my story of innocence with people, I was told 'That's what they all say,' or 'If you didn't do it, you should have.' Never have crueler words been uttered to those who suffer conviction unjustly."

—**Jason Baldwin, one of the wrongfully convicted "West Memphis Three"**

"Our criminal justice system is broken. Broken in so many ways and at so many levels and adversely impacting so many millions. Fixing our system depends in the first place on involving and empowering the American people to begin the process of reform. Alison Flowers's timely 'diaries' provide a powerful glimpse into one broken aspect of the system: the wrongly convicted. Flowers sets a moral example for us all. Having encountered injustice she set about educating and enlisting us in her search for answers. Our thanks to Kristine, Jacques, James, and Antione for having the courage to share their stories on behalf of all those who have been denied that opportunity."

—**US Congressman Danny Davis**

"In *Exoneree Diaries* Alison Flowers walks readers through the wrongful convictions of four exonerees, chronicling the unexpected yet multifaceted difficulties they—and all exonerees—face upon release. Most people, including the exonerees themselves, expect that once exonerated, they will experience a life of ease, joy, and happiness. But reality quickly sets in: they are released with nothing. Obtaining gainful employment is virtually impossible, and compensation from lawsuits, if any is awarded, can take several years. Exonerees also often have post-traumatic stress disorder and other psychological aftereffects. It's difficult if not impossible to repair familial relationships and other past friendships. Technology and culture have passed them by, leading to a cumulative feeling of no longer fitting into the world. *Exoneree Diaries* shines light on this hidden reality, while silently raising critically important rhetorical questions: Should society offer reentry services to exonerees, including short-term housing, cost-of-living expenses, mental health services, job training and placement, and other assistance? Or instead continue to release them with nothing, offering less help than parolees receive? Is there a way to expedite the compensation process? Should the states that don't currently offer compensation quickly pass statutes allowing compensation? Should states pass laws designed to prevent wrongful convictions? What can each individual citizen in the United States, and indeed the world, do to fight wrongful convictions? As an exoneree, I urge everyone to learn more about this critical subject by reading this important book."

—**Jeffrey Deskovic, MA, exoneree and founder
of the Jeffrey Deskovic Foundation for Justice**

"These are true, horrifying stories of wrongful convictions—and they can happen to anyone. As an exoneree, I can say that I would have never imagined going through the turmoil that I did. The technological, scientific, and medical advancements, along with a lot of work by attorneys and other experts, can take years to overturn cases like mine. The time the wrongfully convicted people spent in prison was very hard time for them and their loved ones. But, as Alison Flowers so clearly writes, exonerees and their families go through more challenges putting their lives together when they are released. The states have varied, if any, compensation, so the exoneree has to start over with little or no assistance with housing, medical insurance, transportation, employment, while they are trying to restore family relationships and friendships. We need more accountability in our criminal justice system. With this book, I hope hearts will be opened to understand the inhumanity of the system and the humanity of exonerees."

—**Audrey Edmunds, exoneree and author of** *It Happened to Audrey: A Terrifying Journey From Loving Mom to Accused Baby Killer*

"*Exoneree Diaries* is a powerful, truthful, and compelling read for anyone who is interested in the world of wrongful convictions. Alison Flowers has reached into the heart of these exonerees to share their joys, triumphs, and sorrows. She is perhaps the first author to delineate the deep agony experienced by exonerees after their freedom has been won."

—**Gloria Killian, exoneree and author of** *Full Circle: A True Story of Murder, Lies and Vindication*

"Well-researched and written, *Exoneree Diaries* captures the essence of lives torn apart by wrongful convictions. The stories highlight the multiple failures in our system intended to deliver criminal justice and underscore the resulting human suffering. Kristine, Jacques, James, and Antione continue to move forward despite the wrongs, leaving the reader with multiple lessons in the human spirit's will to endure."

—**Frances Lee Watson, director of the Wrongful Conviction Clinic at Indiana University Robert H. McKinney School of Law**

"Sadly, most Americans have witnessed headlines, news stories, and dramatizations of failed justice finally corrected, but what happens after an innocent person, wrongly convicted and imprisoned, emerges into freedom following the cruel loss of family, reputation, career, resources, and liberty for years, even decades? In *Exoneree Diaries* journalist and author Alison Flowers tells the largely untold, fuller personal stories of exonerees. Kristine, Jacques, James, and Antione were all convicted of horrific crimes they did not commit, wrongfully imprisoned, and later released into a changed world. *Exoneree Diaries* is a compelling portrait of the many people impacted by flawed justice—the wrongly convicted and their families, victims and their families, and heroes compelled to invest years in unraveling stubborn miscarriages. Flowers provides a fascinating read with inspiring lessons in courage, hope, and endurance eventually rewarded in bittersweet victories. Because these four cases represent the much larger universe of the wrongly convicted, *Exoneree Diaries* is ultimately a powerful call to Americans to reform our criminal justice system."

—**Jim Petro and Nancy Petro, coauthors of** *False Justice—Eight Myths that Convict the Innocent*

"*Exoneree Diaries* is a unique chapter in the great American tradition of prison writing: Flowers gives us the view from both sides of the bars, each story a transition that is both tragic and triumphant. Stripped of clinical language, this is one of the very best exoneration collections. Flowers' writing is clean and lively, teaching without preaching. Recommended for anyone who wants to understand the Innocence Movement and the quiet heroes who untangle the razor wire of flawed prosecutions."
—**Greg Hampikian, PhD, forensic DNA expert, director of the Idaho Innocence Project**

"In gripping detail, Alison Flowers takes you deep inside the lives of the exonerated, showing the real people behind the headlines. Her accounts of their hopes, dreams, sorrows, and pain help to restore their humanity and reveal the true depths of the injustice of wrongful convictions."
—**Alden Loury, investigative journalist and policy analyst**

"Written with grace and insight, Alison Flowers captures the sadness, tragedy, triumph, and joy reflected in the wrongful conviction stories of Kristine, Jacques, James and Antione, who collectively spent seventy years in prison for crimes none of them committed. Alison is the best kind of eyewitness—a journalist with a keen eye for truth, an abundant heart, and a true talent in sharing what she sees."
—**Anne Driscoll, Irish Innocence Project**

"Alison Flowers dispels the myth that innocent people leaving prison after a long incarceration will become rich as a result. In fact, people who walk out the prison door often have nothing: their family ties have been destroyed, their friends have disappeared, their lives as they knew them no longer exist. And we release them with nothing. Not a cent. *Exoneree Diaries* focuses on four people who were found innocent and follows them after the press leaves, as they attempt to rebuild their lives after a decade or more in prison. Flowers's powerful narrative is a much needed wake-up call to society. We must recognize the damage inflicted, on individuals and society, when we wrongfully convict people. We must work to ensure that innocent people are never put in prison, and when they are, that they are given compensation. Every one. Every time."
—**Alan Mills, executive director, Uptown People's Law Center**

"*Exoneree Diaries* is a book every member of Congress, every state legislator, and every district attorney should read. Although it may seem counterintuitive, exoneration after serving sometimes decades in prison for a crime you did not commit rarely ends in 'happily ever after.' Policymakers above all need to understand this. Flowers reveals a system that creates very high barriers for exonerees to rebuild their lives after already having lost almost everything most of us take for granted. They reenter society as traumatized 'Rip van Winkles' who must even fight the state for some compensation—and much more."

—Florence Graves, founding director, The Schuster Institute for Investigative Journalism & The Justice Brandeis Law Project, Brandeis University

EXONEREE DIARIES

The Fight for Innocence, Independence, and Identity

Alison Flowers

Haymarket Books
Chicago, Illinois

Published in 2016 by
Haymarket Books
P.O. Box 180165
Chicago, IL 60618
773-583-7884
www.haymarketbooks.org
info@haymarketbooks.org

Sections of this book were originally published for Chicago Public Media
on WBEZ.org.

ISBN: 978-1-60846-675-7 (trade paperback)
ISBN: 978-1-60846-587-3 (trade clothbound)

Trade distribution:
In the US, Consortium Book Sales and Distribution, www.cbsd.com
In Canada, Publishers Group Canada, www.pgcbooks.ca
In the UK, Turnaround Publisher Services, www.turnaround-uk.com
All other countries, Publishers Group Worldwide, www.pgw.com

This book was published with the generous support of Lannan Foundation and Wallace Action Fund.

Cover design by John Yates.

Printed in Canada by union labor.

Library of Congress Cataloging-in-Publication data is available.

10 9 8 7 6 5 4 3 2 1

Contents

Untitled

Reaching out into space, from space

to touch your radiant face I was seized
by an inward terror
twas error, on error

Sadness a malady of heart
strikes even from dark to dark
strikes even to dark

"We do not want a thing because we
have found reasons for it, but we find
reasons for it, because we want it

To you who praise the happy
medium, to me as the way
of life and love"

I reply:

"Who wants to be lukewarm
between cold and hot, or tremble
between life and death,

or be jelly,
neither fluid nor
solid?"

—David Keaton (1952–2015), the first person
exonerated from death row in the modern era

AUTHOR'S NOTE ON SOURCES

The narratives in this book are built on a foundation of hundreds of hours of interviews with exonerees, their families, and their friends; criminal justice experts and officials; lawyers, investigators, and students. More than ten thousand pages of records—some more than a quarter of a century old—support these accounts, including original trial transcripts; court filings, orders and dockets; police reports; letters; news stories; affidavits; and other evidence. Quotes were either witnessed by or said to the author, or they were corroborated wherever possible by those interviewed for this book.

INTRODUCTION

This book gives a name to those who do not have one: *exoneree*.

The word doesn't exist. No dictionary I have found, other than on-line references such as an English Wiktionary, lists *exoneree*. We have the words *exoneration, exonerate, exonerated*—but no word for the people freed from prison, innocent of the crimes that sent them there.

The age of mass incarceration has taken many prisoners—not just those behind bars. Families and friends are affected by the loss, as are neighborhoods and communities. More than 2.3 million people are held in thousands of state and federal prisons, jails, and juvenile correctional facilities, as well as military prisons, immigration detention facilities, civil commitment centers, and prisons in the US territories.[1] In a country

1. According to the Bureau of Justice Statistics, jails are locally operated, short-term facilities that hold inmates awaiting trial or sentencing or both, and inmates sentenced to a term of less than one year. Prisons are long-term facilities run by the state or the federal government and typically hold felons and inmates with sentences of more than one year. Definitions may vary by state.

that locks up more people, per capita, than any other in the world, many systemic abuses of citizens exist. Wrongly convicted men and women are inevitably caught in the dragnet. An exoneration happens, on average, every three days in America, a record high. While it is impossible to know how many innocents are languishing behind bars, according to the Innocence Project, studies estimate that between 2.3 percent and 5 percent of all prisoners in the United States did not commit the crimes of which they have been accused—tens of thousands of people. However, formerly incarcerated people, including exonerees, will tell you they believe the actual number is significantly higher. They would know. Alongside those falsely convicted are the multitudes who have accepted plea bargains. This applies in more than 90 percent of cases, as the accused plead guilty to lesser offenses in exchange for more lenient sentences— or, in some cases, so they can leave county jail and continue on with their lives, unable to post bond. In 2015 alone, sixty-five exonerations were for convictions based on guilty pleas, more than in any previous year, according to the National Registry of Exonerations.

For nearly three decades, lawyers, journalists, and innocence advocates have exposed flaws in the criminal justice system and identified the factors that contribute to wrongful convictions: perjury or false accusations, eyewitness misidentification, official misconduct, bad science or misleading forensic evidence, and false confessions. But while exoneration marks a new beginning for those who were unjustly convicted, life on the outside can also be fraught with difficulty. There is no infrastructure or aftercare to help exonerees come to terms with all they have suffered, to teach them how to patch together their shattered lives. The lack of support for those wrongfully convicted is an issue that has long been overlooked by the media, which tend to focus on the multimillion-dollar lawsuits won by a very few. Little is known about how exonerated prisoners struggle to rebuild the lives and the livelihoods they have lost. Indeed, release from prison is not the victory it is often perceived to be. It is not the end of the story. It is simply a new chapter.

I realized this as I was investigating potentially wrongful conviction cases at Northwestern University's Medill Justice Project, where I worked as a journalist from 2011 to 2013. One day as I prepared to head into my basement office, it occurred to me: *We're doing all this work to uncover new evidence that could free innocent people, but what happens when those innocent people are finally set free? Where do they go? What do they do? Who's left in their lives?*

In early 2013, I decided to follow the lives of a handful of exonerated prisoners. Living in Chicago, I had a front-row seat to the experiences of many exonerees, as Cook County leads the country in the number of exonerations since 1989. A long history of corruption in the Chicago Police Department, which has led to many wrongful convictions, has also given rise to a number of law clinics and projects in the city that are dedicated, pro bono, to freeing the innocent.

Beyond Chicago, scores of other innocence projects, both national and international, work on wrongful conviction cases. Among this network is deep concern for what happens to exonerees once they leave prison. Newly released, they encounter a world where they may have no place to sleep and no way to feed or clothe themselves; where family and friends have grown up, grown apart, or died. They frequently struggle to find employment, as they are unable to shake off the stigma of lockup, and they struggle to overcome the years of institutionalization. The Innocence Project estimates that about a third of exonerees have not been compensated. Only thirty states have passed statutes that provide monetary compensation to exonerees, and many of these state laws fall short.[2] In Illinois, where three of those profiled in this book were convicted, exonerees must prove their own innocence to a judge in order to earn a certificate of innocence and thus become eligible for compensation. It is usually much harder to prove innocence than to prove guilt: over the years of an incarceration, people who could testify on exonerees' behalf may have died; evidence may have been destroyed. In addition, in many states, criminal records—many of which are searchable online—are not automatically cleared when judges overturn convictions. This interferes with exonerees' ability to find housing and work and to successfully reintegrate into the community. Meanwhile, to win a civil lawsuit in connection with

---

2. The thirty states include Montana, which provides education aid in the form of tuition waivers and reimbursements but no other monetary compensation. The District of Columbia and the federal system also provide monetary compensation.

a wrongful conviction, it is not enough to prove that an exoneree was imprisoned for a crime he or she did not commit. Rather, the exoneree must show that the wrongful incarceration was caused by a narrowly defined sort of official misconduct. In most of these cases, prosecutors have total immunity from liability for civil damages.

Over a period of three years, the exonerees profiled in this book made themselves open and vulnerable to me. Diverse in many ways, Kristine, Jacques, James, and Antione offer a glimpse into the many faces of exonerees—as of this writing, more than 1,750 known individuals since 1989. As Jacques, James, and Antione hail from Cook County, their cases reveal the patterns of misconduct in Chicago that have led to wrongful convictions. Kristine, in contrast, is an exoneree from Indiana, a state that lacks a compensation law. Her story also highlights some particular challenges women face in our judicial system, especially wrongly convicted women who, in their roles as caretakers or mothers, are accused of harming a loved one. In the majority of these cases—as in Kristine's, in which an accident claimed her child's life—no crime actually occurred. An additional cruelty to many women incarcerated for lengthy sentences is the loss of the chance to have children—a situation that has haunted Kristine.

Throughout our time together, Kristine, Jacques, James, and Antione all revealed their imperfections, failings, and anxieties. While the personal tragedies that they have overcome are heroic, they are not one-dimensional characters. They, like most of us, are complex yet ordinary people. But they are also extraordinary people who beat remarkable odds to return to us here in the visible world. Still invisible are the many tens of thousands more innocents languishing behind bars.

Some exonerees die before receiving a dime of compensation. Glenn Ford spent almost thirty years on death row at Angola prison in Louisiana,[3] convicted in 1984 by an all-white jury of a murder he did not commit. At the time of his release in 2014, he was one of the country's longest-serving death row inmates. In late 2014, Ford applied for compensation under a Louisiana law that would have paid him $25,000 per year for ten years plus as much as $80,000 to help with "lost life oppor-

3. Originally a plantation, Angola was named after the area in Africa from which the plantation's former slaves had come.

tunities" and medical costs. By that time, Ford had been diagnosed with terminal cancer. In March 2015, Ford's compensation application was denied, even though the district attorney had moved for Ford's release after concluding—and stating publicly—that Ford was innocent of the murder for which he had been sentenced to death. In separate federal lawsuits, Ford sued for civil rights violations in connection with his wrongful incarceration and the prison system's failure to provide him adequate medical care. Supporters of Ford launched several fundraising efforts—to help with general needs after his release, to offset the cost of hospice care, and to provide support for a cruise with his family that he was never able to take. In June 2015, a little more than one year after his release, Ford died of lung cancer.

But concerted efforts by the growing network of criminal justice reform advocates have resulted in promising new initiatives in recent years. In 2012, the National Registry of Exonerations launched its database as the most comprehensive tracker of exonerations, further illuminating the flaws that create the conditions allowing for wrongful convictions. In 2014, for the first time, a prosecutor was sent to jail for his direct involvement in wrongfully convicting an innocent Texas man, Michael Morton, in 1987.[4] Also in Texas, in July 2014, former Dallas County district attorney Craig Watkins led the way, showing how prosecutors are supposed to get it right by exonerating a former prisoner through his office's own systematic DNA review of old evidence. It was the first exoneration of its kind. In 2007, Watkins's office was the first prosecutor's office to open a conviction integrity unit to review old cases. Now the Dallas unit, as well as the Brooklyn District Attorney's Conviction Review Unit, has become a national model for other projects. In 2014, the US Attorney's Office in Washington, DC, announced it would open the first federal conviction integrity unit in the country. In December 2015, the US Congress passed a bipartisan bill to prohibit the federal government's taxation of wrongful conviction compensation, excluding these funds from income, where the IRS position had previously been unclear.

---

4. Prosecutor Ken Anderson was sentenced to ten days but was released after only five days "for good behavior."

Change is happening, but much remains unaddressed. Through the stories of these exonerees we can see the larger blight of mass incarceration itself, a system that pulls apart families and destroys communities. In this system, punishment does not diminish harm. Yet the increasing public and political focus on our broken crime-and-punishment machinery provides some hope that lasting reforms might take root, as more people recognize the damage caused by police misconduct, harsh sentencing laws, the economic injustice of monetary bail, and other judicial ills.

In telling these stories, I have often asked myself how people can ever be made whole after surviving both prison and a wrongful conviction. The exonerees featured here have answered this question for me quite clearly: They can't be made whole. They won't be made whole. They can never make up for lost time. "It is a burden, and it continues to haunt you," says exoneree Antione Day.

They can only move forward.

PART ONE

KRISTINE

Convicted in 1996
Exonerated in 2012

Indianapolis Star

I.

"It feels great when you walk out, and you can hug your family, and no one is telling you don't touch 'em."

Kristine took soft, steady steps down the courthouse hallway on a late August day. On her shackled feet, she wore crisp, white sneakers her family had ordered from Walkenhorst's catalog, a company that specializes in products for inmates. Her dyed blonde hair fell to her shoulders in smooth layers, the result of diligently wrapping her strands underneath a do-rag, setting it while she slept—a beauty trick learned behind bars.

Outside, the Indiana sky appeared cloudless above the courthouse clock tower, on top of which grows a storied mulberry tree, a point of pride for Greensburg, the county seat of Decatur. Nicknamed "Tower Tree Square," the area around the courthouse is lined with Civil War–era buildings, with mom-and-pop shops like Storie's Restaurant serving "made-from-scratch pies" and "pork tenderloins the size of your head"—that is, any day but Sunday.

Inside the pre–Civil War era courthouse, the words "Decatur County Circuit" are squeezed together on one side of the double doors to the courtroom. On the right-hand door, the single word "Court" is etched in metallic decal.

Decatur County sheriff's deputies escorted Kristine to the courtroom, blocked by a huddle of local reporters and TV cameras on hand for the latest twist in the case. As the cameras clicked, Kristine offered a shaky half-smile as she braced herself for the hearing. Inside the courtroom, her family waited. Some childhood friends also looked on. Kristine wasn't sure if they were there for spectacle or for support.

Kristine had walked those halls before. Almost seventeen years earlier, in 1996, she was wearing a chunky knit sweater over her growing belly, tears staining her cheeks, after being sentenced to sixty years for murder. The nine months leading up to her trial were a painful blur—the trailer fire, the loss of her three-year-old son Tony, the swift investigation and arrest five days later, the grim months in a jail cell, the discovery of a pregnancy while on bond. With not so much as a parking ticket on her record at the time, she struggled to believe the nightmare she was living.

Now something else was happening, and it also felt like a dream. She was about to walk free.

A few months before her release, she had been reading *Jesus Calling* on her bed at Indiana Women's Prison (IWP) in Indianapolis when her daily devotion was interrupted.

"Bunch!" the counselor hollered her last name down the hall. "Phone call. My office."

On the line was Jane Raley, one of Kristine's pro bono attorneys from the Center on Wrongful Convictions at Northwestern University, who had been laboring on her case for five years, with assistance from two law firms and another attorney. For more than a decade, Jane had helped free the innocent. With about a dozen exonerations, a human rights award, and some death-sentence commutations under her belt, Jane was a pro. Known for her empathy, Jane was beloved by her clients, who took to her like a best friend or parent. But she was also a relentless, fierce advocate for them, and Kristine was no exception. The work was slow, and positive developments for her clients were scarce. But this time, she had good news to share. She told Kristine the State Supreme Court had ruled in her favor, awarding her a new trial. She was to be released on her previous bond.

Kristine was shocked. "You wait for that moment for so long and it gets there, you feel like they are going to jerk it back and say, 'We're keeping you,'" she says.

Scared and overwhelmed, she called her friend Donna. "I'll be home in forty-eight hours," she said over Donna's shrieks. "I have so much to do, and I don't know how I'm going to do it." Kristine didn't know what to expect next. But with her freedom imminent—what she thought would be immediate—Kristine prepared for her release.

She purged her belongings, passing them out to all her friends in prison. Kiera got her black drawstring shorts with the pockets—a coveted item no longer available in the overpriced, privatized prison shop known as commissary. Her bunkie Leslie got her small TV that had cost $179. Her radio went to Rhonda. She distributed a couple pairs of illegal earrings to some others. Another friend got her makeup.

The only thing she kept were her Polaroids and some scanned photos of her son Trent, now sixteen, whom she had delivered three months into her incarceration. Photos were a restricted item in prison, and Kristine had kept too many snapshots from their monthly visits to pass inspections. She had to sneak the photos between her legal papers, rotating them out.

She was ready. And then she waited.

Weeks later, Kristine had still not left the prison. The trial judge's vacation plans came between Kristine and her prompt release. Finally, she was shipped to the county jail for a brief hearing at the courthouse, where her pro bono lawyers were ready for her. At Decatur County Jail, the deputies didn't process her in, Kristine says. "Because there was a good chance I was leaving."

In the courthouse hallway, a man behind a camera asked, "How are you doing today, Kristine?"

"No cameras in the courtroom," a deputy said as the reporters shuffled in.

Kristine sighed, smiled, and looked up as she approached the courtroom.

A fill-in judge ordered her release; Kristine would have to report back in a month's time for a pretrial hearing. A new murder trial had been set for February 2013. Upon her exit from the courtroom, TV reporters plunged their microphones toward Kristine as her hands remained chained. A heavy belt hung around her beige prison uniform.

"What does this day mean to you?"

Kristine looked around through her rectangular, narrow, black eyeglasses. She took a breath. "It's everything right now," she said in a shaky, high-pitched voice, swallowing the tears. She shook her head and took a long sniff. "More than I can put into words. More than I can say."

The reporters wanted to know what she planned to do next.

She laughed. "Probably disturb my son while I watch him do everything. Because I want to see everything he does."

"Did you ever give up hope?"

"No. Never."

A plastic bag with her name on it held a purple-and-blue striped frock, dress shoes, and some tan-colored pantyhose. Kristine's mother, Susan, had managed to get these items into the hands of a deputy inside the jail, where she was preparing to leave.

Kristine chucked the nylon pantyhose. "No way was I going to wear that. That was another prison," she says. But she conceded and put on the "horrible, ugly dress" from her mother.

Clutching the plastic bag and some papers, she walked out into the sunshine. Another batch of reporters greeted her. After years of running file photos and old video on her case, the news crews ate up the chance to capture fresh footage of Kristine, hugging her mother and the lawyers who had helped her. Kristine smiled and pivoted to answer their questions.

"Once I'm fully cleared, I'm going to law school," she told them, garnering claps from her supporters.

Kristine had worked in the prison law library for several years, becoming a paralegal and helping other women with their cases. She was one of the first inmates at IWP to take the LSAT. She had done much of her own legal work in prison, sending ideas and tips to her local attorney.

"You seem so happy," one reporter noted. "It would seem like you might be tempted to be bitter about waiting this long to get out. You don't seem to show that. Can you explain that?"

Kristine turned to him mid-question, and her face dropped. "I think because this entire time I haven't been by myself," she answered. "I've had a family that has stood by me. I've had people that believed in me and stepped up. And you can't receive blessings like that and be bitter."

Away from the reporters, her teenaged son Trent was a little standoffish. His striped polo shirt hung on his frame. His wavy hair was cut into the shaggy, swooped style of teen pop star Justin Bieber, and Trent was now several inches taller than Kristine, at about five foot seven. He gave her a hug but said nothing.

Maybe it's something that happens with boys, Kristine thought. *They don't want to be hugged and kissed.* Plus, she knew that he understood her legal victory could only be a temporary reprieve from the difficult life he had known. A retrial could snatch Kristine back into captivity.

Still, Trent posed with his family for a photo, arms linked, flashing a wide camera smile, frozen in time.

At a bistro in nearby Columbus, Indiana, Kristine ordered a glass of champagne, scallops (not on the menu, but made specially by the restaurant for her first night free), and some peach ice cream. As she sipped her champagne, a TV camera captured footage around the table of Kristine breaking bread with her lawyers and family.

It was a quiet, pensive ride back to her mother's apartment, where her son had been living. This would be her home, too.

Kristine walked through the door and stopped. To her shock, the space was packed, with only small pathways of linoleum separating the junk. There was garbage strewn about. Cigarette smoke had yellowed the walls. During her years in prison, Trent had never mentioned these conditions. The disorder hung in stark contrast to the orderliness of prison, though both settings concealed a certain chaos.

"Something broke in her," Kristine says, attributing her mother's hoarding behavior to the pain of losing her daughter for seventeen years. She clings to what she can, Kristine reasons. "Now she can't seem to clean or throw things away."

Inside, everyone else went to bed. Kristine didn't know what to do; she didn't have a toothbrush or pajamas or a place to sleep.

She took off her dress, changed back into her beige prison uniform and cleared off a space on a recliner. Then, Kristine got back up. She went to Trent, who was conked out in his bed. She watched her son closely. He was almost a grown man. For hours, Kristine stayed awake: "I always wanted to check on my baby as he slept."

II.

"The only best friend I had sometimes were books. That was the only true escape. That was a saving grace in prison as well."

Born in 1973, Kristine grew up on her grandparents' land near Connersville, Indiana, a small manufacturing town about sixty-five miles from Indianapolis. Her family operated a bakery in town that her grandfather, a retired design engineer, owned—his second career of baking cakes and donuts. Later, under new ownership, the bakery burned down. Now all that remains is a parking lot, and the rest of the town, save the stately Masonic lodge to which Kristine's grandfather belonged, is mostly dilapidated, having lost thousands of manufacturing jobs. Amid the town's changing fortunes, some small businesses have hung on—a discount cigarette shop, a car dealer with fewer than a dozen vehicles, a gun shop selling a box of fifty 9 mm ammo for $13.99, and the Plaza Lanes bowling alley, which, though scarcely patronized on a Saturday night, upholds a retro, space-age sign that has since faded into pastel, its changeable letterboard now incomprehensible, tiles having fallen away.

Kristine remembers her grandparents as being well off financially—"very wealthy," even. They raised corn and owned two cattle farms—one in nearby Everton, Indiana, where she attended school, and one west of town in an area the kids called Hillbilly Hill, on account of a junkyard that had a picture of a hillbilly in the window. Her grandparents drove a Chrysler with big hood ornaments. "It was freakin' huge," she says with a laugh. "You'd never get a cheeseburger to eat in the back seat." But at times, Kristine's own parents struggled financially. Her father worked odd jobs before becoming a welder; her mother managed the family bakery. Kristine tended to her brother Michael, who was four years younger. When money grew tighter, her family—Dad, Mom, Kristine, and Michael—lived with her grandparents for a while.

An active and bright kid, Kristine was a Brownie and a Girl Scout. She sang in the choir and earned top grades statewide. She dreamed of becoming a teacher. A voracious reader, Kristine loved classic children's book series like *Nancy Drew*, *Hardy Boys*, and *Little House on the Prairie*. In the fourth grade, she earned a youth author award for penning a story about an alien named Tecumseh (she was studying Indiana history about Native Americans at the time) who had come to earth. Tecumseh, in her story, was trying to return home. As her prize, Kristine got to meet Norman Bridwell, the famed Indiana author of the *Clifford the Big Red Dog* books. Bridwell praised Kristine and the other award recipients. They, too, could become writers someday, he told them. Kristine's dad, Arthur, had come to the ceremony. "Yeah, this is a good hobby," she recalls his telling her, brushing off the achievement. Deflated, she stopped writing.

When Kristine was nine, her parents divorced, slowly unraveling what she otherwise considered a happy childhood. In fifth grade, she stayed at the same school and kept the same friends. Kristine took to mothering Michael. She knew he hated medicine, so once, when he was sick, instead of cough syrup she gave him Worcestershire sauce, which he liked.

Retiring with plans to travel in an RV, Kristine's grandparents sold the farms and the bakery when she was in middle school. In a new relationship, Susan packed up the kids and moved to Greensburg, Indiana, about forty-five minutes away. Kristine grew apart from her dad.

"At least in Connersville, he was an every-weekend dad," she says. They saw him less and less.

At nearby Lake McCoy, Kristine's mother bought a white aluminum trailer with green shutters at Creswood Resort, a mobile home park, "out in the boonies," Kristine says. The hilly, grass-and-gravel property sits amid a canopy of trees off the state road leading back to town. The trailer, several feet short of a double-wide, was built in 1972. Dividers could turn it from a three-bedroom to a four-bedroom. Kristine's family didn't have a view of the lake from their trailer, but she could walk a few steps outside to take in the water's stillness.

Susan remarried a younger man, ten years her junior. At eighteen years old, he was not quite six years older than Kristine. "It was like having a big brother instead of a stepdad," she says. Often left alone in their new environment, Kristine and her brother banded together.

Out of place, depressed and unchallenged at a new school, Kristine started skipping class, as did her brother, who was in elementary school. She would ride the bus into town. Michael would go fishing. They were never caught, never apprehended by the school. "They didn't give a shit," Kristine says.

Kristine dropped out of high school in the ninth grade. "They knew I was going to turn sixteen and quit anyway, and so they just let me," she says. Her mother remembers it differently. "She was too smart to drop out and do nothing with her life," Susan says. "I knew she was going to need her education."

Drifting along, Kristine sometimes stayed with her dad back in Connersville. When she grew tired of living there, she stayed with her mom. By this time, she had acquired a new group of friends, and together they would get drunk and smoke, uneventfully. The most trouble Kristine had with the law was a warning for speeding five miles per hour over the limit.

Susan had divorced again when a neighbor, a factory worker and World War II navy man named Tom Claxton, came into their lives. His romantic relationship with Susan didn't last long, but he stuck around for Kristine and Michael. "He was like my surrogate dad," Kristine recalls. "He was always there." Tom was the kind of man who set curfews and sent you out with a quarter for a pay phone in case there was any trouble.

At age seventeen, Kristine went to the doctor, believing she'd had the flu for months. She discovered she was pregnant with a baby boy, a surprise, as she had been taking birth control pills since before she was a teenager. Kristine turned to Tom for guidance.

"What do you want to do?" Tom asked her.

"I don't know."

"OK, whatever you want to do, I'm going to support him," Tom assured her.

Susan also rose to Kristine's defense, telling family members who might be upset by the news, "I don't want to hear any flapped lips about it. She's not the first and she won't be the last."

During her pregnancy, Kristine earned her GED. She also tried to stay in a relationship with her baby's father. "I don't go to church all the time," she told Tom. "I can't promise I'm going to love him forever and be with him."

"You don't have to," Tom said.

Her baby's dad made Kristine's choice easier when she was five months pregnant and he took off. She was not devastated—her focus was her child. On March 11, 1992, Anthony "Tony" Bunch was born by caesarean section. Remarkably, he slept through the whole first night. Kristine's mom thought something was wrong, but as they soon learned, this was typical Tony—not much of a crier, and an easy baby. Kristine's cat, Felix, liked to curl up next to Tony while he slept.

A new mom, Kristine wanted more space, apart from her own mother. She turned to Tom, who rented one of his trailers to her for a time. Meanwhile, Kristine worked two jobs, a temporary position at auto-parts factories and a part-time job at Kmart so she could get a discount on toys and clothes. Through the government's Women, Infants, and Children (WIC) program, Kristine filled her cupboards and refrigerator with milk, juice, and cereal. Tom babysat Tony while Kristine was at work.

For Tony's first birthday, Kristine bought a bag of assorted-color round balloons and stayed up late the night before to blow them up. She spread them on a sheet on the floor and then thumb-tacked the sheet to the ceiling for a makeshift balloon drop. The next day, when she unleashed the colorful cluster of a hundred balloons above Tony, he threw back his head, thrust his tiny fists in the air, and started laughing.

"He thought it was great," Kristine remembers. "I didn't have a whole lot of money, being a working mom. I wanted something that would have that 'Wow!' surprise effect and didn't cost me a lot."

When Kristine started a job skills program to become a machinist, she moved back into her mom's trailer to save money. Most of the time, Kristine and Tony had the place to themselves. Susan, divorced from a third husband, worked at the Goodwill in nearby Columbus and often stayed on a friend's houseboat. While Kristine was in school, Tom babysat Tony, giving him the nickname "Little Wicker." As a toddler, Tony loved watching *Terminator* with Uncle Michael, and he would mimic Schwarzenegger's deep voice, bellowing "Arnold!" He could dribble a basketball at age two. He loved playing outside, Michael recalls. Like most nineties kids, Tony was a fan of a popular purple TV dinosaur named Barney and, of course, Nintendo. A spirited, blond-haired, blue-eyed boy, Tony would sing along to Bon Jovi with Kristine, holding out the notes on "Always," the only lyric of the rock ballad he knew. Kristine would fill in the rest of the chorus for him:

And I will love you, baby—Always
And I'll be there forever and a day—Always
I'll be there till the stars don't shine
Till the heavens burst and

The words don't rhyme
And I know when I die, you'll be on my mind
And I'll love you—Always

III.

"Why not leave him and take me? He was the best of me."

On June 29, 1995, Kristine reheated chicken and rice with mushrooms and carrots for dinner in her mother's trailer. Susan spent most of her time away from home, which suited Kristine.

It was just like any other Thursday. Kristine had gone to school and then picked up three-year-old Tony at Tom's place, where they were watching *Angels in the Outfield*, Tony's favorite movie.

"It could happen!" Tony would tell Kristine, parroting a line from the movie.

"Maybe," she would smile back. "Yeah, it could."

That evening, Kristine mowed Tom's grass. Tony followed her with a toy lawn mower. He was more than three feet tall.

After Kristine juggled dinner, laundry, and a bath, she and Tony read a bedtime story together, a short children's book adapted from a traditional nursery rhyme:

Ladybug, ladybug, fly away home,
Your house is on fire and your children are gone.
House all afire? Can it be so?
Poor ladybug doesn't know which way to go.
Ladybug, ladybug, blown by the breeze,
Over the wheat field, into the trees.
Ladybug, ladybug, lands in some smoke.
There's really a fire, it isn't a joke.

Together, Kristine and Tony cozied up for bedtime with their two kittens on the living room sofa. He wasn't feeling well, and the air conditioning hadn't been on in the back bedroom all day. Plus, he was afraid of the dark and didn't like to sleep alone.

They sang a song together—Kristine can't remember which one—but it might have been the popular "You Are So Beautiful to Me," during which Tony would have chimed in an enthusiastic "boo-ti-ful."

Tony fell asleep around midnight. He woke up Kristine at 3 a.m. because a dog, Smokey, was barking outside. She took Tony to the bathroom and on the way back hollered at the dog to shut up. She handed Tony his kittens and he drifted right back to sleep. Exhausted, she took two allergy pills, which would make her drowsy, but Kristine shut off her alarm clock with plans to sleep in and go into school late.

A few hours later, something jarred Kristine awake on the couch, where she had fallen asleep. She thought she heard Tony calling "Mommy" from the adjacent bedroom. It was odd that he had moved there during the night.

What happened next is largely unknown, buried beneath memory, hallucination, and trauma. But what is known is that Kristine discovered a blaze separating her from Tony in the bedroom. She remembered him standing on his bed and shouting "It's hot, Mommy!" It was too hot to enter the room and reach him, so she threw a blanket on the fire. It melted. Kristine tried to put out the fire with a pillow. It burned. Then, she frantically searched for the fire extinguisher. She couldn't find it. As seconds passed, the fire filled the room.

It all happened in minutes but felt more stretched out, slow and desperate like quicksand. "It's like I'm underwater. I'm watching and I'm telling. I'm saying you need to do this and you need to do that," Kristine describes.

Barefoot in her nightgown, she ran outside and screamed for Tom. Together, they tried to smash Tony's bedroom windows. Kristine grabbed a tricycle and thrust it at the glass. She started to climb in but someone held her back. "It's too late," someone told her. "He's gone," the voice said.

By the time firefighters arrived, the trailer's ceiling had collapsed. The fire lasted less than thirty minutes.

In an ambulance, Kristine answered a medic's questions. The hair on her forehead was singed. She had blisters on her nose. She was cut up and covered in soot. Her cheeks and nose were red. Later, she would cough up black phlegm in the emergency room.

The firefighters emerged with Tony's lifeless body. He was pronounced dead at the scene. When Tom came over to the ambulance, Kristine asked if they had found Tony. She knew he was gone, but she didn't want him to be lost. Tom, quietly crying, confirmed the news. "Yeah, they found him," Tom said.

At the hospital, Kristine was given a prescription for Xanax. The staff did not run tests to check her carbon monoxide levels. The nerve pills made her drowsy, but she couldn't sleep. The images of the blaze filled her mind.

Someone found a minister at the hospital. He came in and introduced himself to her. Kristine asked him one question: Were there basketball courts in heaven?

"Made of gold," the minister smiled. Then he sat down next to her, held her hand, and did not say another word.

Later, her mom helped her shower and comb her singed hair, but Kristine could still smell the smoke and fire.

She had other visitors—a state trooper and deputy sheriff. Bewildered, she gave a taped statement to the investigators. She didn't ask for a lawyer or realize she was a suspect. But she quickly learned law enforcement believed an arson had taken place. Within hours, the Indiana State Fire Marshal's office had already started to conclude the fire had been intentionally set.

Later, at Tom's place, the sheriff called for her again and told her mom to bring her in. At 10 p.m., the same day as the fire, Kristine walked into the Decatur County sheriff's office. She was barefoot—all her shoes gone in the flames.

Inside, her mother was told to wait while the sheriff interrogated Kristine about the fire and about the gasoline she had used to fill up Tom's lawn mower. Kristine says she was called names and yelled at.

"Kristy, can I tell you something?" asked Sheriff Jon Oldham. "I have worked as a detective talking to people for the last twenty-nine years of my life, and I know when somebody for some reason is not leveling with me. And you are not. So you've got to tell me why."

"You people have accused me, and you tell me it was an arsonist, and then you tell me—"

"I haven't told you anything," Oldham answered. As the interrogation wore on, he asked her repeatedly who had set the fire. Kristine didn't know.

"Kristy, you realize what I'm telling you don't you?" Oldham asked her a few minutes later. "Accelerant was on the thing. There is no way that you—if his room was on fire, the living room would have been on fire too. I mean, it was not an accidental fire. It was set."

Kristine struggled to think who could be responsible.

"Did you set it?"

"No."

"Then who did?"

"I can't tell you."

"You can."

"What am I going to do, make wild stabs at people that just don't like me?"

Hammered about a gas can found near the home, Kristine swore she would never have brought it inside the trailer. In fact, she normally kept anything possibly toxic out in the shed, away from Tony. And she had replaced all her cigarette lighters with childproof ones.

Throughout the interview, Kristine maintained her account with some variance in clarity. On top of the trauma and shock, memory loss and confusion are common symptoms of carbon monoxide poisoning, which seemed to elude investigators. Later, at trial, jurors were never informed of this fact.

"I don't ever want to know the grief that you're going through now, because I know it's horrendous," Oldham said, before ending the interview. "But I feel responsible, because that little boy can't tell what happened to him . . . I think we owe him that, don't you? Are you going to help? You can, okay?"

After the interrogation, Kristine went back to Tom's house. As Tony's babysitter, Tom had some of his toys and clothes around the home. Kristine gathered the objects and curled up in bed, clutching the remnants.

Tony didn't have an open casket; instead, a long infant box. At his funeral, there was only one song to play. This time, Bon Jovi's aching verse:

> *Now your pictures that you left behind*
> *Are just memories of a different life*
> *Some that made us laugh, some that made us cry*
> *One that made you have to say goodbye*
> *What I'd give to run my fingers through your hair*
> *To touch your lips, to hold you near*
> *When you say your prayers try to understand*
> *I've made mistakes, I'm just a man*

For the price of five hundred dollars, Susan says, the funeral home provided the service and burial, with a rectangular, two-by-one-foot, bevel-style gravestone made of Georgia gray granite at Valley Grove Cemetery, off a road leading to Connersville:

TONY

ANTHONY M. BUNCH

TOM'S LITTLE WICKER

MAR. 11, 1992 – JUNE 30, 1995

TAKEN MUCH TOO SOON

In the midst of the Bunch family's grief, investigators kept tabs on Kristine, following her and interviewing her again. Fire marshals believed they had evidence of arson: that gas can found outside the trailer and accelerant "pour patterns" in the burned-out home. While processing the scene, investigators discarded electrical wiring—evidence that could have pointed to an accidental fire. Two days after the fire, they sent other evidence samples to the Bureau of Alcohol, Tobacco, and Firearms (ATF) National Laboratory, stating that the fire had been an arson caused by a liquid accelerant.

A day before the laboratory received the samples for testing, Kristine agreed to take a polygraph test, with investigators telling her the goal was to eliminate her as a suspect. She went into the state trooper's office. Kristine was scared, nervous, and tired from the nerve pills.

Strapped to a chair and facing a wall, she felt like the test administrator kept sneaking up on her. After the test concluded, Kristine says, the polygraph operator told her he knew she killed her son. She asked for a lawyer and, shortly after, was taken to the sheriff's office, arrested, and charged with murder and arson—five days after the fire. Investigators had asked about any insurance policies; Kristine didn't know of any. *I'm just a kid*, she thought. *I don't even have insurance on my car.*

The lack of motive persisted. A forensic chemist at the national laboratory, William Kinard, conducted testing on the samples from the Indiana fire marshals. He determined that none of the evidence from Tony's bedroom tested positive for heavy petroleum distillates (HPDs) or other accelerants. A sample of wood from the living room—where the marshals claimed there was a "pour pattern"—also did not test positive. Kinard, however, did find HPDs consistent with kerosene on other areas of the home, supported by the fact that kerosene heaters had been used in the trailer for several years, as well as insecticides (which also may contain kerosene). Kinard prepared an initial report summarizing these findings.

But, for reasons that remain unclear, after Kinard's report undercut the fire marshal's theory of arson, the document was altered. Two critical, negative samples were crossed out by hand—a sample from Tony's bedroom and one of the wood samples—and changed to positive results. Kinard created a new report and sent it to the fire marshals, who also had a copy of the original findings. But the investigators sent the Decatur County prosecutor's office the second, falsified report. That document would serve as the primary evidence against Kristine at trial. And the original test results would remain buried for more than a decade.

IV.

"I didn't care if I didn't wake up."

The Decatur County Jail sits behind the railroad tracks south of the historic courthouse square in Greensburg. A small, weathered brick box of a building, today it has three back exits, one padlocked shut. Here, in a concrete cell, Kristine languished for nearly four months, grieving for Tony and wishing she was dead herself, before a judge released her on a five-thousand-dollar bond, having found no motive.

On the other side of the tracks, a long, cinderblock, nearly windowless building stretches behind Main Street's row of shops—the *Greensburg Daily News*. Its building painted a sad shade of lavender, walls peeling, the newspaper fueled a relentless campaign of speculation and sensationalism around Kristine's case. The people of Greensburg couldn't get enough of it. People drove by the crime scene to gawk at the destroyed trailer. More than once, Kristine was called a "baby killer." It didn't stop there. When she was buying cigarettes at a gas station, somebody from a building across the street shouted out, "Murderer!"

The media storm was fueled, perhaps, in part by the high-profile trial of Susan Smith, a South Carolina woman accused of killing her two sons by rolling her car into a lake. Smith was convicted the same month Kristine was arrested.

Days before Kristine's trial, the front page of the *Greensburg Daily News* featured a misleading article about her polygraph test: "Bunch told David Motsinger of the Indiana State Police during an interview that she 'didn't know' why she had started the fire." Although her public defender, Greensburg attorney Frank Hamilton, lacked murder trial experience, he understood the impact the media attention could have on jurors. Hamilton tried, and failed, to secure a change of venue. The callous media hype devastated Kristine.

Before trial, the prosecutors arranged a deposition with Kristine. Upon entering the room, prosecutors dropped a file folder of autopsy photos on the table in front of her, allowing images of her son's body to slide into view.

"It took me a minute to register that these are pictures of my kid," Kristine says.

"They were horrible to her. Showing you your baby cut up?" Susan remembers.

The months before trial were a blur for Kristine. Out on bond, she cried and slept and partied. "I didn't give a fuck what happened," Kristine says. "I felt like everything was over. My whole life was built around Tony, and I didn't have him. I wanted to forget and not think about it." To escape the scrutiny in Greensburg, Kristine stayed at her dad's place near Connersville. She called Tom every day; he was concerned about her.

Spaced out on Xanax, Kristine met a man at a gas station.

"Is your name Crystal?"

"You're close!" said Susan, who was out with Kristine.

"I knew this girl named Crystal," the man said. "She had a smile like yours."

They went to a bar, drank, smoked, and later had sex. "For a while I didn't have to feel the loss, and I didn't have to feel the pain," Kristine remembers.

When she eventually discovered she was pregnant, she says she "cleaned up again." Kristine informed her new boyfriend that she was having a baby, but she learned he was married with children of his own. Their relationship ended.

By the time of the trial, which lasted six days in Judge John Westhafer's courtroom, from the end of February to early March 1996, Kristine's pregnant belly was barely visible beneath bulky sweaters. Testimony centered on the fire marshals and Kinard, the ATF National Lab chemist, along with his falsified report, which was entered into evidence. Prosecutor William Smith argued Kristine had started two fires—one in the living room and one in the bedroom—blocking Tony from fleeing the flames, a theory seemingly bolstered by a firefighter's surprise testimony that he had seen a chair placed in the doorway to the bedroom. It was a startling new claim and a departure from his original reports.

When Tony's autopsy pictures were shown again at trial, Kristine finally grasped that Tony was gone. "I thought it looked like a doll, not my baby." But during the trial, Kristine tried to show no emotion. That's what her lawyer had told her to do, she says. She didn't testify; she was in no state to do so. She never spoke. She never cried. After a few hours of deliberating, the jury found her guilty.

A month later, Westhafer sentenced her to sixty years for murder and fifty years for arson, merging the punishments, but not without a shaming accusation. "I understand you have arranged to have yourself impregnated during the period of time that you were out of jail and prior to the trial. I can think of no other reason for that to have happened than that you thought it would work to your advantage somehow in this process. It will not," Westhafer said.

The judge added that he would see to it that the child became a ward of the state and was put up for adoption. "You will not raise that child," Westhafer reprimanded. "You'll have nothing to do with that child."

Kristine shut down when she heard the words. Hearing only two sentences—sixty years plus fifty years—she figured that equaled a lifetime in prison.

"I'm never getting out," she thought. Immediately, her mind went to adopting out the growing baby inside her.

Later, her dad explained the judge had combined her two sentences. Her sentence was sixty years, with thirty years to serve in Indiana, he told her. And they would fight her conviction.

V.

"As soon as you walk in those doors, you're labeled a baby killer. Not only by inmates, but staff. They're trying to humiliate you and demean you."

"We've been waiting for you."

Staring back at Kristine in the main unit at Indiana Women's Prison (IWP) was a teenaged girl, Hope Rippey.

Hope wasn't wearing a prison uniform. The inmates at IWP, under then superintendent Dana Blank—whose philosophy was "You are not your crime"—were allowed to wear their regular clothes, except during the intake process. Kristine was fully showing her six months of pregnancy when she had to put on a blue prison uniform, known among the inmates as the "Smurf" outfit. The uniform separated the newbies from the rest of the population.

Kristine had heard about Hope's case on the outside. And Hope had heard about Kristine.

In 1992, Hope and three other young women were accused of the torture and murder of a classmate, a twelve-year-old girl named Shanda Sharer. The case had become a national news fascination, giving rise to books, a play, TV dramas, and true-crime documentaries.[5]

Hope and Kristine were both facing the majority of their lives behind bars. Believing she would not be released in time to have children of her own, Hope asked if she could share Kristine's baby with her. Early in their friendship, Kristine let Hope rub her belly and sing Madonna and Cyndi Lauper pop songs to her stomach. They wanted the baby to be smart, so Hope also later read poems by Keats and Blake. It was a warm welcome in a daunting place. Hope held Kristine's hand as they walked to the dining hall because she was too frightened to go alone. The gesture granted Kristine a certain level of protection.

Kristine's biggest challenge, especially the first couple of months, was not to break. "Not to let them win," she says. "Not to let them change the person I was. Not to let them tear me up so much that I couldn't recover from it."

She had secretly hoped the delivery day would never come. If only she could stay pregnant forever, she wouldn't have to lose her baby. Again.

"You start thinking a little crazy," Kristine admits. *"What if I hide him in my locker or keep him in my dorm and nobody would know?"*

In late July 1996, Kristine had been having back pain for a week. Hope shifted from rubbing her belly to rubbing her back. Kristine hadn't had a clinic visit for three weeks, due to a scheduling screw-up. When she went to the infirmary, the staff couldn't find a heartbeat and called an ambulance. Unknowingly, Kristine was already in labor.

Handcuffed but not shackled in the ambulance, Kristine was rushed to the hospital. "There's no point in shackling her," a friendly guard said. "Look at her! She's in pain."

At an Indianapolis hospital, a doctor walked in and asked, "What's wrong with you?"

---

5. Hope was released early in 2006, and, five years later, tried to reconcile with Sharer's family on the *Dr. Phil* show, explaining she was a troubled kid, "a weak person" and a follower—not the ringleader.

"They couldn't find a heartbeat," Kristine cried. "I think something has happened to the baby."

He felt her belly, concluding, "There's nothing wrong."

"Yes, there is!" she sobbed.

After a probe was employed, the familiar *boom-boom, boom-boom* came through the monitor. Kristine cried with relief.

When she wasn't dilated enough, the doctors considered an emergency caesarean section. They asked her, "Is this your first baby?"

It was decided. Kristine headed in for the procedure. "I want all cuffs off of her," the doctor instructed. "That's not going into my surgery."

Her family gathered in the hospital waiting room. Hope had used Kristine's phone code to call. They knew each other's codes for family calls as a precaution. You never knew if something were to happen inside the prison.

Kristine woke up from surgery with her leg chained to the hospital bed. The next day, still recovering from the C-section, she was forced to say goodbye to her son, a big-eyed, squirmy, and sweet Trenton Bunch.

"That's the time when you realize *I'm never going to get to cuddle him again*," she says. "*I'm never going to get to change his diaper again*."

At first, her father, Arthur, took care of Trent. But when six weeks went by before Arthur brought the baby to prison for a visit, Susan took over.

When Trent was five months old, Kristine started seeing him every week. The following year, the IWP, under Dana Blank, opened a Family Preservation Center as part of a program to help women retain custody of and maintain responsibility for their kids during incarceration. The "Family Pres" center, considering the setting, was warm and inviting, with beanbag chairs and a floor area where the mothers could play one on one with their babies. The prison hosted picnics, scrapbooking parties, and other programs aimed at connecting, rather than separating, families. Hope couldn't play with Trent inside the recreation area, so Kristine would pass through the hallway so she could see him.

At first, as little Trent grew, a bespectacled kid with a mop of dark hair, he believed his mom was in school. But once he could read—at an early age, like Kristine—he started gathering clues from the prison signage. Trent received counseling, in part due to an ADHD diagnosis, Susan says. With almost every growth spurt, he experienced a medication change as well. In between prison visits, Trent would become antsy to see his mother again, and he would act out. Kristine and Trent saw each other sometimes weekly, sometimes every other week, and sometimes with breaks longer than that, when Susan's eyes were too bad to drive and they had to catch rides to the prison with church volunteers. Her brother, Michael, visited Kristine often at first, then he became consumed with work, toiling for more than eighty hours a week building transmissions. Letters helped fill the gaps.

For years, Trent slept in Susan's bed. He called her "Nanny," as Tony had. Susan saved his baby teeth. She took him fishing, teaching him to cast out at age three. At age four, he caught his first fish—a bluegill. He caught forty-seven different kinds of fish that year. And one turtle, Susan says. As he grew older, Trent and Kristine kept in touch through letters in addition to their visits. Through the mail, they read the *Harry Potter* series together.

On a prison salary, Kristine couldn't provide much for Trent. Over the years, she had different jobs, which paid varying amounts, she says: sixty-five cents a day for cosmetology, a dollar a day for cleaning jobs, $1.25 a day for cooking in the kitchen. With high scores, she was snatched up as a GED tutor, earning a dollar a day. "It's one of those sad moments, you realize *I could have done something so different*," Kristine says. "*I could have been something more.*"

She was determined to create a better life for herself and Trent, should she ever get out of prison. She earned an associate's degree from Ball State University in 2000 and a bachelor's degree the following year. To finish her degrees in prison, she had to cut into her recreation time to accommodate the four to seven classes a week. The time spent studying was unpaid.

She also tried to save for her legal appeals. What she lacked in funds she made up for by studying her case and others like it, determined to prove her innocence.

Early in her sentence, Kristine had taken to mothering the youngest inmate in the prison—Donna, who had entered the system as a scared fifteen-year-old girl. Kristine, then twenty-three, protected her from harm, fighting others off who threatened her. She made Donna special

SPAM burgers with pickles and pizza-dough buns. She concocted ice cream using pudding, creamer, and water from the prison kitchen.

"I've always been her baby," Donna says. "I didn't have a normal life. The most normal I had was prison. I had someone unconditionally love me."

Donna—who, according to court records and social workers, endured a childhood of repeated sexual abuse and beatings—set fire to her family's Huntington, Indiana, home when she was fourteen, a blaze that killed her mother and sister. Her father put her up to it, Donna says: "I would have done anything for my dad."

Pleading guilty, Donna was convicted in adult court and sentenced to twenty-five years in prison, making her a symbol in what became a national saga about the issue of juvenile justice. A judge had urged that she be put in a juvenile facility for therapy and educational opportunities, but the state Department of Correction sent her to IWP. The next youngest inmate on Donna's unit, reported the *New York Times* in 1997, was twenty-one years old. After her attorneys filed suit against the Indiana Department of Correction, Donna was transferred to a private treatment center for young people in Fort Wayne, Indiana, until she turned eighteen and was sent back to IWP as an adult to carry out the rest of her sentence.

The years apart from Kristine were difficult for Donna. The two had fostered a familial bond at IWP. When Donna turned sixteen, Kristine had thrown her a little party, giving her sixteen Tootsie Pops wrapped with a ribbon—a bouquet for her "Sweet Sixteen." During their separation, Kristine and Donna broke the rules and communicated through letters (in Indiana, inmates are not permitted to correspond with one another). When they got in trouble for communicating, the superintendent, Dana Blank, intervened. Recognizing Kristine was all Donna had, Blank allowed the letters to continue at a certain number a month. When Donna came back to IWP after two years at the juvenile facility, Kristine greeted her with a Nutty Bar, a pop, and an embrace. There was a "no hug" policy at the prison, but they didn't care if they were punished.

Donna was released early from IWP at age twenty-one in 2002; a judge had reduced her sentence to twenty years, with only ten years to serve, and she earned time credit for her schooling. Kristine was working in the kitchen when they said goodbye. "Baby, go soar," she said. "I'll always be there. I'm right behind you."

At the time, Kristine's words were but a shred of hope. Ten years later, they became a reality.

VI.

"It was out of my control. That's easier to accept—that it was already done—than the fact that I couldn't fix it."

A few years into her sentence, Kristine found out about a special kind of legal appeal known as a post-conviction petition that could win a prisoner a new trial. For such a petition, Kristine would have to present new evidence that wasn't available at the time of the original trial—evidence that would have made a difference in the outcome of her case.

She cracked open the phone book and launched her own letter-writing campaign to law firms for help. Most often, she received no reply. Occasionally, some sent her the courtesy of a rejection letter. Others responded by requesting tens of thousands of dollars for their services.

In 2001, a journalist named Jennifer Furio was working on a book about women in prison. Through letters, she interviewed Hope Rippey. Hope then suggested Furio talk to Kristine, too. They exchanged a series of letters, and Kristine's case ended up being the subject of a chapter in Furio's *Letters from Prison: Voices of Women Murderers*—a book title that belied Furio's sympathy for Kristine, whose case she described with compelling indicators of innocence.

In her first letter to Furio, Kristine wrote: "Ms. Furio, I am trying to fight to be able to mourn and grieve for my baby, Tony, to be able to visit his grave; and I am fighting to be with my other son, who needs his mom." She explained that she didn't have money for an attorney. Kristine continued:

> My whole life I have been poor. That has been okay; I was working on making that better for Tony and me. But my family had always been

lower-class. There is stigma with that. I just couldn't believe it went into the courtroom with me. As if poor equals dumb. And I love my children as much as anyone, and I know I deserve a fair trial as much as someone with means. But the two seem to go hand-in-hand. I don't think I'll have the money anytime soon, so what else are my options?

Furio and Kristine exchanged a series of letters, and Furio read Kristine's trial transcripts, also interviewing a fire investigator Kristine had tracked down, who had agreed to look into her case for free. He told Furio Kristine had been "shafted." Still, Furio told Kristine not to expect any miracles.

In 2003, an Indianapolis lawyer, Hilary Ricks, performed a small miracle for Kristine. She agreed to take the case for only two thousand dollars up front. Kristine saved up to pay for half, and her family was able to come up with the rest.

Ricks knew the scientific understanding of arson had changed drastically and rapidly in recent years to include a growing body of knowledge that was not widely used at the time of Kristine's trial. Advances in fire science could undermine the fire marshals' quick conclusion about the fire that killed Tony. Theories of burn and pour patterns, among other interpretations of arson, had since been debunked as fallacies.

But for Kristine's case specifically, the troubling lab report had cited evidence of an accelerant—or so she had been told. In closing arguments at trial, the prosecutor left no room for debate in the jurors' minds: "We called Bill Kinard. Bill's evidence is undisputed. There's no dispute whatsoever with this piece of evidence."

Since her case had hinged on Kinard's report, Kristine decided to track down the raw data behind it. She learned about gas chromatographs, squiggly lines of information not unlike those on a polygraph or heart monitor. These would have been the basis of Kinard's analysis. Through the Freedom of Information Act, Kristine submitted a request for the data to the ATF National Laboratory, where Kinard had been a chemist. Her letter went unanswered. Meanwhile, Kristine earned a paralegal certificate in 2005. She urged Ricks to reach out to top fire-science experts whom she had read about, and one of them offered ten hours of pro bono assistance through one of his staffers, Jamie McAllister.

Along the way, Kristine found other helpers who took an interest in her case. A prison minister managed to track down more case documents. In 2006, a college student sent the chapter about Kristine from Furio's book to Northwestern University's Center on Wrongful Convictions. This would prove to be the turning point. Her case caught the attention of the center's powerhouse attorneys Jane Raley and Karen Daniel.

Before taking the case, the women contacted top fire experts for further review, including John Malooly, formerly of the ATF, and John DeHaan, who had authored the leading manual on fire investigation. Both testify almost exclusively for the prosecution in arson cases. But upon reviewing Kristine's case, they did not believe the fatal fire was arson.

"The case was just screaming at us that this was the real thing," Jane told *Indianapolis Monthly* journalist Megan Fernandez in a piece published in 2014. "Here we had a woman with no prior criminal history. No eyewitness. No confession. No motive. And the experts we were consulting with were telling us that there was no scientific basis to suggest arson. We had a perfect case."

Teaming up with Ricks, Raley and Daniel built on Kristine's post-conviction petition in 2007, recruiting two more legal heavyweights to the case—Ron Safer and Kelly Warner of the prestigious Schiff Hardin law firm in Chicago. With the star team in place, the evidence against Kristine started to unravel.

Using their subpoena power, Kristine's lawyers sought the entire ATF file, which included the gas chromatographs from the national laboratory. Remarkably, they discovered the raw data still existed. Then, to everyone's shock, they discovered in the file the long-buried, original ATF report testing the trailer floor samples. The document revealed the handwritten edits altering the original reading to what was presented at Kristine's trial. This type of suppressed evidence amounted to a constitutional violation—what's known as a "Brady claim," from the US Supreme Court case *Brady v. Maryland*. The rule says that when prosecutors suppress evidence that is favorable to a defendant, it violates that person's due-process rights. In Kristine's case, a Brady claim would give serious force to her appeal.

But there was an emotional toll to this breakthrough about the fabricated report. Kristine was furious.

"That was the angriest time," she says, her voice shaking upon conjuring the memory. "I went to prison thinking either somebody did that or that there was a monster inside of me that nobody knew about. I couldn't understand why it was an arson. And to hear that you not only ripped away my freedom, but you lied—that's what fucked me up the most."

For years, Kristine had been led to believe someone had set fire to her trailer—the evidence of an accelerant had been so persuasive. In prison counseling, she struggled with this belief. *Could I have buried a memory of setting the fire?* she thought. Finally, a counselor advised that she stop blaming herself, telling her frankly, "There's nothing there."

Other new evidence developed as well. The "doorway" to Tony's bedroom that a firefighter testified had been blocked by a chair was revealed to be a burned-out wall frame, not the entry to the room after all. Meanwhile, Jamie McAllister, the forensic toxicologist who was offering Kristine pro bono assistance, analyzed Tony's autopsy report. The medical document stated Tony had died of carbon monoxide poisoning, not from burns. McAllister noticed Tony's blood toxicology was at a significantly high level when he stopped breathing—80 percent, well over the typically fatal amount. For Tony's exposure to reach that level, the fire would have needed to blaze for ninety minutes, in which time Tony would have died from burns—but the fire had lasted less than thirty minutes. Tony's unburned trachea and lungs suggested he had been quickly poisoned by carbon monoxide before the fire could reach him. The spike of carbon monoxide, McAllister believed, could have come from an electrical fire accumulating in Tony's bedroom ceiling and seeping into the trailer (poisoning both mother and son) before burning through. This also provided an explanation for the ceiling tiles falling to the floor.

McAllister's revelation about the medical report seemed to conflict with Kristine's hazy memory of waking up to Tony calling "Mommy" during the fire. "I swear my baby woke me up," she says, even today. But under McAllister's explanation of the ceiling fire and the subsequent carbon monoxide poisoning, Tony would have already been dead by the time Kristine awakened. Confronted with the false memory of Tony calling for her and standing on his bed, Kristine was not at odds with this new expert analysis. To her, it finally all made sense. Instead, she understood that something, be it Tony's voice or spirit, saved her from perishing. "He's the reason that I woke up," Kristine says. "Even though logic says no. My heart says that's why I woke up. That's why I made it out."

Her imperfect memory of the fire, however, also aligned with McAllister's analysis. Given Tony's own blood toxicology levels, Kristine, asleep in the next room, would have also suffered carbon monoxide poisoning—the effects of which include memory loss.

This explanation of the fire and Tony's death also meant Kristine's frantic, failed attempts to save her son no longer mattered. He was already gone. She couldn't have saved him. And Kristine could finally begin to forgive herself for something she never did.

The new evidence was so compelling, even to prosecutors, that in 2009, they offered Kristine a way out of prison early, without having to admit their own shortfalls—a plea deal. She could leave IWP in six years in exchange for a guilty plea. Kristine's responsibility as a mother to Trent tugged at her. But she turned down the deal. She couldn't accept it and teach her son to lie—and, worse, admit to something she didn't do.

Kristine earned an evidentiary hearing on appeal, back in the same court—and in front of the same judge, Judge John Westhafer, who had originally sentenced her, calling her "cold-hearted" and "cruel." But this time around, with renewed (and more sympathetic) media interest in her case, the guards and officers treated her more favorably, offering her bottled water at the hearing.

For the better part of a year, Westhafer deliberated on the new evidence from Kristine's hearing and post-conviction petition, which asked for a reversal of her conviction or a new trial. In June 2010, Westhafer shot down the petition in a forty-seven-page ruling, stating, "new experts do not create new evidence."

Prepared, Kristine's lawyers promptly filed an appeal to his decision. A three-person appeals court panel heard the evidence. Kristine was not permitted to attend the hearing. In March 2012, a two-to-one ruling ordered a new trial.

The critical victory was met with a caveat: the state could appeal as well. And it did. Now, the Indiana Supreme Court would have to rule. Months later, the state Supreme Court shut down the state's appeal and ruled that Kristine could finally be released on bond and await a new trial.

By mid-2012, much had changed, inside the prison and out. Superintendent Dana Blank had left in 2006 and retired the following year. To Kristine and many others, the prison culture at IWP suffered as a result. Under a new warden, there were new rules. The prison became more like a business, with cheaper food and fewer programs for inmates. Prison uniforms were reintroduced. Strip searches happened more regularly. Time with family was curtailed. And Kristine's family relationships had suffered as a result. Trent was already at an age where he was questioning the prison environment, unsure whether he wanted to be there, and the administration changes further strained Kristine's bond with him.

Kristine knew times and people had changed while she was in prison. For several years, her only window to the outside world, apart from family visits and letters, had been the TV show *Friends*. When Kristine left prison, the show had long ended, but she was still watching the reruns.

And the makeup of her family had changed. Her grandfather had died, and Kristine was not allowed to attend his funeral. The pair had, however, been able to talk one last time by phone. "You're my only grandbaby that graduated," he told her. "I'm so proud of you, and you keep fighting."

"I will."

Tom Claxton was gone, too. He died in 2001, more than a decade before Kristine's release. Susan had told her the news over the phone. "That was the first time that I realized that there were going to be people that I was never going to get to see again," Kristine remembers.

Up at the Valley Grove Cemetery outside Connersville, Tom's government-style bronze gravestone sits to the left of Tony, his "Little Wicker."

But Kristine had made it out alive, and there was another survivor, too: her struggling sixteen-year-old son. Trent had been waiting for her.

VII.

"I can never make it up to him. I can never step in and take over that role that my mom has fulfilled. For me, that was the hardest. In my mind for sixteen years, I was getting out, and I was going to have my kid."

Hours after being released, Kristine was receiving a lot of calls on her mom's phone. Her story had been in the newspaper, on TV news, and on the radio. Hope had called and left messages. Other friends—some she hadn't heard from since she went in—wanted to talk to her. Overwhelmed, Kristine couldn't call them all back.

"They're on Facebook," Trent told her on the ride home from the jail. "You can just message them."

"What's that?"

Trent explained to her how social media worked, later taking a photo of her using his laptop and helping her to set up a profile. Kristine had no Internet access in prison, so she thought the web was essentially a search engine like Lexis/Nexis, the legal research tool updated from time to time in the prison library. She didn't realize the Internet was a virtual place to stay connected to other people. The world's technological topography had drastically shifted during her incarceration, and she didn't know how to navigate this new landscape.

As she slowly cruised the web, Kristine noticed an appeals court website. She asked Trent about it.

"I know," he said. "I check all the time."

"Where?"

"On the website. On the computer," he said, showing her the docket page.

"Nuh-uh."

"Yeah."

"You don't have to search for it?"

"No, it's bookmarked. I checked to see if there was a decision."

In fact, he had been checking her case daily. And now, there was another waiting game hanging over them, months away—a retrial.

Later that morning, Kristine called her brother Michael from the bathroom so no one would hear. Michael, strangely, hadn't been alongside her family when she was released. Kristine says her mother didn't call him, while Susan and Michael say he was at work.

"What the fuck?" Kristine whispered into the phone. "I don't even have a toothbrush."

"Take a shower. Do some laundry. I'll pick you up after work."

Kristine cleaned the apartment as she waited. The purging process would stretch out for days as Kristine filled ten garbage bags full of trash, gathering sticky cans of pop and crusty bowls of macaroni and cheese from her son's room. She found other strange, foul messes: "I couldn't believe Trent was living in that."

Meanwhile, Susan, who considers herself "neat as a pin," brushed off the allegation that she had become a hoarder. "Trent is a mess-maker. Him and his cat trash my stuff," Susan says. "Trent doesn't take showers. He doesn't keep anything clean."

When Michael arrived from Indianapolis, for a minute the cluttered apartment faded away. "It was the happiest I've been in a really long time," he says of their reunion.

In 1995, when Tony died, Michael was a teenager living with his dad in Connersville. When authorities launched an investigation against Kristine, Michael became filled by a rage that he found hard to control. More than once, his father took his car keys away to keep him from driving to Greensburg.

"Because it wouldn't end well. I was that distraught," Michael says. "I was very angry because not only had I lost Tony, but I had lost Kris, too. I was very angry and I was a very distraught teenager."

For the first several years of her incarceration, Michael would see her as often as he could, taking long lunch hours. Back then, the guards weren't so bad. Later on, under the new administration, it became a lot more troublesome. When his responsibilities mounted—marriage but no kids, overtime hours building transmissions, and taking care of Trent and Susan—the visits became less frequent. Still, Michael kept in touch the best he could through letters. For Kristine, Michael was a part of her that had been missing. "He was the only person that really knew me."

After sharing hugs and wiping tears, Michael and Kristine went with Trent to Texas Roadhouse for a big meal before hitting the outlet mall. Afterward, Trent didn't want to shop, so they dropped him off.

First up, Kristine needed bras and panties. She scooped up all white undergarments. It was all she knew from prison.

"What are you doing?" Michael stopped her. "You get *one* white, and one of every color."

They picked out some clothes and Kristine tried on garments. Michael treated her to a wine tasting, and they stopped by a chocolate factory store. Then, on to Walmart for "hygienes," as she had grown to call them at IWP.

The Walmart in town had been a regular-sized store when Kristine went into prison. Now, it was a "supercenter" with sweet Indiana wines for $5.50. Kristine went up and down the aisles flooded with products and choices. She had trouble knowing which shampoo to buy.

"You just pick," Michael said, advising that she smell the shampoo to narrow down her selection.

Kristine was in awe as Michael put an oscillating toothbrush that required batteries into the shopping cart.

"I'm going to need tampons," she informed her brother.

"What kind do you use?" Michael said. As they turned the corner, they found a wall full of tampons. Every size and scent. Kristine began to cry.

Michael paused. "Megan uses this," he said, referencing his wife. "Put some Tampax in there and some Always liners."

Kristine nodded. "If you don't like it, we'll come back and get something else," he reassured her. "We'll do it again the next day and the next day."

Back at Michael's tri-level home, he whipped up some of the special guacamole that he had brought to the prison during the years when picnics with outside food from family were allowed.

At the kitchen table, Kristine told him, "I can't live there. I can't believe Trent has been living there this whole time."

"Sissy, we were trying to protect you," Michael said. "You had enough to deal with inside."

"But he shouldn't be there either."

"Then you can come stay here. You are welcome. Trent's welcome."

For the night, Michael set up Kristine in a guest bedroom with a new comforter and sheets. She soaked in the tub, her first hot bath in years. In the washing machine, her new clothes were swishing around. Cleaned up and nerves soothed, Kristine sat up with her brother at the kitchen table, talking until the early morning hours. Michael showed her newspaper clippings he had saved and other odds and ends of what had happened through the years. He wanted her to experience them on the other side of the bars.

As they caught up, Michael suddenly remembered something else he wanted to give her. He had purchased a ring at a jewelry store when it was going out of business. He didn't know what it was for or why he had to have it. But he bought the ring anyway. Now, he understood.

Michael went and found the ring—a mint-green sapphire set in white gold.

"It's beautiful," she said.

"We'll go tomorrow and get it sized."

The next day, Michael called off work. Shopping again—this time for watches. Kristine thought something two-toned in gold and silver would be nice, to match both kinds of jewelry.

They decided to see a movie, an R-rated horror movie remake. During the movie, Kristine went to find the restroom. It took her a while before she returned to their seats.

She whispered to Michael in the dark movie theater: "Um, you could have told me how to turn on the water." The automated faucet had thrown her off. She tried to find a way to turn it on, elbowing and hitting the sink. Finally, her fingers caught the motion sensor.

After the movie, Michael drove Kristine back to their mom's apartment, where they found Susan was upset about Kristine's leaving for so long with Michael.

"I'll be moving Trent at the end of the week," Kristine announced to her mother's bewilderment. They would move in with Michael for a fresh start, Kristine said. Trent wasn't happy with the change, but Kristine, reclaiming her power as a mother, forced him.

Donna's SUV hadn't fully stopped in the parking lot of Susan's apartment building when she was already leaping out of it to see Kristine.

"John, stop the car!" she told her husband.

"Hold on! Let me park."

"No—let me out!"

The weekend before Trent and Kristine moved into Michael's four-bedroom home, Donna came to visit with her family—a husband and three kids.

Donna had been out of prison for a decade. About two weeks after her release, in 2002, she found herself dating a guy she had met at the juvenile facility in Fort Wayne, Indiana, where she had been sent from IWP before turning eighteen. The relationship produced two daughters, Mara Jade and Leia. Other than that, Donna described it as the "worst five years of my life." Kristine helped as much as she could from prison, encouraging her to keep herself and her kids safe.

"I'm learning how to be a good mom," Donna says. "I wouldn't be a good mom if it weren't for Krissy."

A few years later, Donna's fate took a turn on her ride home from work one evening when her Citilink bus driver, John, made an impression on her: "I was finding my way home, and I found love." When Donna won a trip to Miami, she took John with her. They later married in Vegas, joining their families in Fort Wayne.

Donna wasn't allowed to visit Kristine in prison, save once, about a year after she had been released. "The rule is if you're an ex-offender you can't go," she says. "But I was pregnant with Mara Jade, and they let me come in."

Determined to stay close, the two kept in touch through letters and phone calls. "I didn't want to be a 'one book of stamps' with her," Donna says. "We always say people buy one book of stamps, but when the book is gone, they're gone."

Once, Donna's daughters had sent "Aunt Krissy" a musical greeting card for Christmas. The prison sent it back. Donna took a picture of the card and sent it to Kristine instead.

At Susan's apartment, Donna's family picked up Kristine and Trent. They found a hotel in Columbus where they all could stay. Trent had already met Donna during prison family visits and the one time Donna was allowed to visit Kristine after her own release.

"Why do you keep touching me?" Kristine asked Donna as they were talking.

"Because I want to pinch you! This isn't real."

"You're supposed to pinch yourself."

"No!" Donna laughed. "That will hurt!"

Donna hadn't slept away from John since they met, but that night, she crawled into bed with Kristine, with her husband in a queen-sized bed next to them and their kids in the next room. Side by side, Kristine rubbed Donna's head like she used to in prison.

As Donna drifted off to sleep, for the first time she finally felt like she was free.

VIII.

"I came out to a very angry, confused sixteen-year-old."

Trent wasn't happy about the move to Michael's house. He would have his own room there, and so would Kristine, but he wasn't good with change and even worse with structure. He didn't want to live without his Nanny or to seem to be turning his back on her.

As Kristine shifted back into her mom routine, a life she had fought so long to regain, she struggled to shake her rigidly scheduled prison mindset. She tried to impose some organization in their new lives. Chores. Dinnertime. Bedtime. The regimen was met with resistance, a "battle every day," Michael observed.

They fought about going to school, doing his homework, taking regular showers, and cleaning up after himself. Kristine was dumbfounded by his lack of discipline and initiative. She questioned the extent to which he was medicated, more than what some women she had known in prison were taking. Trapped in a confusing power dynamic, Kristine sought legal custody of Trent, dissolving her mom's guardianship. Trent was almost an adult, but Kristine wanted clarity and control.

"I wouldn't have fought her either way," Susan says. "I think she went about it the wrong way. Trent doesn't do change well."

Kristine proceeded to juggle school meetings and counselors' visits, but Trent ended up on academic probation. He hadn't been going to school. The stress filled her days, a distraction from her own emotional battle over being free again in a new, unfamiliar world. "It seemed like I didn't deal with my stuff because I was continuously dealing with his stuff," Kristine says, in retrospect.

Still, she needed a paycheck, so she used her paralegal skills to work part-time for Hilary Ricks, her attorney in prison. Someone tipped off the local media about Kristine's job, and reporters showed up to the county building to talk to her. A judge approached her after court was over.

"Ms. Bunch? There's a camera crew here." He let her out back to escape the scrutiny.

The media also left messages for her at home, trying to track her down for a "day in the life" story. Kristine wasn't interested.

When she went out, she could hear people whispering about her. Isolation, that old familiar friend in prison, became her escape.

One month after Kristine's release, a family outing with Michael, Trent, and her sister-in-law, Megan, to a tattoo convention outside Indianapolis was a welcome reprieve from the feuding and uncertainty at home.

Kristine had started getting tattoos when she was seventeen, despite her mother's objections. "'I forbid it,'" she remembers Susan telling her. By the time Kristine went to prison, she had three tattoos—a lion's head on her right shoulder, a black panther on her leg, and a tiger lily on the back of her neck. At the time, she was thrilled with her body art. But over the years, her tastes had changed, and the tiger lily, inked in fluorescent orange, had faded in prison.

At the convention, she sought out a tattoo artist to cover up the old ones. One vendor, Trinity of High Caliber Tattoo in Indianapolis, caught her eye. After Kristine shared her story, they plotted some cover-up tattoo options: the lion's head could become a smattering of purple and blue flowers; the tiger lily, a butterfly; and the black panther could transform into a phoenix rising out of the ashes, covering her calf. The tattoos would take multiple sessions to complete, and it would be painful.

These would be the first of other tattoos Kristine would add to the inventive cover-ups: the word "Freedom" with bird imagery on her right wrist, matching "Siblings' Day" tattoos with Michael, the word "Love" with a heart around it on her right knee. On her neck, notes of music emerging from the butterfly cover-up.

But there was one tattoo that Kristine wouldn't cover up—the one inked on the back of her neck in a dark scrawl: "Rhonda."

At IWP, tattoos could be had with a needle and some gel pens. Dip and poke, dip and poke. Kristine held off until her last few years. Likewise, Rhonda tattooed "Kristine" across her shoulders in tall, red cursive.

They met in the education building. They were about the same age, both from Indiana. Rhonda had seven and half years to serve on a plea deal in a burglary case. In her late thirties, Rhonda wanted to learn how to read and write. Kristine was her tutor.

There were some children's books in the prison library, but Kristine started Rhonda on newspapers, comics, and other reading materials from the prison's day room. Rhonda could write her letters and say the alphabet, but she couldn't read much and was afraid to read aloud. Kristine practiced phonics with her on children's poems by the nineteenth-century Hoosier poet James Whitcomb Riley, who used simple language to pen country tales and famous rhymes like "Little Orphant Annie."

In time, Rhonda had no trouble sounding out words and getting them right. But, as a person with epilepsy, she suffered from seizures, and between episodes would forget what she had learned. The seizures were frightening events that would leave Rhonda injured—a damaged rotator cuff, concussions. The prison also seemed to be changing her medications "at the drop of a hat," Kristine remembers. Once, during a seizure, Rhonda fell in the day room and cut her head open; blood was everywhere. She was wheeled off to the infirmary and back on her feet the same day.

"Everyone else had to take care of her," Kristine says. "She isn't taken care of the way she should [be]."

They were together for five years—a crucial time during Kristine's appeal. "She was there for every crazy, fucked-up moment," she says. At the time, Kristine didn't identify as bisexual, nor did the trope "gay for the stay" apply either.

"It's basic," Kristine says. "You need to get off. You need to be kissed."

Rhonda's humor kept Kristine smiling when she was torn up over her court battle.

"So something happened?" Rhonda asked as they were walking in the prison yard.

Kristine nodded. Rhonda shifted into comedy mode. She stuck her hand down the backside of her pants, to Kristine's confusion. "They just came up with this new perfume—it's called Passion!" she said, holding out her stinky hand. "You wanna smell it?"

Kristine burst out laughing and, for a moment, forgot her worries, as the appeal dragged on for years. When she lost hope, Rhonda cheered her on: "I believe this is going to happen."

Rhonda was a needy girlfriend, but Kristine didn't mind. She liked having someone to take care of, someone to love.

In 2012, when Kristine found out she earned a new trial, Rhonda didn't begrudge her impending freedom. Her own release was only three years away. Until then, she could call collect every week. This did not soothe their difficult parting, but a few guards allowed them to have a proper farewell.

"The guard that was on Building Six opened up the door so I could give her a hug and tell her that I loved her," Kristine remembers. They cried together.

When Kristine walked off to the end of the building, she knew she was never coming back.

IX.

"That's what I fought for. I had this baby. So now, realizing that I'm out here and it's just me? That's a whole new set of challenges."

For almost four months after her release, Kristine and Trent couldn't quite settle into the idea that she was really free. Another trial, scheduled for February 2013, threatened to steal her back into the system. The impermanence created an atmosphere of fear.

Trent's behavioral issues continued to deteriorate, and Kristine was drinking and smoking to dull her growing discontent with their circumstances.

But one positive development occurred during her first trip to Chicago, in November 2012. For the first time, Kristine met other women exonerees, as part of a new initiative focused on wrongly convicted women. She quickly found a new community of people who understood her.

"How are you?" someone had asked her.

"I'm falling apart."

"It's OK. We are too."

An Illinois exoneree, Juan Rivera, who was freed the same year as Kristine (also with attorney Jane Raley's help), reached out to her as they struggled through new experiences on the outside. Their cases were starkly different—Rivera was cleared by DNA of the rape and murder of a young Lake County girl—but as new exonerees they kindled a special bond.

A week before Christmas, in December 2012, when the Decatur County Prosecutor's Office announced it was dropping the murder charges, Kristine felt little relief. New charges could still be filed, and by canceling the February trial date, the county could then reinvestigate the case with more time than before. It wasn't over.

"We have not surrendered," Chief Deputy Prosecutor Doug Brown told the *Indianapolis Star*. "We are still evaluating what [evidence] is available with the intention to go forward."

Kristine turned to her newest civil attorneys, John Stainthorp and Jan Susler at the People's Law Office in Chicago. The first time they met at their humble office digs in Chicago's West Town, Jan asked, "What are you looking for out of this?"

"I want them to know that they can't keep bending me over and fucking me up the ass."

Jan smiled. "We're going to get along."

They would file lawsuits, suing the state fire marshals for suppressing evidence as well as the United States of America, the employer of William Kinard, the ATF chemist whose altered report had contributed to Kristine's conviction. Altogether, they would ask for $17 million—one million for each year of her life she lost.

But beyond providing legal assistance, Jan could see Kristine was struggling when she visited the office. She suggested Kristine find some counseling. Having seen a prison counselor for years, Kristine decided to take Jan's advice and find a therapist.

As Kristine explained her unusual history to a new counselor, the woman seemed strangely distracted. "Who do you think is going to play you in the movie?" the counselor asked, succumbing to her curiosity.

"What movie?"

"Of course there will be a movie. They usually have a movie." The counselor paused. "Who is going to play me?"

Kristine was sick and angry at the suggestion. "It's not going to be Demi Moore, bitch."

"No, no, no! I'm just saying—"

Kristine interrupted her attempt to salvage the situation. "I don't care what you're saying. I don't trust you. You said the wrong thing." And with that, she walked out of the office.

Once her anger faded, Kristine agreed to meet with another counselor. The Center on Wrongful Convictions connected her to a different woman, Heidi, who really listened.

"I was exonerated after seventeen years in prison, and I still don't feel free," she explained in despair. Kristine told Heidi of the daily irony of longing for seclusion and security despite having earned this new, hard-fought independence. She described wanting to crawl into bed and not do anything all day. She told Heidi about plastering a fake smile on her face when she was around other people, only to be exhausted when she would remove the façade back at home. She felt like her feet were in both worlds—one in prison, one not in prison, and she couldn't fit into either of them.

Heidi said their goal would be to make Kristine comfortable with who she was now, given her past. Their goal would be to help Kristine feel normal again.

Kristine's future uncertain, in December 2012 her brother Michael and his wife, Megan, decided to shuttle her away from her present reality in Indiana and take her on a trip to Mexico.

Before leaving, Kristine felt she had exhausted her options with Trent and put him in a residential treatment program to help him get off his ADHD medications at Meadows Hospital in Bloomington, Indiana, about an hour away. She hoped by taking him off as many medications as possible and providing him with additional support and therapy, he could deal with his behavioral issues.

In theory, the time away in Mexico seemed like exactly what Kristine needed—a new environment where she could let go and relax. In practice, it proved more difficult. Her first time on a plane since prison, the post-9/11 security protocols spooked her. They were going to have to pat her down, a TSA agent informed her. Michael could see the dread spread across Kristine's face. It was too reminiscent of prison.

"She was like, 'Oh my God, I just got out of this, and now I have do it again?'"

And then the fear gave way to anger. Kristine cursed out the agent. Michael intervened, giving her ponytail a playful tug and whispering to her. "Yo!" he laughed. "Everybody has to do it."

"Oh. Well. That's fine," Kristine, embarrassed, reined in her anger.

In Mexico, the all-inclusive vacation made everything easy. Kristine loved it. They hung out by the pool and soaked up the sun on the beach. Kristine parasailed for the first time.

"She was ecstatic," Michael remembers. "She could have just stayed up there all day."

Back in Indiana after their vacation, a refreshed Kristine developed a new routine for the next six months, visiting Trent at Meadows Hospital three times a week and focusing on his care. She didn't go back to work. Not yet. Michael wanted her to take the time to adjust to her new environment and work through Trent's issues. With only a learner's permit, Kristine had to drive with Michael before she earned her license. At Meadows, Trent was getting his grades back up, attending counseling sessions several times a week, and figuring out his medications. Kristine would take him out to the movies, out to eat, out shopping. While these outings signified progress in his relationship with Kristine, it also became clear during his treatment that he felt he was betraying his Nanny—"loyalty bond issues," she says—and that he wished the three of them could simply live together, as he had imagined while Kristine was incarcerated.

Kristine had to accept that their visions of the future were drastically different. No amount of family picnics, letters, or playtime at the prison could fill the canyon of missed history between them. "At the end of the day, I'm Mom, and it's my fault," Kristine says. "I should have been there and made things better for him."

When Trent checked out of Meadows, he was almost seventeen years old and more motivated about life. For his birthday, Kristine took him to Chicago to see the big city and to explore the idea of moving there permanently. He was upbeat. So was Kristine. Away from Indiana where people would recognize her, Kristine liked being closer to her support system at Northwestern University. The Center on Wrongful Convictions staff and fellow exonerees had become her friends. In Indiana, Kristine didn't know any other exonerees; there weren't many in the state—fewer than twenty—and with such a small network and little attention paid to them, Indiana lacked laws and policies to compensate exonerees or provide any aftercare. But in Illinois, with seminal innocence projects advocating on behalf of the wrongly convicted, Cook County led the nation in exonerations.

In downtown Chicago, Kristine could easily stop by the Center at the law school, right off the ever-glistening Lake Michigan. There, Jane Raley would greet Kristine enthusiastically when she visited. "You have sandals on!" Jane said, noticing Kristine's uncommon footwear one day.

"I know, and I totally have a blister on my toe!"

"Where have you been?"

"Up Michigan Avenue and all the way back down," Kristine answered her. "I went into every single store. I almost bought these sunglasses at Burberry. They were on sale. But I didn't think $175 was a good enough sale price," she joked.

"You're crazy!" Jane laughed.

Kristine smiled. She loved the city. "It's fabulous."

She dreamed of going to law school in Chicago and helping other wrongly convicted people. As she studied for the LSAT, having taken it once before, in prison, she saved up for the move by working at a Speedway gas station near her brother's house in Indiana. It was her first full-time paycheck since being released, and her boss quickly boosted her weekly hours from twenty-six to forty. Remarkably, her background check came back clear, or so she was told, but she didn't work up the courage to share her real story with the manager for another few months.

Between long hours of cooking food, stocking coolers, and pulling trash, Kristine found a romantic interest, or at least a physical relationship, with a sweet, younger guy. He was in his twenties, and her brother Michael took to calling him "the toddler," but Kristine didn't care about his age or Michael's objections. Something simple and unattached was all she wanted. It was all she could handle.

Living so close to the gas station, Kristine was called in often to cover other shifts. One of the Speedway managers soon realized how hard Kristine worked and how much she knew about running a place. She asked her about becoming part of the management team, a shift leader. Yes, Kristine said, but at one of the Illinois locations. They prepared for her transfer to the Chicago area.

With school back in session in the fall of 2013, an increasingly unmotivated Trent reemerged. He and Kristine began to butt heads again at home. They were both stubborn, and the pressure of the impending move was fraying their already fragile relationship. A few days before the move to Chicago, Trent revealed that he had second thoughts.

"I think Nanny would really die if I didn't live with her," she remembers him telling her. He decided to stay behind. "So you are going to change your plans, right?"

Kristine knew she had to let go. No, she told him. She was going to move away with or without him.

For seventeen years, she had fought for Trent. His wide smile, jet-black curly hair, and hopeful eyes had been her motivation to break free from prison and withstand years of appeals, train for jobs, and earn her degrees, making pennies a day. But Kristine realized that at some point she had lost him. And her mom Susan could have him back.

"She always told him that I was his mom, but that he was her child. I get that," Kristine says. "I understand you fighting to keep your child."

The day before Kristine moved to Chicago, she stopped by Connersville, where she had spent her happiest childhood years. But she was there to visit Tony's grave. She never told anyone when she visited the cemetery. She always wanted to be alone with her boy.

Kristine brought a new bouquet for the grave, some purple petunias with iridescent plastic butterflies dangling from the arrangement. She set them in the granite vase affixed to the gravestone, wishing there had been a hook to hang the bright bouquet and glittery butterflies above his head, like those hundred balloons falling from the trailer ceiling on his first birthday, too many years ago.

"The butterflies would have bounced and sparkled," Kristine says. "He would have laughed about that."

X.

"It's a huge 360 to be wearing that uniform, escorting people around, doing pat searches."

In early October 2013, Kristine moved to Chicago on her fortieth birthday. For the first time in her life, she would be living in her own place. She drove Michael's old car, a 2007 bright yellow Chevy Cobalt he had given her. The Chevy still had a lot of life in it, and it was already paid off. Her sister-in-law, Megan, drove the U-Haul, loaded up with kitchen and bathroom stuff, an elliptical machine, a bed and matching drawers, a rocking chair, couch, big-screen TV, and DVD player—all from Michael's place. Michael drove his car as the three of them caravanned for four hours to Evanston, Illinois, where Kristine had found a place in a vintage brick apartment building, sight unseen. An old friend from an organization that helped women prisoners in Indiana had raised money for the security deposit. Accustomed to the prison system of having to return all favors, Kristine had trouble accepting the help.

Between trips to unload furniture, Kristine caught a glimpse of the laundry room in her building. "Are you fucking kidding me?" she yelled at the Coinmach washers and dryers. The coin-operated machines were just like the ones in prison. "I have to pay for these on the outside, too?"

As they unpacked in the new apartment, Michael started to feel uneasy. It seemed like his sister was unhappy with the place. He gave her a pep talk.

"It's not that I'm disappointed," she told him. "I absolutely like it. I like the quirks. It's just kind of hitting me that I've left everybody and everything."

Michael gave her ponytail a tug and told her everything would be okay. And if it wasn't, he would come and get her. But Michael was scared for her, too.

"I didn't know how fast I could get to her if something happens," he says. "It was like a parent moving their kid out."

When Megan and Michael left, Kristine took a deep breath and started moving the furniture around the apartment to where she wanted it, arranging and rearranging the pieces into different configurations. Afterward, she fell into bed, exhausted from moving and trying to be strong for Michael so that he didn't worry about her.

The next morning in her new place, she sat on her couch. *What the fuck did I do?* she thought. *I left everything. What am I doing?*

With a cup of coffee and a cigarette, she inched outside to her fire escape to sit and take it all in for a moment. *I'm going to do this.* Kristine willed herself to get used to the odd noises around the building or the way the light came in through the windows in the morning. In the quiet of each new day, her daily cup of coffee on the fire escape became a ritual for her, a reminder that she was alone, but free, in this world.

Kristine hadn't been in the Chicago area for much more than a week when she found out her position at Speedway was gone. Her manager had signed off on her transfer and guaranteed her forty hours a week as a shift leader. But by the time Kristine moved to Evanston, the position was filled by someone else.

To make ends meet, she started working temporary jobs at Northwestern across different departments. She did anything that was needed, such as administrative assistance or moving and organizing items from the Social Sciences building. She heard that if she networked enough, she might be able to land a permanent job on campus. Faced with her mounting financial responsibilities, she mentally set aside law school plans.

A lead for a job at Rivers Casino in Des Plaines, Illinois, came from the Center on Wrongful Convictions. The lawyer for the casino had studied at Northwestern and was interested in hiring an exoneree. Kristine interviewed and was offered the job—on the casino's security team. Her skills from prison, watching people and seeing how they try to work you over, could be put to use. Before she started, Kristine was fingerprinted, drug-tested, fitted for a uniform, and interviewed by an officer for the gaming commission, who tried to school her on the huge money and security risks at play. She was upfront about her wrongful conviction, but the officer continued to probe.

"Is there anything in your past you need to disclose?

"No."

"We will find it."

Kristine left the interview composed but soon gave way to crying and shaking. A lady she had met in the process squeezed her shoulder. "They didn't just do it to you," she assured her. "Everybody goes through that. It's not just you."

It took a few weeks before the casino brought her in to start. On her first day, Kristine showed up to the back employee entrance. They handed her a badge, and she signed for a lock. At the carousel, she swiped her badge, found her uniform, and changed into it in the ladies' room. After a debriefing, she was paired with another officer for orientation and training. Her regular shift would be 10 p.m. until 6 a.m.

She learned how the security cameras worked, how transporting money and signing receipts worked. Much of her time was making sure drunk people left the casino safely and calming people down before situations escalated.

Another job responsibility, which ate away at her each of the four times she was called to do it, was overseeing the counting and transporting of cash. It began next to the cashier in a private room. Employees wearing jumpsuits would carry money from one place to another. She would have to shake everything out to make sure no one was stealing, just short of a full pat-down. *I'm a piece of shit,* she thought. *Just like those officers who used to do it to me. It's horrible.* When she got a call on her radio to assist with the cash count removal, sometimes she would ignore it.

Working the overnight shift, she had her days free, and she kept interviewing at Northwestern. Finally, a gig as an administrative assistant opened up at the university's Alice Millar Chapel, a stained-glass-and-stone religious center. She wanted the job. It seemed like a peaceful alternative to conducting pat-downs and hauling off drunk gamblers. After interviewing with the chaplains and organist, Kristine took the job offered to her.

With her new university job in Evanston, Kristine could walk to work. She had healthcare. Dental benefits. She had vacation days and personal days, but struggled to take them for her own leisure. Her counselor, Heidi, encouraged her to set work aside and enjoy herself, moving past the prison mindset.

She visited her family in Indiana often, though the power struggle with her mother and Trent had not improved. He had quit school during his senior year. With each visit, Kristine saw Trent's habits, and Susan's inability to control them, growing worse. Her relationship with Michael, however, deepened as they continued to make up for lost time.

On her downtime, Kristine participated in different speaking engagements and panels when asked by the Center on Wrongful Convictions. She never needed to prepare; she knew her story.

"The *State versus Bunch* isn't just a case," said a lawyer introducing her to a room full of students familiar with the Indiana Supreme Court decision. "It's about a real person. She's right over there."

As Kristine spoke, the assembly fell quiet. She navigated through her life's narrative and its painful twists, eliciting tears from most everyone in the room. Afterward, she was exhausted. When she returned home, she slept for fourteen hours straight.

On a warm Friday in July 2014, Kristine took the day off work, a floating personal holiday. She made her way up to the Chicago campus to cheer on the Center's softball team for their afternoon game. Exonerees, law students, and staff faced off against another school's law program at a baseball diamond steps from the building. Juan, the exoneree she had become friends with, was playing, although he had smashed his finger on some pipes at work.

Little kids and leaping dogs played in view of the game. A dog resembling a malamute sauntered by on the pavement past Kristine. "She has a lot more hair," she remarked, moving to the shade, debating whether the hound was a mix or not. Maybe it was part chow. "Chows look like little lions like that."

In prison, Kristine had trained service dogs, teaching them to open doors and get up on hospital beds for young children. She loved animals. At first, it was always hard to part with the puppies that she had trained for two years before graduating them as young dogs.

Kristine's love of canines had enticed her to attend the Catholic Bible study in prison even though she wasn't Catholic, because the church volunteers brought in dogs. She would sit on the floor and play with the dogs, snuggling them as she listened to a priest named Father Larry. Kristine worried that once Father Larry discovered her real intent, she would be asked to leave. *For sure it'd be over*, she thought, and she grew sad that she wouldn't get to see the dogs anymore.

When the truth finally came out, Father Larry gave Kristine a hug and said, "You don't have to leave. You're home here."

The priest's kindness changed something in Kristine. *That's the kind of person I want to be*, she thought. Having been raised in a smattering of Christian churches, Kristine decided to start attending all of Father Larry's services. She went to mass, took classes, and was confirmed. She picked "Elizabeth" as her confirmation name.

But outside of prison, religion seemed to make less sense to her than it had inside. "The church takes a firm stance on things I don't agree with," she says. "I believe in God, and I try to do the right things." On the other side of the prison bars, Kristine sometimes attended church. "I haven't found a faith community that I feel good in completely," she says.

Up to bat in the softball game was a Chicago man and client of the Center, Johnnie Lee Savory, who had long been awaiting a pardon for a

1977 double murder. He was fourteen years old at the time of the crime, for which he remained behind bars for twenty-nine years before being paroled in 2006. After his release, DNA tests cleared him, and as one of former Illinois governor Pat Quinn's last acts in office, he pardoned Savory in January 2015.

"C'mon, Johnnie! Home run!" Kristine cheered as Savory stepped up. "All right, all right—home run, babe!"

As the game wore on, Kristine talked to Juan. "What's happening out there?" she asked. "I feel like they're whooping us. Who are these people?"

Juan hung around with Kristine, waiting for his turn, and they reminisced about go-cart racing in Skokie, Illinois, near Evanston. "This fool! First place, every single time," Kristine laughed. "Zoom! Zoom! Zoom!"

"Oh, hell yeah," Juan said, feigning nonchalance.

Earlier in the year, Juan had called to check on Kristine when he saw on the news that an Evanston restaurant kitchen fire had wiped out a string of businesses a few hundred feet from her apartment building. Kristine discovered the sirens and smoke as she came bouncing down the street to move her car in the morning. She froze at the sight and the smell.

"I was there all over again," she says of the horror. Somehow she made it back up to her apartment and fell apart, rocking herself and crying in bed.

Juan called her. "Babe, are you OK?"

"Yeah."

"Have you been outside?"

"Yeah."

"Do you need to talk about this?"

"No," she said, hanging up the phone.

Juan came over and knocked on her door. He had once lived in the building and knew how to get in. "Babe? Let me in?"

She opened the door to her friend, and he hugged her. She lay back down and told him she needed to rest.

"But if you need me, you'll call?" he asked.

"I'll call."

She stayed in bed the rest of the day and the following day until noon. Juan moved her car so that she wouldn't have to keep parking it outside amid the smell of smoke.

XI.

"When she got me out, it didn't end there. She continued to be there to offer friendship, support, advice. I catch myself now in the middle of the day wanting to talk to her."

Her friend and former attorney, Jane Raley, was sick. It was cancer, and she knew it was bad. Kristine, like many others, was shattered.

One summer Jane had invited her and exoneree Jacques Rivera to her home for the Ravinia Music Festival in town. Kristine had sat alongside Jane whenever she asked, speaking on panels about wrongful convictions of women. When Kristine dialed the area code "847" on her cell phone, Jane's number popped up as a favorite. Jane was her confidante. They could talk about parenthood. When Trent dropped out of school, she talked to Jane about playing the bad cop while her mom was the good cop: "She had babied him into nothingness."

It seemed like no one could listen quite like Jane. Or smile quite as widely and sincerely. When Kristine shared with her that she planned to try for a baby through fertility treatment, Jane both smiled and listened from a hospital bed, with her own children nearby.

Trying for a baby wasn't a decision Kristine had taken lightly. Parenthood, for her, had been difficult and tragic. After living on her own for a year, though, she knew her heart and its silent desires.

She spent Thanksgiving 2014 alone, turning down many kind offers and even family dinner invitations. After so many years behind bars, to Kristine, the holiday had lost its significance. In prison, Thanksgiving had become just another day of missing out on family memories. "I haven't celebrated it in so long," Kristine says. "It feels like another mask I have to put on."

In the solitude of her apartment, she ate some turkey she'd ordered and watched her favorite holiday classic, *It's a Wonderful Life*.

As the young love of George Bailey and Mary unfolded on her TV screen, Kristine felt as though she, like Mary, wanted the moon. She wanted her own child and the opportunity to raise it. But the chance wasn't going to come to her. If she wanted the moon, she would have to tie a lasso around it and give it to herself.

Kristine met with a doctor and a fertility counselor. Freezing her eggs at this point, at forty-one, she learned, wasn't a good option. Instead, artificial insemination would be the best route. Narrowing down the sperm donor list, Kristine asked her doctor to help her pick between the remaining candidates. She liked one guy because he was raised by a single mother. *Maybe him*, she thought.

The doctors made no promises, except that they wouldn't move forward if they didn't think she could get pregnant. X-rays confirmed everything looked good. Kristine signed up for three vials.

When the fertility counselor advised that twins or multiples were a possibility, Kristine was undeterred. "You won't hear me complain," she said, tears in her eyes. "That'd be such a blessing."

They would shoot for January, with a follow-up appointment before the holidays. Kristine shared her plans with her mom. Susan was encouraging and gracious. She remembered feeling the tug for more children when she was Kristine's age, but for her it had been too late.

"You were always a good mom," Susan said.

"You'll have to clean up your house if we're going to visit."

"Maybe we'll just come over to your place," she joked.

Trent's reaction was mixed. At first, he remarked that he always wanted a little brother or sister. But later he said that he wanted to be an only child.

"Actually, you were never an only child," Kristine reminded him.

As the mother to a now adult Trent, Kristine still had no power over his decisions. He continued to loaf around his Nanny's house, sleeping in and smoking, playing—and beating—video games into the night.

Jane died on Christmas Day. Over the coming months, Kristine would instinctively dial "847" into her phone. She wished she could ask Jane what she should do.

The first round of insemination didn't work. She got her period a few days later. Still, the doctors remained optimistic. Kristine was crestfallen. "You're just heartbroken," she says. "They steal a little something from me every day even though I'm still out."

She decided to take a break from fertility treatment so that she and Megan, newly (though amicably) divorced from Michael, could travel to Mardi Gras in New Orleans. Kristine was ready for a party, but as she discovered on the streets of the Latin Quarter, big crowds made her uneasy. Megan grabbed ahold of her and pulled her through the swarms of people. *I can't see everyone*, she thought. *I can't see what everyone is doing.*

Megan and Kristine had brunch, feasted on beignets, and toured the swamps and cemeteries, as well as the vodou attractions. Three days into the trip, the pair decided to see a tarot card reader.

It had been three decades since she'd had a card reading. In Connersville, she'd gone once with her mother. "I remember her telling me that I was going to have a lot of pain in my life," she says. At the time, she thought the tarot card reader was referring to her parents' divorce. That was the only pain she had experienced in her twelve years.

Megan went in first. Her session lasted about thirty minutes. When she came out to the waiting area, she was flustered—and Megan didn't fluster much.

Kristine entered the room and the reader shuffled the cards. The woman had reddish-brown hair pulled back in a bun. She wore leggings and a skirt. "She kind of reminded you of a gypsy," Kristine says.

The tarot card reader spoke of the blackness in Kristine's life that she carried around like luggage. She saw a lawsuit in the works. When they make an offer, she advised, don't take it. A bigger offer is coming.

"You are meant to be the mother to four children," she said.

Kristine said she had Tony, who had passed. And then Trent.

With a miscarriage in between, the reader said. "You'll have one more."

Kristine was in shock. As she moved to leave, the reader asked about the black spot in her life. Only then did Kristine tell her what had happened. The reader handed her a business card and asked to keep in touch.

After the reading, Megan and Kristine commiserated over "grown-up people's milk"—bourbon milkshakes, with two big straws.

In April 2015, at a law office in Lafayette, Indiana, Kristine sat with her attorneys, Jan Susler and John Stainthorp, for a few hours at a conference room table. Earlier that morning, bundled in a turtleneck and leather jacket, Kristine had gone in for an insemination at Northwestern Memorial Hospital, then she drove across state lines for a deposition in her civil lawsuit.

As in most depositions, Kristine was asked the same question over and over again. She crumbled into tears several times. The painful memories mingled with the fertility hormones. The pressure to become pregnant was mounting.

At one point, her fertility treatment plans entered the discussion. Kristine said she had lost the chance to raise a family.

"What about adoption?" someone on the other side of the table asked her.

With her name plastered across the Internet, including on the site *Murderpedia: The Encyclopedia of Murderers*, she didn't feel she had a good chance at adopting.

Kristine mentioned she was trying to become pregnant. The interviewer was surprised, telling her he didn't know she was dating.

Irritated, she corrected him: "I'm not. I went with an anonymous donor."

Afterward, she drove home alone. The lawyers went out to eat, but she wasn't hungry. On the road, she felt more free: "You can point anywhere and go."

For a couple of hours, she didn't answer Juan's texts and calls. He wanted to see how the deposition went, how she was doing.

"You can either come over here, or I'm coming to you," he told her.

When the April pregnancy test didn't register positive, Kristine was crestfallen. She only needed one egg, one good egg, and it could happen, she told herself. A friend offered to help pay for another round. Determined and humbled, Kristine picked up the check at her friend's house.

XII.

"Nobody had to make a call for me and explain my situation. I did this all by myself. On my own."

In June, Kristine decided to move to a new place across town. When she first started looking months earlier, she had envisioned a bigger space with room for a baby and maybe a dog (to be sure, a little hypoallergenic poodle mix). By the time she had found the ideal place—a garden apartment in Chicago's Rogers Park neighborhood, a bit beyond her budget—she sprang for the two-bedroom spot, even if she would be the only occupant. She fell in love with the hardwood floors, Jacuzzi and glass sink in the bathroom, and, best of all, an ice maker-dispenser on the refrigerator that could produce crushed or cubed ice.

What she loved most about the new place was that she had applied for it without anybody's help, and she got it on her own references and credit history. It had touched her, the many ways a few generous friends and her brother, Michael, had helped her since her release from prison. A friend from the Women's Fund of Central Indiana, a progressive prison organization, had helped her find dental services. This was no small thing, as Kristine had lacked proper care in prison and had seven teeth pulled while she was behind bars. Once released, she needed a bridge, and she accepted the financial help. But landing her own apartment without anyone running interference for her made Kristine realize how far she had come.

The night before her move, she couldn't sleep. By 4:30 a.m., she was out of bed, out on her apartment fire escape, savoring the sweet refuge of a final cup of coffee.

It was pouring rain when Juan arrived with his brother Miguel and friends Ike, Brian, and Angel to help her load up a seventeen-foot moving truck. She had promised to pay them in Heineken and Coors Light. The liquor store around the corner was closed, so she hiked over to the grocery store for the booze.

Juan disassembled a piece of furniture that he had put together at the first apartment—a giant armoire that she used to stash wine and mixers. She had acquired a few other pieces of furniture, including a café bistro table and chairs purchased from Ace Hardware over the Fourth of July the previous year. Michael helped her assemble it while he was in town. He had come to visit because he knew those few days around the anniversary of Tony's death were especially hard on her. He knew she had nightmares.

Within hours of unloading into her new apartment, Kristine had most of the place set up. Dried flowers in vases. A TV above the fireplace.

A jewel-toned patterned rug across the floor. Her rocking chair set up next to a lamp and bookshelf. A framed picture of Trent.

She needed her showerheads replaced, and she knew she would have no trouble getting them fixed. "He said to give you whatever you want," the repairman said.

Kristine's bearded property manager and building owner had taken a fancy to her during the leasing process. They got to talking in his office, and later, he showed her his warehouse building. To her surprise, he had quite the underground BDSM operation. Nevertheless, she wanted some company, so she agreed to dinner at a casual Evanston restaurant.

"I'm a dom," he told her.

Kristine laughed it off—and ultimately passed on the invitation. "After seventeen years in prison, there's not much I haven't tried. But I'm not going to be under anybody's thumb."

In recent months, her romantic exploits had fizzled. One less-than-astute guy she was seeing, who knew little about her, had finally remarked, "You're down at the law school at lot."

She went ahead and told him she was an exoneree. He offered a flip response of "That's cool," so she kicked him out.

There was too much going on to be romantically involved with anyone. Ovarian cysts had delayed her next round of insemination and fertility shots until June. Then, that try was unsuccessful. When the cysts came back in July, the doctor said she needed to rest before trying again. Kristine agreed, and they settled on doing one final round at the end of the month. "Then, yea or nay, I'm stopping," she said.

With law school deferred due to her fear of debt, she filled her time by convening with "her people"—her buddy Juan and the Northwestern community, Donna, Michael, and Megan. She kept up weekly phone calls with Rhonda, though supporting Rhonda emotionally while trying to hang on herself was proving an exhausting challenge.

"Aunt Krissy, are you coming to my birthday party?" asked Mara Jade, Donna's daughter.

"Of course I am," Kristine answered over the phone.

"Are you staying the night?"

"No, I think I'll just come to the party and leave," Kristine jested.

"Are you for real?" Mara Jade asked with a little attitude.

Kristine told her she would stay the night, of course, but she might be getting in too late that Friday night. Mara Jade would already be in bed.

"Maybe you should tell my mom to let me stay up."

Kristine made the three-and-a-half hour drive to Fort Wayne, Indiana, for Mara Jade's eleventh birthday party. Donna lamented that it would likely be the last kids' party of its kind, as her daughter had already requested a more grown-up slumber party the following year. Still, Donna set up a kiddie pool, yard games, balloons, a ring-toss game using two-liter bottles of soda (with more Strawberry Sunkist for drinking), a jumping castle, and a dunking machine in her brother-in-law's backyard. They were expecting ten or so kids at the party. "It keeps growing, but that's all right," Donna said.

Speakers, a mixing board, and laptop were set up on a folding table in the back yard, playing rap music. Her husband, John, who was still driving the Citilink bus where they had met, moonlighted as a DJ as well, going by "DJ Citi." The hobby had paid for the kids' new bikes the previous year.

Kristine had taken Donna's younger daughter Leia to get her hair done. Leia was having a meltdown, jealous over her sister's party, feelings that Kristine quelled: "It's OK. We'll do her hair." The next day, she had promised Mara Jade a pedicure.

Kristine and Donna had visited numerous times and exchanged even more phone calls over the nearly three years since her release in 2012. Donna would ring her up whenever drama hit her marriage. "Babe, you need to tone it down," Kristine would remind her.

When an electrical fire had claimed most of Donna's home and all her possessions earlier in the year, she had lost her sense of security—"It flashed me back. It flashed me back bad," Donna says. She called Kristine. She couldn't go in the burned house.

"You've got to put your big girl panties on," Kristine told her. "You've got to face it. If you run from this, it will be worse."

Donna went inside.

Kristine arrived at the birthday party with Leia and her new French braid in tow, as Donna was testing the water on the dunking machine. "It got warm earlier," Donna said. "I'm going in first." Her daughter pledged to dunk her.

Donna greeted Kristine with a side hug.

"Hi, baby doll," Kristine said. "We had such a good time. We took selfies."

The other kids piled into the jumping castle. Then, a shriek: "Krissy!" Leia ran to her and pointed to a bandage on her skinned knee that was starting to peel off. "I fell yesterday on my bike."

Kristine found three bandages. "Poor little baby. You've had a rough time riding those bikes," she said. "Two might actually do it. Here, you open that up. Here, let me hold on to that third one."

Donna and Kristine chatted and managed the yard of kids.

"At Walmart, they have camisole tops for $1.68 apiece," Kristine said.

"Are you serious? So you got me two of them, right?"

"We gotta go back."

After a full-blown water balloon fight among the children, Donna eyed the dunking machine. "You ready, John?" she asked her husband, as she climbed up to the seat. "Hold out—let me situate it."

Mara Jade prepared to throw. She tossed the ball at the big red button, but John pushed it before the ball could hit. Donna went under. "John!" she said between splashes. In seconds, Donna got back up on the seat. Mara hit the button immediately as Kristine used her cell phone to shoot video of the event, swaying from side to side to get better angles.

Donna wiped the water away from her face, returning to the seat again and again, giving all the kids a try. "I'm glad you all are enjoying this!" Donna laughed. "This is *fun*?"

"When do I get to throw?" Kristine hollered at Donna.

"You'd never want to throw. You love me!"

"I do love you, but I want a try!"

"All right, are you doing a throw?"

Kristine grabbed a softball and waited for the kids to clear from the path. "C'mon—out of the way!"

. Finally, she walked over the machine, and instead of hitting the button, helped Donna climb out. Donna, soaked through, hugged Kristine, dampening her T-shirt.

Kristine laughed, "Oh, that was necessary?"

XIII.

"It's not that I'm grieving that I'm never going to have a child. It's that I'm grieving I'm never going to have my *child. That's never going to happen. I've got three opportunities here that I never got to have."*

Her last round of fertility treatments failed in late July 2015. Kristine was crushed, again. The doctor tried to comfort her. She told her it wouldn't be unheard of to meet someone, get married, and, six months later, find herself pregnant. Or she could always look into donor eggs. That was also an option.

"I don't have the funds to buy donor eggs," Kristine said. She had already put law school on the back burner, not wanting to have to crawl out of debt. Her civil lawsuit lingered on[6]—suing the federal government can take years and years—and she couldn't count on any compensation. She could end up with nothing at all.

The tension with Trent was unavailing. They had argued about money over the summer, exchanging bitter words.

"I don't owe you anything," she said to her nearly twenty-year-old son.

"See, this is why I don't respect you."

"You don't respect anybody. You don't respect your Nanny. Look at how you're living."

As an escape, Kristine made plans to visit Las Vegas with Megan over spring break. She joked with her brother that she might end up drunk and hitched in Sin City: "Maybe I will find Prince Charming and think he's everything and get married and have a little baby."

---

6. One factor contributing to the delays in Kristine's lawsuit is whether Kinard can or should be considered an actor of the federal government. He is deceased and thus cannot shed light on the issue of his falsified report.

After a stretch away from Indiana, over Labor Day weekend Kristine made a quick trip to visit her mom and Trent, who had moved in with Kristine's grandmother. She couldn't tolerate their house very long, not with Trent getting up in the late afternoon. Kristine stayed at Michael's place.

And she had other plans that weekend.

A bit on edge, Kristine drove to a McDonald's in Crawfordsville, Indiana. She got out of her yellow Chevy. Standing before her was Rhonda. Her fifteen-year sentence, seven and a half years to serve, had finally come to an end. She was forty-five years old.

Very skinny now, practically gaunt, Rhonda smiled. Her short, buzzed hair was dyed "purple," but looked apple red. She wore regular clothes again—a pair of jeans, a white tank top, and a matching cross necklace Kristine had bought for them after her release in 2012. Michael and Megan had helped her find the necklaces online.

Kristine hugged Rhonda and kissed her on the cheek. Rhonda was shaking. "You know I can't believe it!" she whispered. "It's crazy, and it feels so real!"

They decided to eat at the Pizza Hut buffet instead of McDonald's. Rhonda's mom accompanied them for lunch, then left them alone. In the restaurant parking lot, they caught up, even though their weekly collect calls had kept them mostly up to date about each other's lives. After a while, Rhonda asked if they could have a relationship on the outside.

Kristine had been waiting for the question. "I don't have anything to give," she told her. "It takes all my energy to take care of me, let alone take care of you. I'm not the same person I was in there."

In the silence, Rhonda asked, "We are going to stay friends? You are always going to be there?"

"Absolutely I'm going to be there."

Over the weekend, Kristine helped Rhonda set up a Facebook account. She took a profile photo of her using her cell phone, as Rhonda didn't have her own phone yet. They went out to Outback Steakhouse for a big meal. Rhonda was going to ask for a half-order of rib tips. With some prodding from Kristine, she ordered the whole thing.

Kristine dropped Rhonda off in Waveland, Indiana, at her mother's house. Saying goodbye was hard. "I didn't want to leave her there just because I feel they aren't going to take care of her," she says. "I know I can't take care of her the way I took care of her in there."

On the drive back home, Kristine could feel the inked etching on her right outer thigh: a new tattoo. It was just the outline—Trinity would fill in the color later.

Kristine had found an image on Facebook of Jack Skellington, the protagonist of the 1993 film *The Nightmare Before Christmas*, her brother's favorite movie. The picture showed Jack with his soulmate, a rag doll named Sally.

"In the movie, Sally keeps falling apart and Jack keeps putting her back together," Kristine explains. Stitched together by life chapters more painful than joyous, Kristine felt increasingly unraveled in her new world. She longed for order and stability, for something familiar. For seventeen years, life in prison, with its casual cruelties and controlled chaos, had choked off her life outside prison like a deep weed. Uprooted and still struggling to survive, Kristine wanted someone like Jack to patch her heart back together: "I'm waiting for someone to come along and sew one in for me."

A week later, in a bar back in Chicago, Kristine was drinking a sugary cocktail in a bar when that old Bon Jovi ballad came on.

She sang along, as she had long before, but not at the top of her lungs. Not like it was with Tony. Never like it was with Tony.

This time, she stared at the ceiling and mouthed the words, with barely a sound: "And I know when I die, you'll be on my mind. And I'll love you—always."

PART TWO

JACQUES

Convicted in 1990
Exonerated in 2011

Courtesy WBEZ/Andrew Gill

69

I.

"I put my head down for a minute, and when I looked up, my kids were running at me. So, that was a very special moment to see my kids there."

Jacques Rivera slid a butcher's knife under his pillow.

The forty-six-year-old man was tucked away in a second-floor apartment bedroom at his sister's bungalow on the northwest side of Chicago. He couldn't fall asleep. The hours crept past midnight.

The previous day, October 4, 2011, had been a remarkable Tuesday. He had finally gained his freedom, 7,841 days after being convicted of first-degree murder. He had been a few weeks shy of his twenty-fifth birthday when he was sent to "Hotel Hell"—Stateville Correctional Center, a maximum-security prison in Joliet, Illinois, just southwest of the Chicago metro area. For more than twenty years, that was his home. A thirty-three-foot wall, his picket fence.

On the Tuesday morning in 2011, Jacques's family and friends occupied the rows on both sides of the courtroom. From the state's side of the room, they could get a better look at him, or so they had learned during the hearings leading up to this one. In the third row, Jacques's three children sat together. Near them, Jacques's older sister, Jeanette, was breathing heavily, praying next to her mother, Gwendolyn. In recent weeks, the two women had shared dreams that Jacques's release would be imminent. In the dream, he would tell them: *It'll come. It'll come. Wait. Wait. Wait.*

"All rise," the bailiff ordered.

Cook County Judge Neera Walsh began the hearing with a stern warning: "I know I don't have to remind anybody in the courtroom that there will be no outbursts of any kind, regardless of what happens today, right?"

Jacques's supporters looked at each other, trying to decode the judge's words. *Did this mean he was going to be freed? Or would he be sent back to Stateville for the rest of his eighty-year sentence?*

"Okay. And if anybody does have a cell phone, they need to turn it off. Not on silent, not on vibrate, but off. And if you don't, there will be consequences, okay?" Walsh instructed.

The state proceeded. "Motion State *nolle*."

"It would be a motion State *nolle prose*," the judge repeated.

Jacques had never heard this legal term. *Nolle pros* or *prose*, short for *nolle prosequi*, is Latin for "We shall no longer prosecute."

The moment fell like dust in a split-second, one of Jacques's sons describes.

"Mr. Rivera, you are released. Good luck to you, sir," Walsh said.

The crowd gasped, trying not to make too much noise. Managing the shock, Jacques shook his head. He didn't want to move around too much, fearing the bailiff would think he was going to run.

Jacques was free, yes—but not quite. There was, of course, paperwork to be done, and he would need to be processed out of the jail where he had been waiting for his new trial on appeal.

Unable to stifle their excitement any longer—like children about to explode into laughter in the middle of church—Jacques's family and supporters burst through the courtroom doors and began to scream, cheer, and hug one another in the lofty hallway. They took out the cell phones they weren't supposed to have in the building and started calling and texting, spreading the news.

Jeanette, who had complied with the no-cell policy, hustled outside to her parked car, where she opened the glove compartment and grabbed her brother-in-law's phone to call her daughter and husband.

"He's free," she said.

Inside the jail, correctional officers escorted Jacques about, buffering his every move. Should he trip and fall or become injured, the Department of Corrections could be held liable.

Jacques had no property. The staff found some jeans and a T-shirt that would fit him. The outtake process lingered for hours. They wanted to be sure, Jacques thought.

In the waiting room at the sheriff's office, his attorneys, Jane Raley and Judy Royal, were waiting for him. Jacques started to weep when he saw their beaming faces. Jane, who was also juggling Kristine Bunch's case, had taken an interest in Jacques's more than a decade earlier.

Jane handed Jacques a Chicago Bears sports jacket, a gift from one of his sons, who was waiting outside.

A correctional officer asked if they were ready. As they headed toward the door, Jacques started hyperventilating. He stooped to catch his breath. "It's okay," the officer calmed him, patiently. "If you want to go back, we can wait."

"I've waited twenty-one years," Jacques told him. "I'm never going to go back. I'm moving forward." With his head slightly down, clasping his mouth to contain the nausea, Jacques walked through gates and chilly air, flanked by his two pillars—Jane and Judy.

A shaky, fourteen-second cell phone video captured the moment at dusk when, amid a cheering and whistling crowd, TV news cameras, and bright lights, Jacques looked up and saw the world before him. Greeting him first, three of his four children—Jacques Jr., who was almost twenty-nine; Richard, twenty-seven; and Jennifer, twenty-three—ran to him, defying orders from officers who had advised the crowd to stand back. As they ran, arms extended, they reached for their sobbing father. *Can't nobody stop us now*, Jacques Jr. remembers thinking. His third son, Joshua, was not there for the reunion.

After breaking free from a string of embraces, Jacques stopped to pose for a picture with his children. Their stance mirrored a Polaroid photo taken of them during a prison visit shortly after his 1990 conviction. In that family snapshot, Jacques held his baby girl Jennifer in his arms, with his younger son Richard to his left, and Jacques Jr., the oldest, to his right. Not pictured: his son Joshua.

"Real strange how that was, you know?" Jacques says of the two photos, which now hang juxtaposed in his bedroom.

News cameras clicked and flickered as Jacques hugged his sobbing mother, her cries ambient in the TV footage. "I was afraid somebody was going to pinch me and say you're dreamin'," Gwendolyn Rivera told reporters as her son draped his arms over her shoulders, as if to stabilize her or soak up her pain. "But"—his mother gasped for breath between tears—"It's a dream come true."

Six microphones with news flags appeared before Jacques. His supporters hovered behind him. Friends toted poster boards featuring fuzzy mug shots of a younger Jacques, in his early twenties. Now his face appeared gray, bearded, exhausted.

"The City of Chicago needs to know the truth. I didn't kill that young man," Jacques shouted over the microphones, his voice brimming with an angry sadness. "And that's the bottom line."

The cameras turned to Jane, and she offered some of the protracted backstory of appealing the case. "I thought, *My goodness! This person should not have been convicted in the first place*," she told the reporters. "And then it took us ten years to find the eyewitness."

Reporters asked Jacques about the eyewitness, a young boy who testified against him at his original trial for the gang killing of a neighborhood teen. The witness, now a man in his thirties living in a different state, had come forward to say it was all one huge, haunting lie.

"I love Orlando Lopez," Jacques said. "It wasn't his fault. He was a twelve-year-old boy. He was misguided. He was manipulated."

Throughout the press conference, Jacques also collected laughs from the crowd, frequently praising his lawyers. "America had a 1996 Olympic dream team. This is my dream team!" he said.

Jane beamed her wide, effusive smile that could delicately stretch over her face in a split second and then vanish into seriousness.

The news photographers followed Jacques as he piled into a car with his kids and ex-wife, Sophia. He hadn't seen or talked to her much since their marriage in prison in the early nineties and subsequent divorce a year later, during his incarceration. But with a fumbling, awkward grace and some small talk, they cut through their ambiguous past, checking the rearview mirror as TV news trucks followed their caravan of cars.

Waiting back at home, Jacques's sister Jeanette ran barefoot from her house to the corner so she could see the makeshift motorcade driving toward her sister's place.

"He was like the president," Jeanette remembers. "He was like an important person."

The honking and wailing of the caravan crescendoed with the approach. Jeanette ran three houses down to fetch her shoes, scuttling back a third time to wait for her brother on the sidewalk. Emerging from his son's car, Jacques embraced his sister.

"Oh my god, I can't believe it," she said. "You're free. You're here."

Overwhelmed, Jacques choked out the words: "Yep, sis. Yep, sis."

Neighbors started popping out of their houses, as though a movie were being shot. An unusual sight, tripods and lights were splayed on the block.

Inside the house, pizza had been delivered. Jacques took only a bite or two, to be polite. He was sweating, and his stomach was cramping into nervous knots as the house packed with people, snapping photos with their smartphones, LED lights ablaze.

They handed him various mobile devices to say hello to old friends. *You sure you don't want a steak or something?*

"You could tell in his face," his son Jacques Jr. recalls. "He was like, *What am I experiencing?*"

A news crew knocked on the door. "Nah, tell 'em to leave me alone," Jacques said.

Back in the family kitchen, Jeanette gave her brother some advice. For starters, he'd need an ID card. She told him to make sure to keep all his receipts this time around. Hanging on to receipts had become a longstanding family joke. *What's your alibi? Where you at? What are you doing? Got your receipts?*

Then, Jeanette became very serious. "Don't hang around the old block," she told him. "Watch your shoulder. Watch your back." They had lost him once. They didn't want to lose him again.

"I know, I know," Jacques assured her. "I'm a grown man. I can take care of myself."

A look of concern spread across Jeanette's face. "Yeah, but this is the real world. It's like you've been sleeping under a rock and all of a sudden you've come back to life."

His family didn't want to leave him, but they planned to reconvene for breakfast the following morning. For the time being, Jacques would live with his mother in his sister Rose's loft apartment.

It was time for bed. Rose studied her brother. "To be perfectly honest, he looked homeless," she observed. "He looked frightened, scared. He was out of his element."

They headed up to the small, confined space through the separate double entrance. "Are you going to put bars on the windows?" Jacques asked her. "You know, people can get in these windows here. Are you going to get an alarm system?"

"Jacques, no one is going to get in here. You are safe here," Rose told him.

Jacques locked the inside door to the double entrance, even though it was made of glass. He figured he would at least hear the shattering noise if someone broke in. Meanwhile, two Chihuahuas, Tigger and Roo, would be on guard as well, yapping if anyone approached the door.

Unable to fall asleep, Jacques pondered finding something to protect himself. He retrieved an instrument, a kitchen butcher knife and, blade in hand, promptly returned to bed.

II.

"The gangs would drive on kids like me. You know, they knew my father had passed away. We lived in the neighborhood. My mom didn't have money. . . . They latched on to me. 'We'll take care of you. We'll be your family.'"

Jacques grew up on the West Side of Chicago, in Humboldt Park. In the 1960s and '70s, the neighborhood was the heart of the city's Puerto Rican community, before it thinned out. Jacques's father, Reinaldo, worked as a car mechanic out of the garage of their family home on Beach Street. Jacques's mother, Gwendolyn, who came from Kentucky, worked at the discount department store Ventures to support their children—five girls (one of whom died) and two boys. In the middle of the birth order was Jacques, whose name alludes to French heritage on his father's side.

The Rivera family was close-knit. The kids attended the neighborhood elementary school, James Russell Lowell, around the block from their home. As a chummy brother-sister pair, Jacques and his little sister Candida loved the variety show pop duo Donny and Marie Osmond. Candida had the Osmond doll figures. An early animal lover, Jacques collected stray dogs in the basement of the family home, much to the frustration of his mother. "I gave her hell as a boy," he says. "Must have had twenty of them."

Just up the street from the Rivera residence sat the sprawling, more than two-hundred-acre Humboldt Park, a hilly, green expanse with gyms, fields, playgrounds, and a lagoon where Jacques used to fish. Today, a $2 million replica of the Chicago Cubs stadium, "Little Cubs Field," stands on the edge of the park, where hundreds of kids play during the summer. Jacques played there, too, before it became a Chicago destination.

Gangs were a part of life. With young kids at home, Reinaldo let off steam by hanging around with the Latin Kings, the oldest and largest Hispanic-led gang, which was formed in Humboldt Park. Part of the "Peoples" gang alliance—as opposed to "Folks," their rival alliance—the Latin Kings originally organized around blocking Black gangs from their neighborhood. Today, the highly structured gang has spread across the United States, with tens of thousands of members, scores of factions, and chapters in about three dozen states. The Latin Kings are often described as one of the most dangerous street gangs, with a reach extending into other countries.

Jacques remembers the early days of the gang, and his father's involvement in it, as more of a political movement. "It's actually not called Latin Kings, it's called Latino Kings," Jacques corrects, likening the history of the organization to that of the Black Panthers. "It's for Jesus Christ, King of Kings." Originally, a three-point crown demarked the Puerto Rican faction, and a five-point crown signaled the Mexican faction. Honor, obedience, sacrifice, righteousness, and love are the five reigning attributes. Now, a five-point crown is used almost universally by the Latin King Nation, with the expression "Amor de Rey" or "King's Love" as the sign of allegiance.

On the Fourth of July 1978, Jacques's family life changed forever. He was thirteen years old, spending the night at a friend's house, where they had been making their own fireworks. In the middle of the night, one of Jacques's older sisters—he can't remember which one—appeared out in front of his friend's house, looking for Jacques. His friend's father awakened him. His sister said he had to come home now.

"What's the matter?" Jacques asked her.

"Dad died last night."

When Jacques went home, the news was confirmed. Unable to process what he was hearing, he turned and ran.

Jacques ran through Humboldt Park. He ran for almost half an hour. At first he thought he might go try to find his dad, wherever he was staying. Perhaps it was a mistake, he thought. The darkness around him was blotted out by the bright park lights. "I finally realized, *Where am I running to?*" he remembers, before returning home.

His mother told him his dad died of an overdose. Reinaldo was thirty-nine years old. Jacques was devastated. He had been close to his father, though he hated that his father abused his mother. "I used to jump on him to protect her," Jacques says. To his confusion, his mother would throw him out along with his dad after the fights. He remembers the words: "You're just like him."

Right after his father's death, Jacques was recruited into the Latin Kings. He made the decision after seeing some gang members bullying his sisters. With his father gone, Jacques wanted to protect his family. "I was born and raised in a Kings neighborhood," Jacques says. "So they called on us. I figured if I can't beat them, I might as well join them."

Today, he hesitates to talk about the initiation that later occurred in the mobile units of the neighborhood school, where many other kids participated in gang life. "Not really an initiation," he says. "You just have to take a body punch. You have to go thirty seconds like that. It's not like the initiation they show on TV."

On the streets, Jacques went by "Ace." The Kings' motto was, and still is, "Once a King, Always a King."

Fatherless and with a mother barely managing to keep her family afloat, Jacques acted out. "I was in pain," he says. He struggles to remember the impact of his father's death on the rest of his family. His fighting landed him in more trouble in court. "My mom told the judge that she couldn't handle me no more," he remembers.

As a young teen, he ended up being sent to a state youth prison, the now closed Illinois Youth Center Valley View, a facility north of St. Charles, Illinois, about forty miles from Chicago. Jacques describes the place as a "school for young boys," and he stayed through his third year of high school, at which point he was released. With only a year left to graduate, his mother tried to put Jacques back in high school, but Jacques says he wasn't accepted back. Jacques's mother told him the school wouldn't allow kids from the correctional system, but Chicago Public Schools lacked clear policies at the time.

At seventeen, Jacques became a father to his first son, Jacques Jr. He lived with his son's mother, Sophia, not far from where he had grown up. Fourteen months later, another boy arrived, Richard. Four years later, a little girl, Jennifer. His kids remember Jacques picking them up from school and racing them home. He would always give them a head start, only to make zooming noises when he passed them up—"Schewwww!" They went to the beach, to the park. Dad, the kids recall, was a total goofball.

But Jacques speaks of darker periods at home. "There were some bad times," he says. "I caused a lot of it. I was doing what I was taught." Jacques had watched his father abuse his mother, and Jacques also became abusive to his growing family, he says. As a young father, Jacques was still embedded in the gang life, with robbery and stolen vehicle charges on his rap sheet. For the latter, he received two years' probation. But in the eighties, the Latin Kings had become too wild for him, he thought, and it was time to clean up their act—and his. He was losing good friends to gang violence.

"I began to realize that there had to be more to life than gang fighting. Something had to be done, and I didn't have the answer. If only we had something to do, somewhere to go, something to get us off the streets!" Jacques wrote in a 2004 letter from prison.

The opportunity first came during the annual Puerto Rican Day Parade in the mid-eighties. The city and other agencies decided to pay gang members, including Jacques, to work security during the parade as a way to control their own members.

This led to more collaboration. When neighbors would come and plead with Jacques to get the guys to cut back on graffiti, they would spend a weekend morning painting over the tags. They picked up trash. Working with a grassroots group, the Puerto Rican Cultural Center, Jacques and his wife helped establish a community center, the Humboldt Park Institute, where he worked as a youth mentor. Jacques encouraged young men to leave the gang life behind and earn their GEDs. Although he maintained his own ties to the Latin Kings, his life was becoming more stable in his early twenties.

From time to time, police detectives would visit the Humboldt Park Institute, looking for suspects. They would ask questions. "They were more than free to come in," Jacques remembers. "We never stopped them."

One Gang Crimes detective, Reynaldo Guevara, would swing by, lift weights, and look around when he was working a case, Jacques remembers. As the detective would later tell the trial judge, he had known Jacques for "quite a while." Guevara, said a retired police sergeant to the *Chicago Reporter* years later, in June 2000, was "one of the best and most aggressive officers out there."

III.

"He's twelve years old! I mean, he don't know no difference. I have nothing against Orlando Lopez. Never have. Not even from the very beginning. I was kind of upset when he did point at me from the bench, you know, but I knew in my heart that somebody had put him up to doing that. I knew that, because I didn't do that crime."

On a late afternoon in August 1988, twelve-year-old Orlando Lopez had a hankering for some candy. A video game store at the corner sold snacks, so he headed down the stairs of his family's tan brick apartment building on Cortland Avenue in Humboldt Park.

As Orlando was leaving, he saw Felix, the sixteen-year-old brother of his sister's boyfriend, sitting in a parked car in the alley. Felix was waiting for his brother, Israel, to pick up Orlando's sister for a friend's wedding.

Some men pulled up in a copper-colored Chevy and stopped slightly down the street. One of them got out of the car, firing shots at Felix. The gunman was close to Felix, only a few feet away, and the shots were so low in noise that Orlando thought at first they were coming from a BB gun. Orlando saw his family friend Felix try to cover his head, then he slumped forward and slightly to the right.

Orlando ran to the store for help. Finding none, he ran back to the crime scene and hid in an alcove, a dent, by his building about twenty-five feet away from the car. From his hiding place, Orlando saw the shooter fire one last time and look around, furtively. For a moment, Orlando saw his face. He thought he recognized him as someone who played baseball at Humboldt Park. The man then hopped back in the passenger side of the car and took off, turning right on Spaulding Avenue, known at the time to be Latin Kings gang territory.

The medical examiner later counted eleven gunshot-related wounds on Felix's body—one in the back of his head, one in his shoulder, and the rest in his hands and back. Six .22-caliber lead bullets from the teen's chest cavity were inventoried.

Remarkably, when Chicago police officers visited Felix at Cook County Hospital, he was still alive. After talking to him, they went back to the station to retrieve a photo album of the Imperial Gangsters, a Folks alliance street gang, said to be feuding with the Campbell Boys and the Latin Kings at the time. (Since the 1970s, the Imperial Gangsters have battled the Latin Kings over territory.) Police reports following Felix's death state that he was a Campbell Boy, which family members have since denied. Trial testimony indicated that Felix was not in the gang, but his brothers were.

In the hospital, Felix was hooked up to tubes and receiving oxygen through his nostrils. He couldn't move his arms, but he was able to motion "yes" and "no" to questions. One of the police officers moved the gang album pages for him. He identified two men, one as the shooter and one as the driver of the getaway car.

Early the next morning, police arrested an Imperial Gangster, a man whose photo appeared in the album. In what remains a mystery, he was released soon after, without being charged with the crime. Police couldn't track down the second man Felix identified. He was never apprehended. Decades later, private investigators working on Jacques's appeal could not locate the men.

But neither suspect happened to be Jacques Rivera, who was twenty-three at the time.

The night of the shooting, investigators visited Orlando's home for an interview. According to testimony, Orlando described the gunman as wearing dark pants and a black jean jacket. More notably, he said the shooter had brown hair and a ponytail partially dyed yellow. Black and gold were well-known Latin Kings colors, so the officers showed Orlando some more albums, full of purported gang members' photographs, about four or five per page.

Orlando didn't pick anyone out of the first album. In the second book of photos, he saw Jacques's photograph. He told police Jacques resembled the shooter. But a few days later, when Orlando's mom and sister accompanied him to the police station, he viewed a lineup—alone. He did not identify Jacques, who had been brought in as a stand-in, just a filler guy, he was told.

Jacques had figured his lack of involvement in whatever the police were investigating would spare him: "I knew I didn't do nothing." But he also didn't feel he had much of a choice but to go into the station because the officer who apprehended him had opened his coat to display his gun, he says. For the moment, given Orlando's lack of ID, it seemed he was safe.

A week later, Orlando saw a man hanging around Funston Elementary School, a few blocks away from his home. In an instant, he recognized him as the gunman, as he was wearing the same black denim jacket as he was during the shooting. Orlando saw him walk up to another man, giving him an Imperial Gangsters handshake. Orlando realized his grave mistake. But he didn't know how to fix it.

Eighteen days after the shooting, Felix died. Orlando was brought in the next day to view a second lineup. Standing there again, Jacques was puzzled, becoming increasingly nervous as he learned the police were conducting the lineup for a murder case.

As he waited, Orlando told an officer with glasses and a mustache, fitting the description of Detective Reynaldo Guevara, that Jacques—whose photo he had tentatively flagged—was not the gunman. The real shooter, he told them, was an Imperial Gangster, someone he had seen in the neighborhood. Ignored, Orlando also told another woman at the police station that Jacques wasn't the right guy. He didn't know who she was, but she looked like a lawyer and had gray hair.

"Don't be afraid," he remembers the woman telling him. "We will protect you. We will keep you safe."

Orlando didn't know what else to do, whom else to convince. Under pressure in his role as the only known witness, when he viewed the second lineup, he went ahead and identified Jacques, subject number three, standing in the middle, as the shooter. The decision set in motion the state's case against Jacques, and it would haunt Orlando for decades.

Guevara made the arrest himself in September 1988.

Jacques bonded out for $100,000, with only $10,000 to post. He was not apprehensive about facing a murder charge, and he knew little about the case, not realizing it was a gang-related murder until his trial. Naively, Jacques believed his innocence would save him.

A year and a half later, Cook County Judge Michael Close—a veteran and often controversial judge, who was at one time accused of accepting bribes, according to federal testimony, and later charged with misconduct for ethnic slurs—presided over Jacques's brief and bizarre bench trial. In this type of trial, a judge alone decides the verdict. For Jacques, there was no jury, save Judge Close, on April 5, 1990. A cheaper and faster way to conduct trials, bench trials are often preferred by many in the court business—except by defendants like Jacques, who did not understand the full impact of waiving his right to a jury trial. Unlike in federal cases, where both sides of a case must agree to a trial by judge over a jury, in states like Illinois the defendant controls the decision. But often, overworked and underpaid defenders urge their clients to take a bench trial.

"I'd rather have twelve people decide my fate," Jacques remembers telling his private attorney Kenneth Wadas.[7] A former marine who served in Vietnam, Wadas is now a Cook County judge himself, known for hard-nosed, no-nonsense demeanor and a pro-prosecution bent. According to Jacques, Wadas advised against taking a jury, telling him that jury members might be prejudiced by the fact that Jacques was in a gang.

At trial, most notably, not a single officer testified for the prosecution, which is unusual as prosecutors heavily rely on police testimony. Often,

---

7. Wadas refused an interview for this book, citing the civil litigation.

police witnesses establish a case's physical evidence. Here there was none, signaling a weak case, and the state called only one detective—Guevara— as a rebuttal witness, meaning he was brought in only to counter evidence that the defense had presented.

By 1990, corruption permeated the Chicago Police Department, but it remained largely unexposed. The most manifest example of the department's culture of cover-up was the decades-long torture ring led by former commander Jon Burge, whose crews beat confessions out of more than a hundred men, mostly African American, resulting in several known wrongful convictions. At the time of Jacques's trial, however, high-ranking officers such as Burge and Guevara, though now disgraced, were perceived to be credible.

Yet Jacques's case hinged not on Guevara but on the state's key eyewitness, Orlando, who had turned thirteen by the time of trial.

"Mr. Lopez, do you know what it means to tell the truth?" Close asked Orlando.

"Yes."

"And do you know what happens if you don't tell the truth?"

"Yes."

"What happens if you don't tell the truth?"

"I'll be punished."

Close decided Orlando was competent enough to testify. And the boy was sticking to his story.

The state led the boy witness through his memory of the shooting: "When you saw him turn around and run back to the Chevy, did you recognize that person?"

"Yes," Orlando answered.

"That was the person you had seen before?"

"Yes."

"Where did you know that person from?"

"Humboldt."

"Humboldt Park?"

"What did you used to see that person doing at Humboldt Park?"

"Playing baseball."

"Did you see that person in court today?"

"Yes."

"Point him out."

Orlando pointed. "The man with the sweater on over there?" the prosecutor asked.

"Yes," Orlando said.

"For the record, the in-court identification of the defendant Jacques Rivera."

"Did you know his name at the time?"

"No."

The prosecutor also asked Orlando to put an "X" over Jacques's face in the second lineup photograph, suspect #3. But missing from the trial was the fact that police had conducted an original lineup yielding different results, where young Orlando had at first not picked Jacques at all.

Wadas called Chicago police officer Craig Letrich to the stand. Letrich was the cop who had shown Felix the Imperial Gangster photo books at the hospital before the teen's death. But because such testimony would be considered hearsay—Felix was dead and could not testify for himself—the rules of evidence meant Letrich could not explicitly say on the record that Felix had made this identification; it was inadmissible. Wadas teased out the information indirectly, setting up for the judge the obvious conclusion that Felix had identified someone else in the photo book, given the subsequent arrest of another gang member.

"After you showed him photographs from the Imperial Gangsters photographic album, did you then leave the house and go back to the area?" Wadas asked Letrich in court.

"Yes."

"Later on that evening, did you have occasion to arrest an individual?"

"Yes. It could have been technically the next day, the thirty-first, I believe."

"In the early morning hours?"

"Yes."

"And that individual's name is José Rodriguez that you arrested?

"That's correct."

"Was Rodriguez a member of the Imperial Gangsters?"

"Yes."

"Was Rodriguez's photograph in the Imperial Gangster book?"

"Yes."

"Did you also attempt to arrest an individual by the name of Phillip Neves? [*phonetic*]"

"Attempted to locate him to place him under arrest, yes."

"Were you able to find him?"

"No."

"So Rodriguez was the only guy you arrested in connection with the murder?"

"Correct."

"Did you have anything else to do with this case after the arrest of Rodriguez and writing the report?"

"Just to go back the next day and see the victim. That would have been on the thirty-first."

"Rodriguez was released the next day?"

"Either released on the thirty-first or first. I can't recall."

"He wasn't charged?"

"No, he wasn't."

"Nothing further," Wadas said.

The prosecutor tried to poke holes in Letrich's account, questioning whether he had actually been assigned to the case and whether Felix had the capacity to identify the Imperial Gangsters in his serious condition. Decades later, it remains unclear why Rodriguez was released after his arrest, and why these alternative suspects (though one is presumed dead) have not resurfaced.

About halfway through the short trial, Jacques took the stand in his own defense, establishing his alibi—that he was at home with his common-law wife, Sophia.[8]

"Where were you?" Wadas asked.

"I was at home with my wife and kids."

"Did you ever go out on that date anywhere?"

"We did laundry, groceries."

"Did you go out alone anywhere that day?"

---

8. Judge Close later pointed out that Illinois did not have common-law marriage.

"No, sir."

"Did you drive up in a car with someone else, get out and shoot Felix Valentin a bunch of times on that date?"

"No, sir, I never shot anybody in my life."

Jacques's hair became the subject of much testimony, as prosecutors sought to support Orlando's original description to the police that the shooter had a gold-dyed ponytail or pigtail.

"During the summer or that point in time, were you like ever in the park playing baseball or anything like that?" Wadas asked Jacques.

"No, sir."

"How did you wear your hair?"

"Back, pushed back."

"Did you have your hair dyed at all, any part?"

"No, sir."

"When you—and you didn't play any baseball at the park?"

Jacques testified that he was a former, not current, gang member—a lie that would come back to haunt him. "Being a part of the gang, there is a code of silence," he says. "That's why I said I was no longer with it. But you can get shot and beat up—anything can happen to you."

Guevara took the stand on rebuttal, the state's attempt to contradict Jacques's testimony. At the time, Guevara was a twelve-year veteran of the Gang Crimes unit, which was later disbanded in 2000, reorganized amid a cocaine ring scandal and cover-up that made national headlines.

The state elicited testimony from Guevara about Jacques's hairstyle.

"Was there anything unusual about his hair at the time you arrested him?" the prosecutor asked.

"Yes, there was," Guevara answered.

"What was that?"

"In the back it was gold, like a little pigtail dyed in gold."

Despite lineup photos that did not support this description, Guevara's testimony about Jacques's hair, coupled with Orlando's testimony about the shooter's "gold and brown" hair, was largely uncontested. But to show that Jacques's hair did not fit this description, Wadas called to the stand a pastor who had known Jacques over a four-year period. He testified that Jacques's hair was brown. He had never seen it dyed gold.

After closing arguments, the judge made his ruling—no explanation or preamble. "The Court, having considered the evidence received on the trial of the case, finds the defendant guilty as set forth in Count Two of the indictment. I'll set it over for sentencing. How is June fourth?" he said.

Jacques's family was present for the matter-of-fact finding of guilty.

"My mom was crying hysterically," Jacques Jr. remembers. Jacques's mother had to take the baby, Jennifer, from her arms.

Three months later, in July 1990, Jacques appeared before the court for sentencing. He entered the courtroom in a Department of Corrections uniform as his family looked on.

The judge grilled Jacques's lawyer about whether his three children were by the same woman or different women, whether they were on public aid, and whether Jacques had ever supported them. Then he delivered a monologue about the epidemic of crime in Chicago, the pluralistic society that the United States had become, people taking the law unto themselves, and the deterrent effect of sentencing individuals to long periods of incarceration.

"I believe that it does have a deterrent effect, as it has a deterrent effect on the defendant as long as he can be locked up and caged like an animal in part of the gulag that we call the Illinois Department of Corrections," said Close, who was notorious for this type of harsh language.

He sentenced Jacques to eighty years in prison, the maximum extended sentence. And he tacked on five years for a firearm charge. Jacques's family, however, remained hopeful he would win the first appeal in his case.

"My mom said he would come out," Jacques Jr. remembers of the time leading up to the trial. "He would be out by the time I was seven."

Jacques Jr. was four months shy of turning eight when Jacques was sentenced. They weren't allowed to say goodbye.

IV.

"I was heading in the wrong direction. Now I can say that my life is headed on the right path, going in the right direction, thinking a lot more and responding in the correct manner than I did before. So, basically, you can say I grew up."

In the early 1990s, the gangs controlled Stateville prison. "Right on the money," Jacques recalls. "It was a place of despair."

Jacques was still shocked to be entering this new world. "I was trying to get my mind set with a hardcore attitude," he says. "Not like, 'I'm bad, I'm bad,' but 'I ain't no punk.'"

A former Latin Kings gang member writing under the pseudonym Reymundo Sanchez, who was once incarcerated at Stateville, put it like this in his memoir, *Once a King, Always a King*:

> The Peoples and Folks knew to respect each other's boundaries or risk an all-out gang war that would likely spread to all cell houses. Those not associated in any way with a gang had to pay for the privilege to use the phone. These payments came in the form of food, cigarettes, arrangement of outside jail favors, or sex, although sex as payment did not apply to the Latin Kings as they had strict rules against homosexual activity, which resulted in extremely severe punishment. Inmates not affiliated with a gang who did not follow the jailhouse rules were severely beaten. Those who were tough enough to fight back usually ended up joining the gang opposing the one that had beaten them. The jail administration and the guards supposedly overseeing the inmates were powerless to stop or even curb the enforcement of jailhouse rules. It was a way of prison life, and nothing could be done about it.

Jacques was a likeable guy in prison. For more than a decade, he worked in the segregation unit, which meant he was like a trustee to some lieutenants and sergeants. He could roam around and show new correctional officers the ropes through the four galleries, double rows of cells on the first floor: A and B on one side, C and D on the other. When Jacques would find cash or the officers' keys lying about, he would turn them back in. When there was an issue with the Kings, the staff would come to Jacques for help—and he enjoyed trying to make peace.

"They didn't want no problems," he says. "We shouldn't make their work any harder; they shouldn't make our time any harder."

Jacques found a best friend in prison—Juan Rivera, who was serving a life sentence for the rape and murder of an eleven-year-old girl from Waukegan, Illinois. Juan withstood three trials, three guilty verdicts, and three life sentences—despite DNA evidence clearing him of the crime before his third criminal trial. Twenty years into his own sentence, Juan would finally be freed within months of Jacques's release. In prison, Jacques and Juan were so close that people thought they were brothers. The fact that they shared a last name only added to this perception. Later, as free men, Jacques and Juan posted on social media a silly photo of themselves in an elevator, captioned, "Scary! We always wanted to be in the same cell together. It never happened, but we got stuck in an elevator together. Ironic."

Jacques had a lot of jobs at Stateville, working in the kitchen for thirteen years. It was a coveted position: sometimes there would be two hundred applications for only three kitchen jobs. Working food in the segregation unit, where prisoners are isolated from the general population, Jacques would unload truck deliveries. Sometimes the shipments would tilt and tip. One day he tried to keep one from falling and something happened in his back. He had surgery to address the bulged disk, but it continued to bother him. Jacques also suffered from indigestion and heartburn, eating soy-based prison meals around the clock, cold and uncooked when the place was on lockdown.[9] He would save the peanut butter and jelly sandwich from breakfast so that he could have something to replace an inedible meal later in the day.

Jacques remembers the brutality of lockdowns: "It was hell for me. When I first got there, the prison was on a ninety-day lockdown. It was hot as hell in there. I didn't have a phone. I didn't have a TV."

As the years wore on, his tolerance for these periods changed, as he would take the time to rest, research his case, and catch up on letters. But, inevitably, a few weeks into the lockdown, he would grow weary.

But what most troubled Jacques was his mental health. A depression set in about a decade into his sentence. He frequently felt despair and

---

9. Lockdowns in prison are periods of time when inmates are confined to certain areas and most activities are restricted.

would cry and cry. He was offered medication, but he refused. He saw what the pills did to people.

His kids vividly remember the crying. In the beginning, they visited frequently, typically on weekends, mostly Saturdays. At Stateville, they would wait about an hour to get past the strip search and lines, being led from one room to another like cattle. His children visited the prison with their mother until she and Jacques separated and divorced. Later, an aunt or their grandmother would take them there.

The visiting area was downstairs. Reunited briefly with their dad, they were permitted a hug or high-five at the beginning and end of the visits. They could stay for about an hour, and Jacques entertained the kids with Hot Potato and table football played with a paper triangle. Fun and games—until the security guard warned: "Five minutes!"

They would try to be the last to leave visitation so that their dad could peek through the window next to the doorway as they exited. The maneuver would earn them an extra thirty seconds of face time. At most, an extra minute. But it was worth it.

One time, as the kids exited and looked back to see if their dad was still watching at the bottom of the stairs, they found him broken in tears. "He was crying so hard," Richard remembers. "I didn't want to leave. He was just crying so hard. He saw us."

They had phone calls, too, and Jacques would write letters to his kids. "I wouldn't say a lot, but several times," he says. But Jacques Jr. remembers more letters from his dad: "All the time, every holiday."

As the kids got older, their visits became less frequent, but they still wrote him letters. "Life went on," Richard says. Jacques missed holidays, their proms, and graduations. The family endured bouts of financial instability. Sophia, who did not remarry, held down two jobs to support them, working at a GED center and her kids' elementary school. As a nine-year-old, Jacques Jr. earned some loose change parking cars, once earning five dollars in a day. His friends spent their earnings at the candy store, but when Jacques Jr. discovered there was no milk or bread at home, he knew what he had to do. "Of course, with my five dollars, I went to the store. I remember crying the whole walk back home," Jacques Jr. recounts in the oral history blog *Surviving Justice*.

His mother asked him where he got the milk and bread, thinking he might have stolen it. Jacques Jr. told her the whole story, and she broke down. "And ever since that day me and my ma were like Batman and Robin," he recounts.

As teenagers, the Rivera kids couldn't afford much. "Us being teenaged boys and wanting these clothes and those shoes, it was hard for my mom," says Richard, who today has his mother's name, Sophia, tattooed on his left arm. "We didn't make it a big deal with wanting the name-brand stuff."

When the kids were young, Jacques warned them about the Kings: "Stay away from the gangs and stay away from the drugs. You get involved in either, and that is going to be your downfall."

After high school, both of Jacques's sons entered the military. When Richard visited prison in his dress blues, Jacques was ecstatic. "Everybody! Look at my son!"

"It was embarrassing, but it was cool, man," Richard remembers. "The look on his face. It was crazy."

Jacques's sisters visited him as well over the years. His youngest sister, Candida, had faithfully visited about twice a year during his incarceration—one time unsuccessfully, on his birthday, when the prison suddenly went on lockdown.

"It's his birthday!" Candida had cried in the parking lot of Stateville. "And he's in this crappy-ass place! I came all the way from California. I'm right here, and I can't get in."

Over the first half of his incarceration, Jacques did not accept that his prison sentence could be permanent. He always thought he was just one appeal away from walking out. He worked on his own case from prison, writing letters for help and filing his own post-conviction appeal. It was quickly denied a month later. Four years later, he tried for a federal appeal. It was denied the following year. He petitioned the court again in 2000. It was dismissed.

That's when it really hit him. *Man, I have eighty years*, he thought. *What am I going to do? My kids!*

Jacques was lost. But one day he found himself at a Christian service in prison. He sat there, agonizing over his situation. *What can help me now?*

He says he heard a voice—not audibly, but in the spirit. *My son, I'm here for you. I have chosen you.*

Disturbed, Jacques answered: "Who's that?"

Another voice: *Oh, you heard that from the minister. That's where you heard that from.*

But, Jacques reasoned, if it was the minister speaking to him, then why didn't he hear it with his ears?

"What I heard was from my heart," Jacques remembers. "It was within me."

The voices went away. A week or so later, Jacques started thumbing through the Bible, starting with the Book of John. He landed on chapter 15, verse 16: "You did not choose me, but I chose you and appointed you so that you might go and bear fruit—fruit that will last—and so that whatever you ask in my name the Father will give you."

Later, he was walking down the segregation unit, where the floors were waxed and clean. Beneath the rolling electric rail door, Jacques found a tiny object peeping out. It was a metal cross, covered in dirt. Jacques picked it up and read an inscription: *Christ has chosen you.* In that moment, Jacques decided to seek God.

Within a few months, the task became clear to him. He would have to leave the gang. Others had done the same, but it was not an easy process. In *Once a King*, Sanchez writes that he had to endure a brutal three-minute beating, what they call a violation.

Jacques knew that leaving the gang would require permission from the Corona—the leader of the Latin Kings. At the time, Gustavo "Lord Gino" Colon was serving a life sentence in federal prison in Colorado. But he still commanded the gang from his cell. In Lord Gino's stead, one of the chiefs had the power to release Jacques from Latin King Nation. So Jacques had to go talk to him.

The Kings met on Sundays in the gymnasium during church services. The guards did not stop them from organizing. "The gangs ran the prison," Jacques said. "If you didn't want to get stabbed, you didn't interrupt the Kings."

One Sunday, Jacques showed up to approach the Kings, but a correctional officer stopped him: "You have to have your religion on your ID.

You don't have your religion on your ID."

The officer let Jacques go inside—only this one time, he was told. But when Jacques went to talk to the chief, he chickened out. The next week, he tried again, running into the same officer.

"Did you get your ID?"

Jacques hadn't.

"I can't let you go over there because if something happens, then they will blame us," the officer told him. Then, he conceded. "One last time," he warned Jacques.

Once again, faced with having what could be a life-threatening conversation, Jacques panicked. Scared, he couldn't go through with confronting the chief.

By the time the next week rolled around, Jacques had forgotten to get the proper ID. But a different officer was manning the entry, and she wasn't checking IDs. "It was for me a divine intervention," Jacques says. "The Lord knew he had to get me over to that gym."

Walking over to the chief, Jacques was starting to lose his nerve again when one of the other Kings came up to talk to him. Jacques's heart raced.

"I heard you want to get out," he said to Jacques. "You want to give your life to the Lord?"

Jacques felt like he was in a trance. The Christian service was going on in the background, and that familiar voice came to him: *Today, you will choose who you will serve.*

Answering the voice aloud, Jacques said: "Yes, Lord, this is what I want to do."

Coming out of the trance, he realized everyone could hear him speaking aloud—including the chief. "This sense of peace came over my body. I had no fear," Jacques remembers. "I went up to the chief and talked to him."

The chief decided to let him leave the Latin Kings. "Ace" was no more. He had no one to protect him anymore. No one had his back—except God.

Unlike other gang members who left after him—some for their Christian faith, or some who wanted out so that they could have sex with men (forbidden among the Kings)—Jacques faced no repercussions.

Soon God gave him a new name, Jacques says. The name "Jacob" came to him in a dream. When he awakened, he searched for the Book of Jacob—there is none in the Bible. Jacob's story, he discovered, is in the Book of Genesis.

Before he could dive in and read the story, Jacques needed help. He had been having trouble with his back, and he complained to the warden about the pain. He ended up in the hospital several times. Laid up on one of the visits, he had some time to read about Jacob. In Genesis, he read about an angel of the Lord hitting Jacob in his hip, a sign that he was chosen of God. Later in the story, God renames Jacob, calling him Israel.

Jacques took this as a sign to abandon his street name and his birth name, and to assume a new spiritual name—Jacob. "And I'm looking forward to the day when he tells me you're no longer called Jacob. You're called Israel."

Jacques's cellmate of nine years never once called him "Ace" again, not even by mistake. He accepted him as Jacob, as did others in the prison—save one lieutenant, who ran transport from Stateville to Cook County Jail. He wouldn't call him Jacob. It was always "Ace" with him.

"You're not going anywhere," he taunted Jacques after he later earned a new trial.

When he did prevail, Jacques yelled for the lieutenant to come down. "Where is he? Where is he?" The lieutenant wouldn't face him.

Jacques remembers his kids being happy that he had found God and left the gang life behind him. Sometimes they referred to him as Jacob. But his depression did not subside. Now, he believes these symptoms were Satan's handiwork: "There are certain things that come into your life that are from the Devil."

V.

"The Lord was telling me that, to remain faithful, that soon your freedom and justice will come. . . . If it wasn't for the grace of God, I wouldn't be here today. I wouldn't be out of prison today."

In his correspondence from prison, Jacques still used his birth name, as he did in 2004, when he wrote to one organization for help:

> My name is Jacques Rivera, Register No. B-04431, and I am currently incarcerated at the Stateville Correctional Center. My situation is that I have been wrongfully accused by Detective Reynaldo Guevara of the Area 5 Grand and Central police station. Detective Guevara along with several other detectives at Area 5 have been under scrutiny before for police misconduct at Area 5. I am just one of many of the young and Latino men from the Humboldt Park area who has been wrongfully accused and convicted of murder by Detective Guevara.

By the early 2000s, Chicago police detective Reynaldo Guevara had acquired a citywide reputation for manipulating lineups and coercing witnesses. The *Chicago Reporter* published a story in June 2000 that called into question several cases Guevara had investigated. The allegations of beating suspects and forcing confessions mounted. A grassroots group of Latino families, Comite Exigimos Justicia (We Demand Justice), had long been raising awareness about their loved ones, who they maintained had been wrongly convicted because of Guevara's practices. A picture of Comite Exigimos Justicia members rallying at Daley Plaza, a courtyard next to a federal building downtown, appeared on the cover of the *Chicago Reporter.*

Jacques attached a copy of this article to his letters as he searched for help on the outside. To him, the news story proved he was not alone in his injustice. One recipient of his correspondence was Jane Raley at Northwestern University's famed Center on Wrongful Convictions.

His file landed on Jane's desk during the Center's inquiry into other Guevara cases. Leaving work one day, Jane grabbed the file to read on her train commute home to Highland Park, a suburb of Chicago. As Jane settled in for the more than forty-five-minute haul, she read the original trial transcripts. Unlike most cases, in which a transcript consumes reams of paper, Jacques's trial was a thin stack, indicating to Jane that it had been a surprisingly short trial. She read through the entire proceeding by the time the train reached her home station.

Jane thought it was highly unusual that the prosecution had not called a single police officer to testify on direct examination. Then she realized the only evidence was the kid. That would be the place to start. Jane asked the Center's private investigator, Cynthia Estes, and Jennifer Linzer, assistant director of the Center, to help track down Orlando Lopez.

The two women also visited Jacques at Stateville. At first, Estes thought the case seemed like hundreds of others in Chicago, a run-of-the-mill gang case. "But Jacques himself was so compelling to Jennifer and to me that we just felt like we had to take the case," Estes, a thirty-year veteran investigator who now lives in Washington State, reflects. "We couldn't walk away from that man."

Until Estes and Linzer could locate Orlando and see what he had to say, the Center agreed to take Jacques's case on a provisional basis only, for "investigative purposes," he was told.

But Orlando Lopez was nowhere to be found in the city of Chicago. Every search and lead seemed like a dead end. At the time, Estes was also working on Juan Rivera's case, and he had won a new trial. When Juan was reconvicted in 2009, he urged the Center to forget about him and try to get Jacques, whom he called Jacob, out of prison instead.

A few months later, a tip finally catapulted the investigation forward: Orlando could be in Ohio.

In the late afternoon on a snowy Sunday in February 2010, Estes, along with Linzer, knocked on Orlando's front door in the Cleveland area. The two women had driven more than five hours to try their luck. One door knock could fling open the case again—and they were nervous about it.

"We didn't know if we had the right guy," Linzer remembers. "We just knew that this case was going to live or die by this witness."

One of Orlando's sons answered the door. He told Estes and Linzer his dad was out shopping. The women left a card and said they would come back in an hour.

Ten minutes shy of the hour, they returned and parked within view of the house. Orlando and his wife arrived home. Estes and Linzer waited five minutes for them to get inside the house.

Orlando saw the card. "Right there I knew right away. It was my past catching up," he later said.

When the women knocked at the door a second time, a tentative Orlando stuck his head out.

"Are you Orlando Lopez?" Linzer asked.

"Yes."

"Did you live at 3320 Cortland in the eighties—"

Orlando stopped her. He said he knew why they were there. Then, he invited them inside. They walked into his living room.

"Everyone was kind of on edge," Linzer remembers about the small talk and glances bouncing around the room.

Orlando suddenly stood up and suggested they go somewhere they could talk privately. Linzer drove, with Estes in the back and Orlando in the front seat.

Orlando started mumbling something. Estes couldn't hear him and asked him to repeat himself. "Redemption," he said. "This is all about redemption."

He looked up at Estes. Tears came down his face, and he began to sob. Orlando told them the truth before they made it to Starbucks, where they sat and talked for close to two hours. Orlando asked for a pen and paper so he could write to Jacques.

In his mid-thirties, Orlando was now a father of four children. He had left his gang ties behind in Chicago and moved away from the city in the mid-nineties. He earned an honest living at a high-rise window-cleaning company. But Jacques's case haunted him. It nagged at this conscience. Apart from talking to a pastor, Orlando had kept the memory to himself.

After their long chat, Orlando seemed nervous and suggested they go home because his family would be worried about him. Estes and Linzer dropped him off. They agreed this would not be the end of their conversation.

The following Tuesday, Jacques was set to call the Center. Linzer congratulated him by phone: "You're now a client of the Center on Wrongful Convictions."

It was like winning the lottery, only better.

Less than four months later, a State of Ohio notary watched as Orlando signed his affidavit for Jacques's new appeal. Sentence by painful sentence, he tried to undo the lie that had haunted him for almost his entire life. "At some point I made the decision that it was just easier to stick with my original identification of Jacques Rivera as the shooter," Orlando wrote. "I then proceeded to identify Jacques Rivera in the second lineup knowing that he was not the killer."

Orlando explained his family's relationship to Felix, that he was the brother of Orlando's sister's boyfriend, Israel. Israel and Orlando's sister later had three children together before Israel himself was the victim of a fatal shooting. Orlando had looked to Israel as a brother. He didn't want to let anyone down by confessing he had lied.

"I am coming forward with the truth now because I feel terrible about identifying Jacques Rivera as the shooter when in fact he was not the shooter," Orlando wrote. "I have been waiting for years for someone to find me so I could tell the truth. I want to set the record straight. My coming forward is all about redemption."

But the redemption was almost too late. Because Jacques had exhausted his post-conviction appeals, Jane had to argue that another petition was warranted, which meant finding new evidence to show that it would likely change the result on retrial.

Estes, the private investigator for the Center, was hard at work. She tracked down and interviewed several of the men who had stood in line with Jacques at the first live lineup in 1988. The existence of this lineup, in which Orlando did not pick Jacques, was never raised at Jacques's trial. Two of the men from the original lineup signed affidavits for the case.

"I just found it extraordinary because Jacques had told us there was a first lineup, and I have to say that we were skeptical," Estes said. "We didn't have all the pieces to that puzzle."

But when the men she interviewed volunteered the information about the lineup without her asking, Estes knew it was true.

Another affidavit came from a former law student, who interviewed Chicago police detective Craig Letrich. In the student's affidavit, Letrich confirmed that another lineup may have occurred. He also stated that he had spoken to Felix in his hospital bed before he died, where the teen had identified two Imperial Gangsters as the perpetrators.

Estes had long tried to locate these men. "We were not successful," she says. "One of the people we thought maybe had already died. We spent time looking for alternative suspects for sure."

But armed with new, strong evidence for Jacques's case, he earned a hearing. A judge would consider the uncovered facts and decide if he should have a new trial.

For the second time, Orlando got the chance to identify Jacques in court—more than two decades after he pointed him out as a bewildered child witness. In June 2011, back in Chicago, Orlando took the stand. He had flown in the day before, missing work. Media attention had generated more interest in the case, and Jacques remembers being surprised to see the courtroom so packed. His family attended the high-stakes hearing.

"As you sit here today under oath, is it your testimony that you consciously lied when you identified Jacques Rivera as the shooter of Felix Valentin?"

"Yes," Orlando answered.

"Mr. Lopez, do you see the man at counsel table who is wearing the yellow jumpsuit?"

"Yes."

"And do you know who that is?"

"Yes."

"Is that Jacques Rivera?"

"Yes."

Temples grayed, hair thinned, Jacques was twenty-one years into his eighty-year sentence at Stateville Correctional Center for murder.

Jacques's faith sustained him in the final years in prison, even as a debilitating depression overcame him. He believed the truth would prevail—so much so that after the hearing, he rejected a potential plea deal from the prosecution.

Jane had been reluctant to bring it to him. She didn't want him to think his appeal wasn't strong enough to win. On top of that, there was no firm offer, she remembers. "It was strange," Jane noted. "Rather, the state approached me and said that they were interested in resolving the matter, but wanted me to make the proposal!"

Estes remembers how adversarially the prosecutors treated Jane. "It was really shocking to my senses. It bothered me so much," she says. "They were cruel to her. In court and outside of court. It was awful."

"It's not about me," Jane would tell Estes.

Jane thought the vague plea deal was offensive and so did Jacques. Given Orlando's recantation and the other new evidence, they decided to pass on the deal. And Jacques prayed really hard.

As he waited to find out about the new trial, Jacques was prepared for the worst. The writing was on the wall, he was warned, that he would likely be denied. Rarely do judges reverse convictions or order a new trial. "I don't know what writing you're seeing on the wall, but I don't see no writing on the wall," Jacques said.

Pacing back and forth in a holding cell, waiting on Jane to visit him one day, Jacques caught a glimpse of the wall in front of him. There was something scribbled in graffiti. "Oh, how ironic," he thought. "The writing really is on the wall." When he went back to see what the graffiti said, he stopped pacing.

It read: *Soon.*

Cook County Judge Neera Walsh granted Jacques a new trial the following September. Jacques cried out in court when Walsh read her ruling: "Oh my God. Thank you." The state was to decide over the coming weeks how it planned to proceed. Until then, Jacques waited in a Cook County Jail cell.

The story about his chance for freedom hit the media before Jacques's family members found out the good news. After years of appeals, keeping track of developments in the case had proven exhausting. And almost all the time, they had been left disappointed.

His son Richard was working security at a high-rise building on the West Side of Chicago when his aunt texted him that Jacques had been on the news. Richard rushed to the corner gas station to find a newspaper. The store was sold out.

He pleaded with the lady working at the store to help him find a newspaper: "My dad is in the paper!" The employee found him an extra copy, and as Richard began to cry in the aisle, she hugged him. He sobbed on her shoulder. For years, growing up, Richard had wondered if his dad was actually innocent, or if his grandmother and aunts just wanted ed Jacques's kids to believe their dad was a good guy. "But I thought, *You*

know what? He's guilty. I never really knew that he was really innocent."
As he grew older and understood the case better, Richard's confidence in
his dad's innocence grew, especially after Northwestern took the case. He
replaced his doubts about his father with hope.

After he calmed down at the gas station, Richard posted the article
on social media, catching the attention of his brother, Jacques Jr., who
found the full newspaper story in the Irving Park Public Library, where
he had been looking for a job. "I read it, and I was just in tears," Jacques
Jr. says. "I could not believe it."

A month later, the state dropped the charges against Jacques instead
of retrying him. The prosecution's case had crumbled with Orlando's recantation, and there was no more evidence with which to keep Jacques
imprisoned.

Amid frenzy and fanfare, he was freed.

VI.

"My troubles just began. You know, I appreciate, you know, my freedom.
I appreciate justice, but my troubles are just beginning. You just can't
throw someone into the wild and say, 'OK, make it.' They just threw me
back out into the wild and said, 'OK, you're on your own now.'"

Jacques's mother, Gwendolyn, shared his sister's second-floor apartment
with him. When she realized the butcher knife was missing from the
kitchen, she asked him about it.

"I'm just scared," he told her.

"What are you scared of?"

He couldn't answer her. But he kept the knife, later moving it from
his pillow to underneath the mattress, with the knife handle protruding,
where it remains today.

One of his only comforts, he discovered, was his sister Rose's French
Vanilla coffee with French Vanilla creamer. She let him drink out of her
red Disney coffee mug with a bird on it, a cup he later claimed as his own.

The caption on the mug said something about a first cup of coffee. It wasn't Jacques's first cup of coffee—but it was his first cup of good coffee in more than two decades. He craved it after his release.

That first morning, Rose made him a fresh cup. She served him some Lucky Charms, his favorite cereal. To Jacques, cereal had been a commodity in prison. It helped fill the gaps between meals, especially when inmates couldn't stomach the chow they were offered. Jacques hoarded boxes of cereal, stacking them up around his cell. They were his currency. Working in the kitchen, he also used to reserve taco meat and give extra to guys in return for what he wanted.

A TV news team came to Rose's door. She called for Jacques. He let them in.

They were eager to know how he was spending his first full day of freedom. Could they follow him? What was he eating for breakfast? Could they go upstairs and see his bed?

"Nah, I'm not going to show you that. C'mon," Jacques told them, defensive and annoyed.

"What's your next move?"

Jacques was bewildered. He was busy contemplating that very question as friends and family poured in for visits. As his children sat before him, Jacques studied their faces. He stared at them, watching as their expressions and mannerisms shifted into new forms unknown to him. Years of poring over their photos in prison had failed to capture who they really were. Jacques felt the gravity of what he had missed.

"I was just looking at them," he says, weeping at the memory. "How much they grew. How much they had changed."

They sat and talked under a canopy in the backyard. Jacques's mind continued to race through the constant activity surrounding him.

What was *his next move?*

Before he could think of the answer, a voice message from the Department of Corrections populated his mother's answering machine. It happened about twice a day for his first few days back. "INMATE J-A-C-Q-U-E-S-R-I-V-E-R-A, register number B-0-4-4-3-1 has been released. . ."

He realized he was no longer B04431. He wasn't Ace. He was Jacques Rivera, exoneree. And he was Jacob—but what did that mean now?

"A Christian from in jail versus a Christian in real life—I think they're two different Christians," his son Jacques Jr. notes. "He's trying to transition himself from being in prison."

For a stretch of months after his release, Jacques attended church a few miles away with a friend, also a former gang member. But Jacques's attendance lapsed as free time became more scarce. "I need to get back into it," he would say. As his sons took him around town, they snapped photos of his "firsts"—like his first haircut. Jacques appeared nervous in the barber's chair. "A couple of the barbers had their hats cocked," his son Richard recalls. "He didn't want to be around no gangbangers."

"Wow, look! You're in the paper!" Rose said, eyeing a newspaper article at their local IHOP, where she and Richard had taken Jacques the day after his release.

The manager swung by the table, saw the picture in the paper and looked up, realizing it was Jacques himself. "You know what?" the manager said. "You don't have to pay for your meal today. Good luck to you."

The next day, there was even more media attention, but this time a TV news crew showed up at another home across town—the Valentins'. A reporter had tracked down Felix Valentin Jr., the twenty-three-year-old son of Felix Valentin.

"I'm angry. Really angry. I don't know who did it," said Felix Jr., father of three children, to Chicago's ABC affiliate.

Having spent two decades with the belief that Felix's killer was behind bars, the Valentin family was left without answers and closure when Jacques was suddenly released. "It just opened up old wounds that I thought were healed," cried Daisy Valentin, Felix's sister. "I'm really very angry about it."

The case having long turned cold, prosecutors announced no plans to reinvestigate.

Jane Raley told Jacques he would need a state ID. Without documentation of his identity—not even a proof of address or bill in his name—it could be an ordeal, she warned him. Jane introduced Jacques to Johnnie Lee Savory, who helped exonerees sort through these logistics. Jacques thanked Savory for his offer but felt safe enough with his family's help to figure out his state records.

"I don't have nothing like that," Jacques said, instead pulling out the *Chicago Sun-Times* article about his wrongful conviction to show a government employee. The clerk left for a minute and then came back. "We'd be more than happy to give you your ID," she said, directing him to the front of the line.

Getting his driver's license was less seamless. "How come you haven't had a license in twenty years?" the driving test proctor asked. Jacques told his story. He would be telling it a lot.

Behind the wheel again, Jacques was nervous. His older sister, Linda, had let him take her car around the block a time or two for practice before his driving test. It felt strange. All the buttons on the dashboard surprised him whenever they lit up. Just like riding a bike, he kept saying to himself. But the parallel parking wasn't so easy.

"Let's just go back," the proctor assured him, giving him a break. "You'll do just fine."

The written portion of the test, however, infamously difficult in Illinois, was the most challenging. "The signs were hard!" Jacques says.

He passed his test. As a reward, Linda let him drive back to Rose's.

At home, Jacques sat on Rose's front porch. She watched him for a minute. "What are you doing?"

"Just sitting on the front porch."

"OK," she said, leaving him alone. "Just sit on the front porch."

For the first week or two, it was as far from home as he would go by himself. He stayed indoors, filling the time by watching sports on TV. Rose had to teach him how to use a remote control again. He was overwhelmed by the number of stations. "It was literally like having an infant child," Rose says.

Rose would ask him things like, "You want to go to Subway?"

"What's Subway?"

She showed him her iPad. "What's this?" he asked. He touched the strange glossy screen. Everything was a tap of a finger away but felt so foreign to Jacques. In a world where technology had created the illusion of ease during his long incarceration, everything seemed more difficult to navigate.

His brother-in-law, an investor, helped him out financially, giving him $300 a month to live on. Jacques accepted the support on the condition that he would pay it back eventually.

A family friend, his grade-school sweetheart who had long ago given him his first kiss, also gave him his first cell phone after his release. "This is something you're going to need now that you're out," she told him. It was a simple phone at first, but a month or two later, she came by and upgraded him to an Android, having put him on her plan. A kind gesture, given their history. After years of being his pen pal and love interest, she had visited him at Stateville after he earned his new trial. Excited about his possible release, Jacques told her to start getting a place ready for the two of them. That's when she broke the news that she was living with another guy. Jacques was crushed. He broke it off.

Jacques continued to secure Rose's house, locking all the windows and doors around him. He felt like someone was watching him. Like someone was coming after him. During his first few days home, Jacques was so troubled by what seemed like a lack of security and by the decisions and responsibilities of being a free man that he was almost ready to go back to Stateville Correctional Center. "I was comfortable. That was my home for twenty-one years," he says. "Came at me too soon. It was all the hype."

When Jacques finally ventured out on his own, he didn't go far, only to the laundromat a block away.

In prison, he used to wash his underwear, T-shirts, and socks by hand. He would scrub them in the shower or in his cell because he didn't want them thrown in with everyone else's uniforms. At the laundromat, he put his dirty clothes in the washer—he had the whole machine to himself. As he added detergent and some coins, he stopped to take it all in. The simplicity of washing your own clothes. The magnitude of his newfound freedom.

There was no going back. This was his new life. So he hit the start button and watched as the machine took off.

VII.

"I love the snow. Wintertime is my favorite time of year. It was just beautiful, standing around the rocks, standing by the edge."

When his little sister, Candida, the youngest, flew in from California after the New Year, a few months after Jacques's release, it took some getting used to seeing him in the flesh. No pat-downs, no long wait.

Over the phone, they had planned out a cross-country trip. They called it their "Donny and Marie Adventure." They were close, like the Osmonds, and people used to tell Candida that she looked just like Marie. Jacques felt ready for the undertaking, eager for some open air away from the cramped apartment he shared with his mother, whose smoking bothered him. She had also taken to criticizing him and treating him like a child again. "I don't like yelling," Jacques said. Apart from their quarrels, he still appreciated the chance to take care of his mother as she aged, as she had taken care of him as a boy. Without grumbling too much, he rubbed Icy Hot on her back when she asked.

The brother-sister adventure started at the airport. Jacques had never been on a plane before. "He was very nervous," Candida remembers.

Jacques sat next to the window, headphones on, eyes shut. He didn't ask for anything to drink. "You're not going to get anything to drink?" Candida asked him.

To stay calm, he chewed his gum. His gum chewing had emerged as a nervous habit not unique to the plane ride. In prison, gum was restricted. And Jacques loved gum. For the next three months of the Donny and Marie Adventure, he chewed gum almost incessantly, which Candida barely tolerated.

Their first stop was the Grand Canyon. It was snowing, magnificently. He couldn't believe the cacti everywhere. It seemed more like a movie than real life. He loved it.

But Las Vegas wasn't quite as awe-inspiring to Jacques. He didn't gamble, and the crowds put him on edge. He didn't feel secure. He was overwhelmed, paranoid. Even more of a damper was put on the trip when Jacques left his cell phone in a taxicab. They called every Las Vegas cab company they could find but had no luck recovering the phone. "I was furious because I have no phone," Jacques remembers. "I lost my contacts and everybody that I called." He also lost pictures of the new memories he had created since being out.

A chance meeting and photo opportunity with famed Chicago Bears player Brian Urlacher cheered him up. "Hey, Brian!" Jacques casually said as the linebacker passed by a taxi stand outside Caesar's Palace.

His sister didn't see the celebrity football player. "Brian? Who's Brian? Who do you know named Brian?"

"Brian Urlacher!"

"Brian Urlacher?!" Candida exclaimed, immediately jumping out of the line to find him.

The night of his release, Jacques had been wearing a Chicago Bears jacket, while one of his sons wore an Urlacher jersey and the other gave him a Walter Payton jersey as a homecoming present. The TV news camera had captured the swag-worthy moment. Shortly thereafter, a Chicago TV sports program hosted Urlacher and asked him about having that kind of impact. He was blown away by the story.

In Vegas, Candida was determined to find Urlacher for her brother, after he slipped away past the taxi stand. "You go this way! I'll go this way!" she said. Jacques followed orders but was wary of separating. They were told Urlacher went inside a tent in the hotel courtyard where a Vaudeville-style show, *Absinthe*, was to go on.

Candida bought tickets for the show. They got inside, but couldn't spot him. Finally, an usher helped them out. "I'm not supposed to tell you, but there's a gentleman meeting that description right behind you," the usher whispered.

Candida approached Urlacher and apologized for interrupting. Would he let them have a photo? Urlacher obliged. Thrilled, Jacques and Candida stayed for the show.

After Vegas, the final leg of Donny and Marie's Adventure was in Dana Point, California, where Candida lived. She took him to Hollywood and Venice Beach, where they stopped in a souvenir shop. Jacques spotted a trophy. It was shaped like an Oscar, inscribed with the words "World's

Best Lawyer." He bought it for Jane.

Candida welcomed Jacques into her church in nearby Laguna Beach. The parishioners of Saint Mary's Episcopal Church had been praying for Jacques over the past year as he neared his unexpected release, and they were excited to meet him. "They were expecting a thug," Candida remembers. "A lot of them have never encountered somebody like Jacques. They were expecting what you see on TV. So when they saw him, they thought he was well-mannered, polite, well-spoken. They were very amazed."

When the bishop visited one Sunday, she brought Jacques up to the altar to join her in the final blessing. He was touched, almost in tears.

Candida's priest was able to pull some strings and get Jacques a brief meeting with Father Greg Boyle, the famed Jesuit priest who founded Homeboy Industries, a program that works with former gang members, helping them break free and move on with their lives. Candida had bought him a signed copy of Father Greg's book, *Tattoos on the Heart*, in which the priest recounts his two decades working with homies in Los Angeles.

The gang life years behind him, Jacques still encountered ghosts from his past on the outside, old friends in Chicago who were eager to catch up with him: "Hey, what's up, brother? Amor!"

"Don't say that to me, man," Jacques would answer, shaking his head. For him, there was no more King Love. It turned out their tour guide at Homeboy Industries in Los Angeles had the same kind of story.

"Before I was this thug and gang member," he told them. "Now I'm the assistant director of this place. I used to have gang members in my cell phone. Now I have the mayor of LA in my cell phone."

A new kind of rank, Jacques thought, picturing himself. One that reforms, redeems. "Everybody wants to be a part of something greater. At least I do," he says.

The Donny and Marie Adventure had lasted three months when both brother and sister knew it was time to bring it to an end. Candida needed to get back to her day-to-day life, and Jacques missed being home in Chicago. The two had been practically inseparable, except for a men's Bible study that Jacques attended with Candida's church folks.

Jacques made the trip back to Chicago alone. At the airport, Candida talked to an agent to try to accompany him through the concourse before saying goodbye. "He really doesn't want to be by himself," she explained. "Can I go through security with him?"

Candida saw him off at the gate. As Jacques walked away from his sister and on to the jetway, she envisioned herself walking away from him during prison visits, as she had many times, painfully. "Every time we would go visit him, I hated leaving," Candida says. "We would go up the stairs. He wouldn't leave until he couldn't see us anymore."

Like Jacques's children, Candida would always turn around and look back at him from the upstairs window. Below in the visiting area, Jacques would still be there, waving and saying, "Bye! I love you!" with a wide grin stretched across his face.

From the jetway, Jacques turned around, looked back at his sister and waved. Candida waved back. And she watched until she could no longer see him.

VIII.

"You know, people don't understand me. People expect me to catch on right away. I've been gone for twenty-one years! You know what I mean? How do you expect me to catch on to something I don't know nothing about?"

The Center on Wrongful Convictions at Northwestern University's School of Law in Chicago became a hangout for Jacques and other exonerees. On the eighth floor of the sparkling law school overlooking Lake Michigan, it was a refuge from the constant activity and unpredictability of the real world.

For Jacques's first birthday back home, the Center threw him a party. He donned a black sombrero with purple feather fringe, which matched his Northwestern Law T-shirt, clothing that had become almost a uniform to him. Jane lit the sparkler candles on a Chicago Bears birthday cake decorated with white-and-blue frosting, Jacques's name piped under the sports logo. Jacques cut the cake and placed it on paper plates. His teeth turned blue from the frosting. Someone snapped a photo of Jacques with Jane, who had put on a glittery purple top hat. Streamers twisted whimsically behind them in the background. A gift table teemed with presents. Jacques's best friend, Juan Rivera—only recently released from prison himself, a few months after Jacques—held a bouquet of cheery balloons. About a week later, the Center treated Jacques to a baseball game at Wrigley Field. He held a handmade sign: "My first Cubs game in twenty-one years!"

Jane introduced Jacques to social work supervisor and attorney Marjorie Moss. An empathetic person, Moss had helped exonerees like him find work, seek counseling, and adjust to life. When Jacques wasn't goofing around, smiling and laughing, Moss could see his paranoia creep out. She knew other former prisoners who struggled with the same. "They're scared," she says. "They're conditioned to look around the corner."

Like Jacques, Moss's clients were tough guys who had spent years surviving behind bars, only to suddenly find themselves struggling to adjust to life on the outside, petrified of the world around them. But in her office and around the clinic, they could breathe. They knew they would find the very people who helped free them in the first place, people they could trust. "Just getting someone free is the very first step in another long process," Moss says.

After their first meeting together at the law school, Jacques wanted to come back to talk with Moss some more, but he found public transportation overwhelming, and he lived about ten miles from Northwestern's Chicago campus. Some graduate students helped him a few times, meeting Jacques at his sister's house, then walking with him to the bus stop and taking the train together downtown. But he could not bring himself to take public transportation alone. He understood how to get from point A to point B, but being surrounded by strangers overwhelmed him. At first Jacques considered taking the kitchen knife with him on the bus, but he quickly dismissed the idea as a poor one. *What about if I overreact and, you know, hurt somebody, or somebody sees and the police come and that's causing trouble?* Jacques reasoned. So he left the blade at home. Instead, he sat with his back to the window. Or he found a seat at the very back of the bus, so that no one could sit behind him. Then he could watch doors. He could see who got on. He could see who got off.

At the Center, Jacques was more comfortable with himself. He would walk from office to office, chatting with people. He would speak at classes and tell his story.

Unlike other exonerees, Jacques didn't want a job right away. He wanted to take his time. But after returning from Donny and Marie's Adventure with Candida, he had warmed up to the idea of finding work. He had grown tired of sitting around and watching TV all day, and he wanted some structure, somewhere to be. Jacques also wanted to be able to provide for his family rather than be provided for. He had found himself embarrassed and frustrated when his daughter's car broke down and he couldn't help her pay for it. "I want to be a dad," he told Moss. "That's what dads do."

So he and Moss set about finding him some work. Some students helped him with his computer skills. Moss gave him a book to study for the GED. "I think he's a little terrified of getting it," Moss says, noting his history of having trouble in school. Together, they crafted his resume. Jacques was worried about the two-decade gap in his work history. His last job had been as a security guard in 1989.

"What did you do in prison?" she prompted.

"I didn't do anything."

"Jacques, you must have done something for those years."

He had. Jacques worked in the kitchen, cooking daily meals for three hundred inmates. He had done maintenance, buffing the floors around the prison. He also worked as a groundskeeper, landscaping at times and clearing out scraps and rocks that cluttered the walkways.

Moss decided to send him to Patricia Messina, a staffing consultant at Northwestern University's human resources department in Evanston, Illinois. She was known for making resumes shine, even though she had only been on the job a few months when Jacques came to see her. Coming off two years of unemployment herself, a victim of the tanked economy, she knew how important work was in a person's life.

Messina first spoke with Jacques on the phone. Very few visitors came to her office, and she was accustomed to screening candidates by phone. But Jacques proposed he make the trip to Evanston to see her. He had the time. "Sure, come in," she told him. "Face to face. That'd be great."

The white cement office building on Maple Avenue in downtown Evanston was slightly off campus, on the corner by a movie theater frequented by students and townies. Messina's sixth-floor office was quiet when Jacques popped in. He was dressed nicely and flashed his bright smile. *A good first impression*, she thought. They sat down at a small interview table. Messina chatted with him a bit and tried to put him at ease; she had been warned he might be jumpy.

They both had worked in big kitchens, she learned. Messina had been a caterer, so, like Jacques, she knew her way around giant pots that could feed hundreds. As a result, they both found it difficult to cook for just one person at home. They laughed about that.

Jacques would be the first exoneree Messina assisted in finding a job, and she listened as he told her about his case—the eyewitness misidentification and the long journey to finding freedom. She was amazed by how quickly his life—and anyone's—could be snatched up. "That's what the scary part of this is, is that it could be any of us. We all look like somebody. It could happen to any one of us."

For homework, Messina gave Jacques some interview preparation questions to fill out. Give an example for each one, she instructed him. There were about a hundred questions.

> Tell me about a time when you had to learn something new.
> Tell me about when you reached a decision by an organized methodical review of the facts.

And so on. Jacques promised he would dedicate some time to it, drawing as best he could from his skills and work experience in prison.

Meanwhile, there was other work to be done. His lawyers at the Center were trying to clear his background. The State of Illinois still considered him a convicted murderer.

IX.

"They would never accept the fact that I was innocent. They would have never admitted to that fact."

Jacques was hanging around the law school when Jane explained to him how a certificate of innocence worked in Illinois—that he would have to petition the court and prove his innocence again to become eligible to receive about $200,000 in state compensation. This would also allow him to clear his record, Jane told him. With employment in view, a first-degree murder conviction was more than an impediment to being hired. It made securing employment almost impossible.

When Jacques was first released in 2011, a spokeswoman for Cook County State's Attorney Anita Alvarez told the *Chicago Tribune* that prosecutors "could not go forward in good faith" with a retrial. But when Jane filed Jacques's certificate of innocence petition, the state opposed it. "Really? Really?" Jacques fumed, incredulously.

As Jane prepared for the legal battle, Jacques, separately, had to decide who should represent him in a civil lawsuit. Unlike the majority of exonerees, who receive no compensation, Jacques's case had the elements that could lead to a hefty payout. The stakes were high. Allegations of police conspiracy, coercion, and a cover-up could mean millions of dollars. A civil lawsuit would be a long process, spanning years, with depositions to be conducted, subpoenas to be served, and other fact-finding to be done.

At first, Jacques thought he would stick with the Northwestern folks, but some advisors there assured him he could choose any lawyer he wished. Jacques understood, but his loyalty to Northwestern tugged at him.

He had first seen Chicago attorney Jon Loevy on the news. A chronically disheveled man and a fierce advocate in court, the famed lawyer of the Loevy & Loevy law firm had won more than $100 million in jury verdicts for his clients. "He's got this thing about him," Jacques describes the man. "I hate to say this, but it was like meeting Jesus!"

So when Locke Bowman, director of the MacArthur Justice Center— a clinical offshoot of Northwestern's law school, with its Chicago office housed alongside the Center on Wrongful Convictions—proposed to work with Loevy on the case, Jacques was on board. *Man, these are some down lawyers!* Jacques thought. *They fight. Man, it's a privilege.*

In 2009, Loevy won $21 million for exoneree Juan Johnson, whose case was remarkably similar to Jacques's. In Johnson's case, retired Gang Crimes detective Reynaldo Guevara had been accused of framing him and coercing eyewitnesses, who later recanted their testimony, to identify Johnson and his brother. In other cases, Guevara was accused of beating confessions out of suspects. Back at home, Jacques had started having nightmares about Guevara tracking him down and shooting him in the back. "Because he won't do it from the front," Jacques said.

In June 2012, eight months after Jacques's release, Loevy and Bowman filed Jacques's civil complaint, suing eleven police officers, the estate of another, Chicago police detectives in general, and the City of Chicago. Guevara topped the list of defendants.

"They knew from the twelve-year-old witness in this case that Jacques was not involved in the shooting of Felix Valentin," says Steven Art, one of Jacques's attorneys with Loevy & Loevy. "They ignored that fact. They ignored Jacques's alibi. They fabricated evidence. And they withheld evidence in order to frame him for a crime he didn't commit."

Facing off against Loevy & Loevy was the Sotos Law Firm, a high-powered group of lawyers who often defended the City of Chicago in such lawsuits. One of Sotos's lawyers had represented the notorious retired Chicago police commander Jon Burge in a number of cases. Under Burge and his rogue gang of officers, more than a hundred people, nearly all African American men, endured torturous interrogations and detention. Burge's reign of terror lasted for decades, starting around the 1970s, representing one of the most heinous examples of police brutality in US history. The torturers performed mock executions and used electrical shock devices, among other violent tactics, leading to false confessions and wrongful convictions. After years of grassroots and activist pressure, the City of Chicago agreed to create a reparations fund for Burge's victims, apologizing in 2015 for the city's long history of abusing citizens.

Like his predecessor Burge, who repeatedly refused to testify by pleading the Fifth, Guevara did the same as he faced his own misconduct allegations. In his answer to Jacques's lawsuit, sentence by sentence, claim by claim, Guevara's response echoed throughout the document: "Defendant Guevara, on the advice of counsel, asserts the rights guaranteed to him by the Fifth Amendment of the United States Constitution, and therefore declines to answer at this time."

Jacques had been following the news as Guevera made an appearance in court on a different case. Two men convicted of murder, Armando Serrano and Jose Montanez, were seeking new trials after waiting twenty years to prove their innocence. A jailhouse snitch and the widow of the murder victim had recanted in the case, accusing Guevara of inducing them to testify against the men, misconduct that dozens of others had alleged in cases against the notorious detective. The defendants hadn't seen Guevara since their 1994 trials in Chicago, and now he appeared before them in what was expected to be a showdown between cop and snitch. Instead, it was an anticlimax, as Guevara refused to testify.

"Mr. Guevara, are you currently employed?" asked Jennifer Bonjean, Serrano's lawyer.

"I take the Fifth Amendment," Guevara replied.

"Did you ever coerce [witnesses] to provide false testimony against Mr. Serrano and Mr. Montanez?"

Again, he pleaded the Fifth.

"Did you give [a jailhouse snitch] money to offer false testimony?" Same answer.

In a *BuzzFeed* news series, reporter Melissa Segura dug into the city's official investigation into claims that Guevara framed at least forty people for murders they didn't commit. In 2013, Chicago mayor Rahm Emanuel and Cook County State's Attorney Anita Alvarez called for the investigation, which produced a report that was not made public. Obtained by *BuzzFeed*, the report revealed in October 2015 that investigators found at least four cases in which defendants, including Serrano and Montanez, were likely innocent of the murders for which they were convicted.

Guevara played a key role in all the men's cases. In spite of these findings, the Cook County State's Attorney's Office announced it would not reopen any of the men's cases, Segura reported.

Three months after Jacques filed his federal civil lawsuit, in a different Chicago courtroom, a Cook County judge was to decide whether to declare Jacques officially innocent of the murder of Felix Valentin. Jane and Judy stood by Jacques at the hearing. It was September 5, 2012, almost a full year since Jacques had walked free, when the state dropped the charges against him.

But deciding not to retry the case and conceding to Jacques's innocence were two different matters, and prosecutors argued before Cook County Judge Michael McHale that Jacques should not be awarded anything. They said he had lied at his 1990 trial about being in a gang. Under the Illinois compensation law for exonerees, people seeking certificates of innocence are ineligible if they contributed to their own wrongful conviction in any way—a tough standard for wrongly convicted people, who may have falsely confessed or, like Jacques, perjured themselves, often on the advice of their own attorneys. Since Jacques portrayed himself at trial as having already left the Latin Kings gang, the state argued, he was responsible for his own downfall.

McHale was unmoved. The fact of Jacques's gang allegiance, had it been known, could not have contributed to his conviction, the judge said. McHale also challenged a left-field assertion by prosecutors that Felix Valentin had identified Jacques from his hospital bed before dying. There was no testimony to back this up, only a "suspiciously incomplete and questionable police report," McHale said. On top of this, police had arrested an Imperial Gangster after the hospital bedside interview, indicating Felix had not identified Jacques at all.

At the end of the hearing, McHale declared what Jacques had been waiting to hear for almost a quarter of a century: "This petitioner has proven by a preponderance of the evidence that he is innocent of the murder of Felix Valentin."

Upon hearing the words, Jacques cried and hugged Jane, then reached for Judy. "It was like, 'It's been said, let it be done,'" he remembers. "That's final."

Perforating the judge's words, however, the prosecutor intimated that the State's Attorney's Office would be appealing the decision. "Judge, could I get an October third or fourth date for an appeal check date?" he said.

Go ahead, Jacques thought. *You keep losing. That's the second fight you lost. Can't you get it through your head?*

After the hearing, Jane and Judy took Jacques out to lunch to celebrate the victory at a fancy restaurant near the law school.

X.

"It's constant work, constant work. I could take fifty packages upstairs and come back down, there will be another fifty waiting."

There was no telling when Jacques's nearly $200,000 state compensation check would come in the mail. Months passed, and Jacques was eager to start contributing to his living expenses. He wanted to be able to pay for his own pricey prescription refills every month, medication for his indigestion and blood pressure. He also had vowed to repay his sister Candida for the monthly allowance she and her husband had been giving him. He needed a job.

With Jacques's story still catching headlines, old acquaintances, a few of them from the Kings, emerged, asking for handouts—just a few G's here and there, assuming he had millions to spare. But he had almost nothing to his name. When his kids called, sometimes they also asked for money. Jacques didn't mind their requests too much. He figured he owed it to them. And he felt lucky to hear from them. They would invite him over for barbecues, filling up Jacques's plate again and again, as his healthy appetite had returned in full force. They took him out for occasions like Father's Day. A new grandparent, Jacques loved spending time with his newborn granddaughter, Jeniah. But still, his children were all grown with lives of their own, their familial bonds long torn. "They were young when I left them, so they really don't know me and I don't know them," Jacques says. "It basically ruined my life with my children. Because they don't know me."

When Northwestern University's medical school had an opening for a storekeeper position, Jacques went in to interview for it. He was nervous but prepared, thanks to poring over interview questions with Patricia Messina in human resources.

Messina was excited and anxious for him. "When you can, give me a call after you're finished," she told him, wishing him luck. Before she had the chance to follow up with Jacques, the hiring manager had already called her. Jacques was at the top of the list. Messina called Jacques right away to share the good news: "You have the offer and someone will be calling you soon to schedule a start date."

"Great! Thank you!" Jacques answered, a little forced and raspy. Messina detected some fear behind his enthusiasm. *Now his life was really going to start,* she thought. And she was nervous, too, wondering if she had made the right decision on advocating for someone she had just met—whose murder conviction had only recently been cleared. *Would he disappoint?*

"I feel that way any time I recommend anybody," Messina says. "They're people. I'm not selling Xerox machines or computers. People—their lives change and things happen."

She promised to check back in with Jacques by email, as she wanted to make sure he was keeping his inbox current and getting used to operating a computer. Jacques thanked her, but Messina gave him the credit. "Well, I didn't do it. It's really up to you to get the job," she assured him. "You're the one that has to show up to work every day."

And so he did. On his first day of work in October 2012, Jacques arrived an hour and a half early, at seven in the morning. He was supposed to report to the delivery dock, but couldn't figure out where exactly to go. Puzzled, he walked over to the law school for help. On the way, he bumped into his new supervisor, walking down the hallway.

"Oh good, you're early!" he said, directing Jacques upstairs to the eighth floor, where they needed to set up for a speaking engagement. A colleague would show him the way back.

The next day, Jacques showed up early again, around 7:30.

"You don't need to come in that early," his coworkers advised.

"I wanna be here," Jacques told them.

After running dozens of deliveries a day, moving supplies to the medical school labs from the loading dock, Jacques was exhausted—

mentally and physically. "I was beat that first week," he shakes his head. "They had to train me, so I had to learn the routes. That was real difficult."

As Jacques learned the protocols, his colleagues helped him along: "If you don't know, just ask."

The building seemed full of friendly people. On one of his first deliveries, Jacques met Annette, who worked on the thirteenth floor of the Tarry Research and Education Center, part of the medical school. Jacques barreled into the neurology research office, pushing a dolly of packages somewhat clumsily.

"Your license needs to be revoked!" Annette teased her new delivery man.

Jacques laughed, and they became quick friends, chatting during his daily route to her office. Having worked at Northwestern for more than twenty years, Annette knew better than to play favorites with her delivery guys. But soon she grew to know Jacques much better than the rest of the crew.

Not long after he started, Jacques plopped down on a chair across from her desk and took a break. He handed her an article, a write-up the law school had done about his case. Annette was shocked that her new delivery friend felt comfortable enough to tell her his story. "He doesn't hide his background at all," Annette says. "Unfortunately, he's had a pretty tough life, but he's not ashamed of it. He wants people to know him."

During office small talk, she would ask him what his weekend plans were, and he wouldn't have any. Annette noticed he hadn't yet grown accustomed to scheduling his own free time. He was used to the structure and limitations of prison. "He has to adjust every day," she says. "A lifelong process."

By June 2013, Jacques was eight months into the physically demanding job. Nine months after the judge granted him a certificate of innocence, he still hadn't seen a dime of compensation from the state. His civil lawsuit was already a year under way and yet a long way from resolution.

By summer's end in 2013, after waiting almost a year for the check, Jacques received his compensation from the State of Illinois. The maximum for those wrongly incarcerated for more than twenty years, the check was just shy of $200,000. For almost two years, his family had propped him up financially, which he had found embarrassing at times. Jacques knew that the support he received was a distinct privilege, foreign to many exonerees. One death row exoneree, Ron Keine, remembers sleeping in abandoned cars, unable to find a job. Ashamed, he hoped snow would cover up the car so that nobody would see him. "I became a recluse," Keine read aloud to a teary crowd at a conference in Portland, Oregon, in 2014. "I did find work only because I made my own job. I would bag up rock salt and go house to house and sell it for a dollar a bag, and later on I got a pickup truck and later on it became more successful."

For Jacques, the state compensation money would only go so far. He knew that. It wasn't nearly enough for him to stop working. The labor of his delivery job took a toll on his body, a tired shell from the trauma and toil of incarceration. His old prison injury, the bulging disc in his back that surgery hadn't resolved, was catching up with him as he unloaded and hauled boxes every day. The medication for the pain made him antsier than usual. He needed physical therapy.

But $200,000 or thereabouts was still some serious dough, and now that he had some cash, Jacques felt more suspicious of others—even his well-intentioned dentist. When she told him he needed an onlay instead of a crown on his tooth, he grew concerned about the more expensive fix. Then, when the dentist began communicating in another language to her assistant about him and he couldn't understand what they were saying, Jacques's anxiety only heightened. "I mean it was just red flags," Jacques said. "It's just little things like that throw me off."

From the chair, he explained his situation to the dentist—that he was an exoneree and didn't know whom to trust. She calmed him down by explaining insurance would cover the pricey cosmetic onlay because it was a partial crown.

A lot of people had ideas about what he should do with the money. One friend set him up with a financial advisor at Morgan Stanley. Jacques thought about using the money to move out. He didn't mind living with his mother most of the time, except when she didn't clean the dishes or when she pushed microwave dinners on him when he wasn't hungry.

The tension with his mother aside, Jacques didn't feel ready to be on his own. "I know he was having a difficult time sleeping," said Rose,

Jacques's sister, whose upstairs apartment he still occupied. "He was afraid that somebody was going to come up to the house."

One night, Rose saw Jacques outside her home, waving a cell phone in his right hand and preparing to throw a rock with his left hand. Jacques had tried to call her, but her phone was on silent.

"What are you doing?" she hollered.

"There's something there!" Jacques exclaimed. "It's right there. Can you see it?"

A small black mass moved through the walkway. Jacques was convinced it was a possum. His son Richard, who used to live at Rose's, had told his dad he once saw a possum just outside the house. The innocuous detail roused Jacques's fears every time he walked home at night.

Finally, one night, he saw something dark scamper through the walkway. Rose told Jacques that if it was a possum, it wasn't dangerous. Jacques asked her to send down one of the dogs to scare it. Rose said no, because the possum might have rabies.

"I thought you said it wasn't dangerous!" Jacques yelled at her. He called to his mom upstairs to see if she could scare it away. Rose went to get a flashlight. She pointed it at the suspicious creature, revealing its true form. "It's a bag, dude," she said, laughing, relieved. Jacques's heart pounded as the garbage bag gulped the air around them and kept moving.

Friends and family urged Jacques to use his new chunk of cash to do something nice for himself, like buying a fancy car. He was uneasy about that. Living with his mother at his sister's home, he wasn't sure parking a flashy car on the street was a good idea. But Jacques finally caved to the pressure. He settled on a new Kia Cadenza. It looked slick but was modest enough in price. On the dashboard of his new car, he kept an old photo of two of his sons, asleep as babies, brothers. Within days of making the purchase, however, Jacques walked down to his parked car. It was riddled with bullet holes.

He was upset, but there were heavier things on his mind. Jane Raley was sick. It was cancer.

The two had remained close. As they both worked at Northwestern's Chicago campus, Jacques would visit her office. She invited him to her home, serving him her special guacamole dip on her deck, going to a music festival, and walking around her neighborhood.

"It's serious," Jane said. "It's metastasized to the liver." In the privacy of her office, she would throw her hands up in the air: "Why me?"

Jacques was flattened by the news, but he believed the faith that had freed him from prison would free his friend of this cancer. "Jane, this is the time where you've got to exercise that same faith, you know, to believe that you can be healed from this," he told her.

Despite the bullet holes, Jacques's new car still caught some attention. "Nice wheels!" a friend shouted to Jacques across a parking lot at the North Austin Library. Jacques was there to join a panel and talk to neighborhood kids about wrongful convictions. On a weekday evening, Jacques made it through rush-hour traffic after work to get there on time.

"You know!" Jacques laughed.

"You earned it! It was just on layaway!"

"Slave labor!" he joked.

Jacques looked in his rearview mirror at a gash on his forehead. He had been rear-ended over the weekend and hit his head. The next day was his granddaughter's birthday, but he missed out because of a headache.

Hopping out of his vehicle, he popped the trunk, where he kept pamphlets from the Center on Wrongful Convictions. He was prepared, rehearsed, having told his story dozens of times: "A young boy witnessed a shooting. He wasn't sure who it was. He didn't identify me. The victim died. They brought me back in. The young boy said it was me. He lied on the stand. I was sentenced to eighty years."

Inside the library, he took his seat on the panel next to two long-time friends and former prisoners, Juan Rivera and Daniel Taylor, both exonerees and clients at the Center. Daniel had only been free for a month. He was Cook County's ninetieth known exoneree since 1989, having spent more than two decades of a life sentence behind bars for a double murder he had confessed to as a teen. A false confession, it turned out, as it was impossible for him to have committed the crime because he was in police custody for disorderly conduct when the 1992 shooting took place.

In 1995, Daniel had tried to take his own life in prison. An inmate named Brick saved him. Brick, housed a few cells away, called Daniel "Black T." One day Brick told him, "Just because you in prison doesn't mean the fight's over. It just knocks you down a little. Whatcha going to do?"

"I'm going to fight for my life," Daniel told him.

At Daniel's homecoming celebration a few weeks before the panel, Jacques had spoken to a crowd of supporters who had assembled for the Center's rose ceremony, a tradition in which each person takes a turn to say a few words and give the exoneree a rose, one for every year he or she spent in prison.

"Where's your mother?" someone asked Daniel at his ceremony.

"My mom couldn't make it," he answered. "She had to work."

When it was Jacques's turn to speak, he jokingly grabbed all the roses from the basket holding them, garnering laughs from the assembly. "This is my brother Daniel," he said proudly. "We met in Stateville Correctional Center. If nobody in the City of Chicago will say this, I apologize that it took this long."

Jacques handed him a rose: "Watch out for that thorn!"

Daniel mumbled something about being stabbed before. He held the bouquet of roses up and brought it to his nose, slowly breathing in the fragrance. Daniel walked up to the podium, telling the crowd he was shy but that he would try to get through a speech. He was not going to miss his chance to take the mic. In prison, there was none. Daniel said he knew it wasn't going to be easy, whatever was to come. "The only way to get it done is to get started," he declared.

Jacques told Daniel they should kick around at the beach. He had his number, he reminded him. "I got your number," Daniel nodded.

"I'm in this with you," Jacques reassured him. "You're not alone."

XI.

"The prison is full of young Black men. I mean, they're young. They are pulling them in there. Some of them are guilty. But the range of sentences

they are giving to them when someone else is doing the same crime, I hate
to say it, but Caucasian, and getting a lesser sentence. That's racism."

Jacques arrived at the security area of the Cook County Juvenile Temporary Detention Center on a Saturday afternoon in March 2013, wearing
gray-on-gray sweatpants and short sleeves. Tracksuits were his usual garb
when he wasn't suited in a delivery work uniform or free Northwestern
University swag.

For a few months, he had been mentoring boys—some of them
young men—in juvenile detention. A law professor at Northwestern had
introduced him to some community leaders who practiced restorative
justice, which seeks to repair the harm caused by crime. The kids were
waiting to appear in court. Jacques joined a team of three other mentors,
some with rough pasts of their own. Together, they would visit kids from
one unit at the detention center.

Clearing security took about forty-five minutes after a mix-up over
visitation dates. As they waited, Jacques told the mentors about his new
ride, fresh bullet holes and all.

"What!?"

"That's what you get for buying a new car!" one of the group leaders
laughed.

"I didn't want to get a new car without a garage," Jacques told them,
shaking his head.

The men waited as security officers filtered through their program
supplies piece by piece.

"What's the blanket for?" one officer asked abruptly.

"To bring them the comforts of home!" Jacques whispered sarcasti-
cally, turning his head so the officer couldn't hear him. In fact, the small
quilted baby blanket would be placed in the center of the group as they
discussed a theme in a circle. Nothing they talked about was meant to
leave the circle of trust. They taught the boys to respect this code. Huddled in the security area, the mentors went over the game plan for the
day. Previously, they had covered values, gangs, and race. They often talked about doing the time and celebrating a second chance. But that day,
the theme was domestic violence, focusing on treatment of women and

children—a tough one for Jacques, who had as a child witnessed abuse and as a young man committed abuse.

"Die to self daily," Jacques says, quoting a scripture about spiritual rebirth. "It's like being in the hole. You got to try every way possible to get out of it. There's only one way to get you out of it."

Jacques and the mentors signed in, went through the metal detector and headed over to the unit of more than a dozen boys they'd be working with that day. The hallways looked more like a middle school than a detention center. Inspirational quotes and pictures adorned the walls.

Inside the dim, brick-walled meeting room, the boys sat on plastic chairs in rows facing the front of the room, supervised by three security guards. They all wore long-sleeved navy blue "JTDC" shirts and gray pants with rubber shoes. They seemed full of energy, ready to burst. Their unit had experienced a month of peace—no fights—and the boys had just found out they would be rewarded with a party and food catered from outside the facility.

One of the mentors asked the kids to help set up the room, and they all jumped up to arrange the chairs in a circle. A ball bounced into view, and soon the group was running and playing an icebreaker game of Presidents and Assassins, a variation on dodgeball.

"Move the ball! Move the ball!"

"Y'all gotta jump for it! Make it easy."

"Spread out!" Jacques shouted, getting in the game. "Gotta take a shot sometime!"

The kids hurried to corner Jacques and eliminate him from the game. Out of breath and beaming, he took a seat at the side of the room by the group leader, who was preparing materials.

After the game, the sixteen boys circled up and were invited to share the latest "rose and thorn" stories in their lives, the high points and low points, passing a sacred object for each to hold when it was his turn to speak.

The mentors handed out pens and sheets of song lyrics. At key moments in the discussion, they took the opportunity to reflect on the theme of the day by playing popular songs on a boombox. The kids underlined the words that spoke to them, moving to the beat. Jacques tapped his foot.

He shared his own story, flashbacks of abuse, snippets of pain and regrets. The boys raised their eyebrows and looked at each other as Jacques spoke. He was both a cautionary tale and a source of inspiration. His past was familiar to them; it was a future they didn't want. But he was proof that it was possible to start over.

In the lobby area after the session concluded, the leaders gathered their personal belongings from the lockers. They huddled once more and went over what went well, who was engaged, and what they could have done better—for next time. They scanned through the program curriculum and realized they hadn't managed to hit all the points, but the diversion was well spent, allowing more time for the kids to talk about their hopes for the future.

Freedom.
Beating their case.
Going home.
Taking care of their families.
Moving out of the country and living happily ever after.
Disappearing.
Leaving the hood.
Stopping the violence.

Across town about two miles away, an inmate stared at Jacques through the glass at Cook County Jail. Jacques was on the other side of the glass, a visitor.

Outside the same jail, about a year and a half earlier, news cameras had been rolling as three of Jacques's grown children ran up to him, a free man after more than twenty years of wrongful incarceration. But one of his kids had been missing that night.

Back at the jail, Jacques peered through the glass. Before him appeared a twenty-five-year-old man with features similar to his own. He was Jacques's son, a fourth child, Joshua.

Joshua had not grown up alongside Jacques's other children, his half-siblings. With the greater emotional distance, Joshua had visited Jacques in prison two or three times as a toddler, when his mother brought him to Stateville. Now, Joshua had been locked up for a few years waiting for a trial or a plea deal in a serious criminal case, having entered the system as Jacques was fighting to get out. With dark, unruly hair and a goatee, Joshua resembled a younger Jacques. Throughout the years Jacques had kept his goatee, which had turned to silver in prison. As a free man, sometimes he would cover the patch with a touch of Just For Men hair dye. Other times, he didn't mind trading in a little gray for some respect, finding that punks on the street tended to leave him alone when he looked older.

Jacques knew little about Joshua's case. All he knew was what was missing—himself, a father who was absent from most of his son's earliest memories. Court records show Joshua was charged with holding up two women in 2009, hijacking their Jeep, grabbing one of them by the hair, and detaining them both. A couple of weeks after the crime, the stolen Jeep crashed with two of his friends inside. They were killed. Joshua, severely injured, was hospitalized for months before being transferred to jail on a slew of charges. While in custody, he racked up another charge for assaulting an officer in 2012.

Jacques's other sons had little sympathy for their half-brother. "Everybody knows right from wrong," Jacques Jr. says. "You should know that to be in a gang, it's not going to get you anywhere. You know right from wrong, regardless of your parents."

Joshua was considering a plea deal when Jacques visited him. Joshua was already familiar with the Illinois Department of Corrections, convicted of a weapons charge in 2007 when he was nineteen years old. As they spoke, Jacques couldn't tell if they were being recorded.

"The public defender lady is supposed to call me," Jacques said. He encouraged his son to learn as many skills as he could in prison, to do the time and make the most of it. Jacques preached this and another gospel to friends who called him from prison. "I accept phone calls from them," Jacques says. "All of them are Christians that do call me. They're not gang members."

He would urge them to minister to the young kids in prison. "You see what the Lord can do for me? He can do the same for you."

Joshua ended up taking the deal, pleading guilty to the car hijacking in exchange for serving half of an eighteen-year sentence, with some credit for the time in jail. A judge sentenced him to three more years for assaulting the officer.

After sentencing, Joshua was booked at Robinson Correctional Center, a four-hour drive south of Chicago. For his mugshot, he had stared straight ahead, blankly. His thick dark hair was slicked back in a thick ponytail, his goatee neatly trimmed. At more than six feet, he stood taller than his dad.

The intake officers noted in his file the presence of several tattoos. On Joshua's left forearm there were several, including "RIP Julio" and "Trust no bitch." On the right, one tattoo showed a pitchfork and horns.

On his back, he tattooed a clown, inked with four words: "Would you love me."

Now, twice a month Jacques gets a call from Joshua. He phones on the weekends, mostly on Sundays, for thirty minutes. On opposite sides of the prison walls, it is the most the father and son have ever connected. They talk about classes Joshua is taking. They talk about creating a better life, doing the time.

"We've been through the process," Jacques says. "We understand each other."

XII.

"People's been telling me that I have anger issues. I don't see it, but you know, of course, you never look at yourself in that manner. But now I'm starting to accept it. Maybe a therapist or somebody could sit down and talk with me. But they [the state] don't provide you nothing. They don't provide me no healthcare, no type of therapy, no counseling, nothing."

The fall of 2013, Jacques's ex-wife, Sophia, hosted a thirty-first birthday party for their oldest son, Jacques Jr. The liquor was flowing, and Jacques was trying to fit in and goof off with his sons.

In the middle of the Hennessey-fueled night, Jacques pulled out a knife in jest, scaring some of his family and friends. His sons understood the long-standing prison joke—but no one else would have known what Jacques meant by the gesture.

"We would make a joke like in movies," his son Richard explains. "Phone check! If you're on the phone too long, they'll come and stab you. He was saying 'phone check' to somebody."

Richard told his dad to put the knife down. Jacques obeyed. And then he left. "He wasn't mad," Richard recalls. "He just felt that he wasn't wanted there."

Jacques was embarrassed. The incident didn't help alleviate the recent admonitions about his "anger issues," as his sons had told him. In prison, losing his temper was commonplace. When he had shared a cell with a Muslim man in county jail, Jacques respected his prayer schedule—but he drew the line when the cellmate washed his feet in the sink before praying, without cleaning it out afterward. The carelessness ate away at Jacques. "You motherfucker!" Jacques would scream at him. Finally, a guy from another cell suggested Jacques's cellmate simply wipe his feet before prayer. That solved it.

But on the outside, Jacques sometimes alarmed the people around him. His paranoia, coupled with his passionate, raspy voice, came across as frantic and frenzied at times.

His drinking also concerned his pal, the Center's assistant director Jennifer Linzer, who had tracked down the grown Orlando Lopez in Ohio. Linzer and Jacques had grown so close that he called her "Ma." But after he lost control at a holiday party—Jacques hadn't eaten all day and threw up—Linzer scolded him, which she later regretted, knowing the yelling he often faced at home. "It was probably a mistake on my part," Linzer says. "You worry that somebody is going to have one too many, and this is exactly what the Chicago police would like."

Jacques insisted his behavior wasn't a regular occurrence, that he had just worked too long and hard that day, taking the booze a little too far. "That's why I don't drink," he reminded himself. Being incarcerated for so long had affected his tolerance. An occasional drinker, he couldn't handle it well.

With his civil lawsuit in the wings, Jacques was under a microscope. Insinuations were flying that he still had gang ties—with the city's lawyers eager to find evidence of any indiscretion.

Meanwhile, Jacques's lawyers were busy collecting evidence to prove what they had long suspected to be true—that for years, in many cases, the Chicago Police Department had kept separate street files from its regular investigation files when investigating a case, never to be turned over to a defendant's trial lawyers. This pattern and practice would mean the City of Chicago had violated the constitutional rights of potentially many more citizens, just like Jacques. It could mean many more lawsuits— and millions of dollars—for his lawyers.

"Gang Crimes doesn't exist anymore," the city's lawyer, Eileen Ellen Rosen, told Judge Mary Rowland at a hearing for Jacques's case in 2014. "CPD does not know of any, doesn't require or maintain any files that are unique to Gang Crimes."

The city's old Gang Crimes files—dozens of file cabinets—could not be found. Jon Loevy wanted access to a room at Area North headquarters. He believed the gang files would be there. "What's missing are the notes," Loevy insisted. "The gang officers are still operating in the Jones Wild West. Those gang files existed. They have not been located. They are just simply missing."

In court, Rosen was frustrated. "We're proposing going to a room that has file cabinets and hundreds and hundreds and hundreds of files and weeding through and going through the paper and going back to what, 1960, to 1962, then based on a hunch or whatever, and then what?"

Rowland granted the request with some limits, satisfying neither side of the case. Rosen, she decided, would get a first pass at the room, checking "every nook and cranny," and then would report back so Loevy could review anything she uncovered.

"We had hoped that we would be part of the search process," Loevy chimed in. "There's no downside to letting us observe it. Maybe we don't touch anything? Maybe we just look over her shoulder? What is the downside to having us observe the search?"

The judge paused, hesitant. "My thought in having her down there is so your search could be more efficient," she answered.

"This is an important search and it seems weird that we wouldn't be there," Loevy reasoned.

"It's not weird," Rosen insisted. "There's no reason that anybody needs to be looking over my shoulder. I'm an officer of the court!"

"We would like to participate! We could go faster!" Loevy negotiated.

"There's no reason they can't take my word for it," Rosen told the judge.

"We could help! What's the downside?!" Loevy volleyed for Rowland's attention.

"We don't want other people rummaging through the files," Rosen said.

The judge cut in the back and forth. "This is my main concern. If there is a single piece of paper about this case, I want it in his hands." Rowland offered to go herself to check it out, eliciting chuckles from the room. But Rosen, she decided for the second time, would get to go alone to the file storage room.

"Can we get some kind of index? Get some kind of record?" Loevy asked, grasping for a win.

The judge proposed sticky notes to keep things straight. The hearing had stretched later than anticipated. Loevy thanked Rowland for the allowance. She nodded and called up the next case on the docket.

It would ultimately take years for a system to be developed to inspect the old cabinets for these old Gang Crimes street files to be found. Finally, in mid-2015, the court ordered the City of Chicago to turn over 138 files to Jacques's attorneys. They were also granted another extension, allowing five more months for the investigation of key facts in the case and for setting a schedule to line up fact and expert witnesses. If Jacques were to win his suit, it was not going to be anytime soon.

The end of 2013 brought more frustrations for Jacques. He had some harsh words with his daughter when she called him explaining she needed six hundred dollars to repair the car he had given her. She asked him what she should do.

"Take the bus!" Jacques said, exasperated, offering no help.

The following morning, he called to apologize. It wasn't her fault, he explained. He was upset with himself because he was cited for two tickets in one day—parking and speeding—so he was stressed about money.

Jacques had been losing his temper at work too, a few episodes. Finally, he recognized that he needed help and so he found his way to a therapist.

Her office was nestled somewhere inside the Merchandise Mart, Chicago's labyrinthine office and shopping space. They were to meet once a week, on Tuesdays. "I knew I needed it," Jacques said. "She's really accurate about a lot of things."

Jacques learned about "misdirecting" his anger. Soon, he would talk about how admitting you have a problem is the first step. He would learn about making healthy decisions.

Six months later, the July sun lit up a softball park near Northwestern's Chicago campus on a Friday afternoon. Law school students and a few exonerees were playing another team from a nearby school.

Jacques showed up in the early afternoon in his Northwestern delivery uniform to watch the game. "What's happening?" he said, side-hugging, chest-bumping, and then back-slapping his longtime friend, fellow exoneree Juan Rivera, who had just been up at bat.

"You on lunch break?" someone said.

"Lunch break?" Jacques echoed, as if to ask, "What's a lunch break?"

In fact, he had just wrapped up an eight-week hiatus from work, having smashed his hand on the job. He'd fractured his pinky finger, the type of injury that will put a delivery guy out of work for a bit.

"Watch your hand!" the supervisor had warned as they were moving a table. Then, *bam*.

Jacques wore a cast for six weeks and went to physical therapy for another two weeks before returning to work. During his time off, he had learned about the professional social network LinkedIn.

"I want to learn how to get in the LinkedIn thing."

"LinkedIn?" someone watching the softball game asked.

"This young lady, I want to try to get ahold of her," Jacques explained, collecting stares from his friends. "She's a nonprofit organization professional. We're trying to start a nonprofit organization."

Innocence Demands Justice would be the name, Jacques decided. He wanted to save the innocent—or at least try to. "Maybe she can assist us, help guide us," he said.

He never got in touch with that young woman, but slowly, Jacques built a small group of allies to look into cases, meeting monthly for updates and sending letters and holiday cards to inmates. Jacques later connected with a mother with two sons in prison, whom he believes to be innocent.

Jacques paused to watch the softball game. He liked hanging out at the park, being with people he trusted. A month earlier, he had stopped by Chicago's annual Puerto Rican Day parade, which was known for its gang presence. When some friends invited him to join, he was hesitant. His buddies assured him the old guys wouldn't be out. Just some new Latin King kids. It's not like it used to be, they told him. Afterwards, they went over to the old neighborhood in Humboldt Park. Police cars were all around. "What happened?" Jacques asked. When he heard some people had been shot, he immediately left.

The dangers felt like they were closing in on him. For this reason, Jacques avoided going out in public with his family. He didn't feel it was safe. He also didn't like being recognized around the old neighborhood. Did people remember his face from the news of his wrongful conviction— or from his past life in the gang? Jacques didn't like being left to wonder.

"See ya!" he told his buddies.

Since his release, Jacques had been putting off getting baptized. He says his faith wavered when his church attendance lapsed. Working a physically exhausting weekday job meant free time on the outside was more precious to him, and church had become less of a priority. But once he was ready to focus on his faith again, Jacques knew whom to turn to for his baptism—the chaplain who had ministered to him in prison.

A silver-bearded man with kind eyes, Bishop George Adamson had always promised to baptize Jacques if he ever got out. Adamson had a long history with the Illinois Department of Corrections, serving on the Religious Practice Advisory Board for almost a quarter of a century.[10]

The baptism would have to be in the river, like Jesus. The closest river to Aurora, Illinois, where Adamson had a congregation, was the Fox River.

"That river is nasty!" Jacques lamented.

On the road trip about forty miles west of Chicago, Jacques spied a bumper sticker on a van in front of him: *Jesus Loves You*. A believer in signs from God, Jacques took this as an indication that he had made the right decision. Jacques tried to take a picture of the bumper sticker with

10. When Jacques's mother, Gwendolyn Rivera, died in February 2016 at the age of seventy-two, Bishop Adamson presided over her memorial service.

his camera phone, but it was too wobbly on the road.

Surrounded by congregants on a Sunday morning, as part of the ritual, Adamson asked Jacques why he came.

"The spirit of the Lord brought me here," Jacques answered.

He was told to pick up a stone from the bottom of the river to symbolize his tombstone, being dead to the world. Reborn in Christ. Jacques put the stone in the trunk of his Kia Cadenza, with plans to engrave the stone with the date of his baptism.

Jacques's former lawyer Jane's condition had been gradually worsening. The last time he saw her had been some months before in her office. After treatment, she was back at work and appeared to be fighting through it. As he passed by Jane's door and caught a glimpse, Jacques didn't want to bother her. She looked so absorbed in what she was doing.

Jacques had prayed and prayed for Jane to be healed. "Whatever you ask in my name," he recited from the Bible. In therapy, his counselor told him, "I don't think you're satisfied with God's answer."

On Christmas Day 2014, Jacques sent Jane a text message: "Merry Christmas, Aunt Jane. I miss you so much."

Jane never read the message. She had passed that morning.

"Why Jane?" Jacques cried, again and again. Engulfed in a crisis of faith, Jacques agonized over whether he had told Jane enough about God and the power of prayer. When Jane would say things like "Keep your fingers crossed," Jacques would become upset and correct her. "Jane! Haven't I told you? You have to have faith!"

He wanted Jane to be resurrected, willing it to be possible through his faith. But on the road to her funeral in early January 2015, he wept as he confronted the reality of her death.

"There was nobody like her. She was the most empathetic and altruistic lawyer—and even human being—I ever knew," says longtime colleague and friend Jeff Urdangen. "She's my muse."

The funeral service was low-key with beautiful music. "Of course, music," Urdangen says with a soft laugh. In addition to being a successful lawyer, Jane played the piano and violin. Years earlier, she had encouraged Urdangen to put his three-year-old son Nathan in lessons.

She recognized in him a certain musicality. As young boys, Jane's son Tom and Nathan had played duets together, violin and piano. "He's now an amazing piano player," says Urdangen, whose son is studying at the Berklee College of Music. "That's going to be his career. Without Jane, I don't know if I would have pursued that for my son."

Jane's loss was felt deeply across different communities. Lawyers and students—and exonerees like Jacques, whom she helped deliver from prison, were distraught. They lost a champion and friend.

After Jane's death, one of her colleagues texted Jacques some pictures of the two of them. In one snapshot, they are walking out of Cook County Jail. Jane is smiling next to Jacques but is looking down, pensively.

Years after that flicker, Jacques peered at the photo on his smudgy cell phone screen with watery eyes. "I wished I had asked her what she was thinking," he said.

Jacques paused, then asked again: "What are you thinking, Jane?"

PART THREE

JAMES

Convicted in 1989
Exonerated in 2012

Courtesy WBEZ/Andrew Gill

I.

"It was one of those life-altering moments. I went from not knowing when I'd be free for a quarter of a century, serving six life sentences and three fourteen-year sentences, to knowing I'd be leaving in twenty-four hours."

"Dude, it's a mistake," he said to the officer. "My call is tomorrow."

It was May 31, 2012. James Kluppelberg, forty-six, was doing some research in the law library at Menard Correctional Center, Illinois's largest maximum-security prison, when an officer told him he had a legal call back in the cell house. James knew his lawyers were supposed to be in court for him that day, about 350 miles away in Chicago's Cook County. But usually he wouldn't get a call until the next day to hear the latest.

"You gotta come now," the officer said.

Escorted into a bullpen, or holding cell, he waited to go to the call room. His counselor arrived to take him, and James again waited for the phone. When he picked up the line, there were several people on the call, including Karl Leonard, a young attorney at one of Chicago's most prestigious law firms, Winston & Strawn. Karl had been working on James's case for about three years, starting as a summer volunteer for the Exoneration Project at the University of Chicago, where he had graduated from law school in 2009.

"It's over," Karl said.

James's heart sank. He thought Karl meant he had lost his latest appeal, his second post-conviction petition, one of various legal routes a prisoner can take to overturn a case. Glancing over at his counselor, James noticed she had a knowing grin on her face.

"We'll be by to pick you up tomorrow," Karl said.

The phone slipped through James's hands. He started crying and shaking.

After a few minutes, back on the line, Karl asked, "What size pant do you wear?"

James had no clue anymore. "DOC don't go by sizes," he told him. "They got elastic."

By the time the call wrapped up, it was getting close to the gallery-officer shift change. News had spread quickly around the prison.

"Couldn't have happened to a better guy." One of the gallery officers wished him well.

The incoming gallery officer counted the guys. Having heard the news, he told James he should go hang out in the shower, even though it was an off-shower day. He could have the whole room and all the hot water to himself.

Alone, he was afraid of what was to come: the unknown. "Scared to death," James remembers. "Scared something was going to happen at the last minute."

His worries cascaded. *Is this really happening? How am I going to survive?* Inside the shower room, he let the hot water hit him, and he took in the rare moment of peace, quiet, and privacy. It was soon dinnertime, and an officer told James he didn't have to go eat with the others. This suited James, who wanted the security of his cell, not wanting to be swept up in a riot or get stabbed, which in prison was always a possibility.

"When you're within twenty-four hours of being free, the cell becomes your best friend," James says.

James started packing. He decided he would take his records and letters but would leave behind the rest of his possessions: a TV, Walkman, typewriter, some clothing and food.

He gave most everything to his cellie, an elderly gentleman who was deep into his sentence. "He just didn't have anyone," James says. "He was the one in most need who was nearest to me."

The next morning he was processed out, a lengthy procedure that began around 8:30 in the morning and lasted four hours. James had to ship out his records and letters to the front gate of the prison, where they would be waiting for him in cardboard boxes. He turned in his bedding and clothing, keeping only the garments he was wearing—gray sweatpants, a T-shirt, and chunky black boots that he had purchased from the prison commissary. His glasses were strung around his neck on a lanyard.

Inside his gray sweatpants pocket he kept the rest of his assets—$14.17.

Karl was waiting for him at the visitor sign-in area in the gatehouse. He told James some reporters were outside. One print reporter, one TV reporter. It was up to him whether or not he wanted to talk to them.

James was happy to answer their questions, leaving behind his belongings to go across the street.

The lone news camera framed him up with historic Menard looking stately in the background. Founded as Southern Illinois Penitentiary in 1878, the prison sits so far south in the state that it's closer to Mississippi than Chicago. Menard is Illinois's largest maximum-security prison, and it was once one of three sites in Illinois where executions were carried out by electrocution. In 2011, Illinois abolished the death penalty, following the 2003 commutation of death sentences.

The news camera captured James and Karl walking from the gate-house. In the footage, both are smiling. Karl is tall and lanky, wearing a dark suit and shiny shoes, with a youthful head of hair. James, considerably shorter and stockier, is bald. His pale skin looks fresh and clear, largely untainted by UV rays for most of his life. But behind his eyes you can see the years and the sadness.

"It's been a long time," James told the media. "January of '88 was the last time I walked free without chains."

James told the reporters he still believed the United States had the best justice system in the world—he had just slipped through the cracks. "Unfortunately the atmosphere when I was arrested, there wasn't a lot of care about it that they got it right," James said on camera. "There was a lot of corruption in the Chicago Police Department."

What did he miss out on? The reporters wanted to know.

He had three grown children. Some of them had children he had never met. His mother, whom he had lost touch with, had died during his incarceration. "There's just so much that I'll never be able to get back," James said, looking down at the pavement, scanning through the last quarter of a century. "It is what it is. I'm blessed to keep waking up each day, and as long as God keeps waking me up, I'll keep moving forward."

He wrapped up the interviews, then went back to the gatehouse for his file boxes. Car loaded, James hopped in. Karl drove. A paralegal sat in the back. They headed to Lambert–St. Louis International Airport, a ninety-mile trip that took about three hours. About four times on the way, Karl had to pull the car over so that James could throw up. James attributed it to motion sickness, having not been in a car in such a long time. Karl believed James's nausea was due to nerves and shock. "I doubt he slept that night at all," Karl later said.

The first time he pulled over, a woman stopped her car beside them. "Looks like you could use this," she said, handing James a bottle of water from a cooler in her car. He accepted it, and she took off. "A random act of kindness from a woman who had no idea who she had just helped," James remembers.

At the airport, more reporters were waiting. James gave some interviews, all the while captivated by the strange environment with heightened security—more akin to prison than the free world. "I mean, you used to be able to walk into an airport, put some money down on a counter and say, 'Give me a ticket. I want to go to so-and-so.' They frown on that now," James says, chuckling.

Karl got a call on his phone just before boarding. It was Sarah, one of James's daughters, a grown woman he knew only through letters from the past thirteen years. Sarah had found out the news of James's release from an aunt.

They didn't have much time to talk. "I'm talking on a phone that gets email!" he told her.

"Yeah, they do that now!" Sarah laughed.

The flight left late due to bad weather. Airborne, they had to circle around Chicago's O'Hare International Airport for a while, arriving about two hours late to find more reporters seeking interviews on the other end.

At a Holiday Inn just outside O'Hare, James spent his first night as a free man. His lawyers at the Exoneration Project had arranged to put him up for a few nights. No one knew where he would stay permanently.

Inside his hotel room, the TV menu teemed with "XXX" amenities. To his shock, James discovered porn was readily available. To his greater shock, the cost of a pulled pork sandwich at the hotel bar was about fifteen dollars. Not including the drink and fries. He carried his meal to his room and ate on his bed.

In the quiet of the space, he reached for the bedside phone.

He dialed her number. She answered.

It was Rena', his longtime prison pen pal. In her late forties, she lived in Silver City, New Mexico, where she managed an Econo Lodge Hotel, some 1,500 miles from Chicago.

"It's Jim."

"Tim who?" she asked.

"No, it's Jim," James said into the phone.

"OK . . . Jim who?"

James told her it was him. From the letters.

Rena' had first reached out to James through a prison correspondence service almost twenty years earlier. She picked him from a list of inmates. His last name started with a "K," and so did hers. When Rena' learned he was serving six life sentences, she felt safe he wouldn't get out and come find her.

Rena' wasn't looking for a romantic relationship—or any relationship at all. Rather, she needed advice that only a prisoner could give. She had a question about prison correspondence services. She was looking to relieve herself of writing letters to four inmates, all sons of a late friend. The frequent letter-writing had become burdensome to her. Rena' thought she'd look into a prison correspondence service and see if an inmate on the other end found it valuable. James was that inmate.

His then wife Donna intercepted Rena's email inquiry and put them in touch. James gave Rena' the information she needed to get her friend's boys set up. Ten years later, when she was passing through Chicago before moving to the Southwest, Rena' took the weekend to visit James and say thanks. Donna accompanied her. It was the first and only time during his incarceration that they met face to face. The trio had one hour. James felt a little apprehension about meeting someone new, but by the end of the visit, he had a new friend.

After he and Donna divorced, James sent Rena' a letter. He told her he didn't have many connections on the outside, and the two became pen pals. For every letter Rena' wrote, James would write five more, sometimes telling her the same story twice. She became curious about his case.

"Ask me any question you want, and I'll answer it," he would write.

The more Rena' read, the more she realized her pen pal was in the wrong place. Assured of his innocence, she wrote to him and asked: "What do you look for in a woman?" This was the first hint that Rena' might be interested in a romantic relationship, but James didn't register the change in tone.

She gave him her phone numbers in case he needed something, someday. On his first night as a free man, he called her from the Holiday Inn.

James and Rena' had been talking for almost an hour when she stopped to ask, "Wait a second, who's paying for this?"

"The attorneys!"

She hung up and called James back, explaining to him that costs had gone up since he'd been in prison. "Well, it's too bad that I'm in Chicago," he said.

"Dude, they make airplanes for a reason," Rena' said.

They agreed she should request time off work and visit in a week's time. Rena' would have to explain to her boyfriend back at home why she was taking off to visit a released prisoner in Illinois. She and her boyfriend had been drifting apart and were becoming more like roommates. Jealous, he had thrown away all of James's letters about two years earlier.

After James got off the phone with Rena', he took a long, hot shower. He lay down for a while, then walked around outside in the morning air to feel the dawn.

II.

"Imagine how badly they must have beaten me for a Cook County judge not to be able to look the other way."

Born to a single mother in Michigan City, Indiana, in 1965, James grew up mostly on the South Side of Chicago. The oldest of five siblings, James never knew his father. He doesn't even know his father's name. But he remembers being close to his mother.

While he was growing up, James's family was on public assistance. Other than that, his mother received support from whomever she was dating at the time. James's last name, Kluppelberg, came from one of her husbands, who adopted him. He has no idea where this man is today.

Once a month, when James was little, his mother would shop in the middle of the night at a twenty-four-hour Jewel grocery store. She would take James with her as she stocked up for the whole month with the family's food stamps. "That used to be our time," he says.

James attended Carter H. Harrison Technical High School, shuttered in 1983. He didn't finish school because of a pushing match with the assistant principal, but he earned his high-school equivalency in 1985.

At the age of seventeen, James had a serious run-in with the law. His mother had thrown a party in a storefront recreation room. As it was wrapping up, one man didn't want to leave. James remembers the inebriated man striking his mother. James grabbed a two-by-four block of wood and hit him. The man ended up in the hospital in critical condition, and James was arrested and held on a $100,000 bond for the battery.

About a month later, the man died at the hospital from complications from his injuries. James was charged with involuntary manslaughter for the death. At trial, Chicago attorney Marshall Weinberg represented James. He was found not guilty.

He stayed out of trouble for the next couple of years, until 1984, when James burglarized a couple of stores—a Radio Shack and a currency exchange, he says—and he attempted to knock over a third. James was found guilty the following January. At nineteen, he was shipped to Joliet to be processed, spending the next eighteen months in Illinois prisons before he was granted work release. Although the prisons weren't nearly as dangerous as he would later experience, James was nonetheless determined to stay out of trouble this time.

Amid these legal situations, James also married before he turned eighteen. The five-year marriage to Donna produced a daughter, Samantha. James also fathered three more children outside his marriage: another daughter, Sarah, born in 1984, whose mother James had dated for a few weeks and didn't tell him about the pregnancy; a son, James Jr., whom he had with a girlfriend, Dawn, in 1985; and, with another woman, a daughter who passed after her birth in 1985. Fresh off a divorce from Donna in 1987, James remarried in 1988, to a woman named Bonnie. The couple had no children.

It was James's relationship with Dawn in the mid-eighties that would determine later events that led to his wrongful conviction. In 1984, Dawn had briefly left her boyfriend and father of her three other sons, Duane Glassco, for James. During their relationship, Dawn and James lived together, and James helped take care of her kids. Duane, a drug addict with nowhere to stay, shacked up in the home, too.

In the early Saturday morning hours of March 24, 1984, a blaze overtook a three-story wood-framed apartment building on the South Side of Chicago. No one lived on the first floor. Two related families occupied the rest of the home. They were asleep in their beds.

Elva Lupercio woke up her husband, Santos, to tell him the house was on fire. He scrambled to gather their five children around him: ten-year-old Santos Jr., eight-year-old Sonia, six-year-old Crisabel,[11] four-year-old Elva Yadira, and three-year-old Anabel.

The family on the third floor was able to get out. But when Santos tried to escape through the front and back doors, flames prevented him. In a back bedroom, he looked out the window to see lashes of fire coming together and separating every few seconds.

Santos decided to exit through the window so that Elva could pass him the children. He explained to her what he was going to do. But as he tried to go down, the floor gave way and he fell from the second floor. Santos screamed for help. Someone carried him to the outside, and an ambulance took him to Holy Cross Hospital. He had fractured his skull, burned his back from the mid-hip to his rib cage, and lost hearing in his right ear. He was treated in Chicago for about a week, then was taken to Mexico, where he continued to be treated for the burns.

He never saw his wife and kids again. They were all pronounced dead at Mercy Hospital within hours of the fire.

Living several doors down from the fire, James, along with many other neighbors, had watched as the flames consumed the building.

"It was rolling pretty good," James remembers. "You didn't know if they were going to get a handle on it."

---

11. Also spelled Cristabelle, Christobel, and Cristobel in various records.

The blaze was so intense that he and Dawn had packed the kids in the car in case they needed to flee to safety.

That night, James had been playing cards with Dawn and Duane. It had been a frustrating night. James had come home to find the pair high on angel dust, a nickname for the hallucinogen PCP. The kids had not eaten, and the house was a wreck. To cool off, James walked his collie-shepherd mix, Bootsie.

When he returned, he quarreled with Dawn and left again with the dog.

The community reeled from not one but two fires in the neighborhood. A *Back of the Yards Journal* article, just a few days after the incidents, reported: "Two Tragic Fires; Six Perish, Many Homeless." In the same paper, a columnist wrote about an "arsonist on the loose," asking, "Who is burning these houses?"

The Back of the Yards Council sponsored a fire victims' fund and planned to sell smoke alarms for $8.15.

The city's only fire investigation unit at the time was the Chicago Police Department's Bomb and Arson Unit. Investigators could not determine how or where the fire started because the building had collapsed. They tested the debris to see if a fire accelerant was used, which could have indicated arson. The results came back negative. The case was ruled an accident and closed.

James hadn't heard that the Lupercio family perished—not until nearly four years later, when Duane contacted police.

Duane, then twenty-three, was facing burglary charges, arrested on felony probation, and he saw the opportunity to get a break on his case. And he could finally retaliate against James. Duane's jealousy over Dawn's leaving him for James in 1984 had not subsided.

Duane made up a story, telling police he had witnessed James going back and forth to the apartment building the night it burned down in 1984. Duane added to the lie, saying he could see James about a block away through the attic window of the home. Another building obstructs the attic view, a fact that would not fully emerge for more than two decades.

Their landlord also kept the attic window boarded up in the winter to retain heat, Dawn would later reveal.

In January 1988, twenty-two-year-old James was repairing frozen pipes at an apartment building on South Hermitage Avenue when police came for him in the evening. A family man who also largely supported his mother, James was accustomed to long ten- or twelve-hour workdays, trying to get his home remodeling company off the ground. He had also recently moonlighted as a security guard over the holidays and had reported two car fires on Christmas Eve 1987. The officers said they wanted to show him some photos pertaining to his report, back at the station.

They took him to the Bomb and Arson squad office on South State Street at the Central Police Station. (The thirteen-floor steel building, with a small moat separating the south wall from the parking lot, was demolished in 2003 to make way for condos.)

They put James in a ten-by-twelve-foot interview room with a tinted one-way mirror window. The space had two doorways, one leading out and the other leading to a lieutenant's office. "I got scared. I got real scared," James says.

He called his lawyer, who wasn't in. He then agreed to take a lie detector test, but just beforehand, police handed him a waiver that stated he would be asked questions about homicides from 1984. James stopped. "I asked them what they were trying to do, and that is when the officer got violent and slammed me up against the wall and put a pair of cuffs on me and dragged me back upstairs," James later would testify at a hearing leading up to his trial.

The interrogation turned into a beating, which led to James's confessing to having set the fires, he says. "They laid me face down on the floor and they started punching me in my back and using the heel of their feet in the back kidney area," James described.

At one point, the beating had stopped long enough for James to use the bathroom, and he realized he had urinated blood. "There was blood in my underwear," James remembers.

Disoriented, he had lost his sense of time when an assistant state's attorney showed up to jot down nine sentences, summarizing James's "confession" to police at about half past midnight. He was not left alone with the assistant state's attorney to divulge he had been beaten. The police kept him in custody, claiming that James had intentionally set the car fires he had reported, constituting a parole violation from his 1984 burglary convictions.

Marshall Weinberg, James's lawyer from his first case, woke up to a phone call. His clock radio and watch told him it was 2:15 in the morning. On the line was James's fiancée, Bonnie. She placed him on a three-way call with James. "He was incoherent. He was hysterical," Weinberg, who would later work to suppress James's confession, said in court. "I could barely understand him. He was crying. He was in a hysterical state. I had to stop him, yell at him, and calm him down before I could understand exactly what he was saying."

In between cries, James told Weinberg he'd been beaten. Weinberg instructed him not to make any more statements to police or prosecutors. James was taken to the county jail, being held for the car fires until a murder indictment could come down.

The booking officer at the jail noticed bruises on James's lower back and kidney area. James told him he was urinating blood. An intake form showed two large markings on a diagram, right where the kidneys would be. When Weinberg visited James in lockup, James pulled up his shirt, revealing several large bruises on his lower back. Weinberg asked a judge to send him to the county jail hospital for treatment, and the court ordered it, but James says he was never sent. It took another week before James received medical attention in jail. He was found doubled over in the bathroom. "They ran some tests, gave me some meds, and sent me back to the deck."

About a week later, Chicago police commander Jon Burge, now infamous for his decades-long torture campaign, announced to the media his department's triumph over the 1984 case. They had obtained a confession, he reported.

"Klupperberg [sic] told us he had been setting fires since he was nine years old," Burge told reporters. The statement was a total fabrication, one that did not even match the forced confession that was beaten out of James.

The beating wasn't the first under Burge's crew, and it was far from the last. In 2010, after decades of civic denial and public outcry, Burge was convicted on perjury charges related to the torture cases. In 2015, the City of Chicago finally agreed to create a $5.5 million reparations fund for Burge's torture survivors, to include a formal apology, among other assistance and memorials.[12]

Indicted for the Lupercio family murders, James's hopes were high that the truth would prevail and he would be set free to return to his family. He sat in county jail for a year and a half waiting for his trial, waiting for justice.

Weinberg continued to represent him, and, before the murder trial, he succeeded in having James's forced confession tossed out. "We cannot have statements that are the result of mistreatment by the police," Judge Robert Collins said after a lengthy hearing in November 1988. "There is no disagreement in that area."

But the case itself would still go forward on the testimony of a single alleged witness, Duane. A few weeks before he faced his fate in court, James turned twenty-four. He marked the day, but after such a long stretch in the jail, it felt like any other.

At a bench trial in July 1989, prosecutors presented a purported arson expert, Commander Francis Burns, who had worked in the Chicago Fire Department's Office of Fire Investigations, which was not operating at the time of the fire. Burns had not conducted an official investigation of the fire. In 1984, the Chicago Police Department's Bomb and Arson Unit handled such investigations and had ruled the fire an accident, closing the case. But for a training exercise, Burns had visited the site of the fire, taking no notes and making no reports. At trial, relying only on memory, Burns told the court about V-shaped burn patterns he had observed, which made him think the fire was an arson.

Having made a deal with the prosecution on his own case—three years in prison considered time served—Duane testified. After a burglary conviction, he was due to be sentenced for a probation violation, and he wanted leniency. In the US criminal justice system, backroom deals like

12. Now released from federal prison after less than four years behind bars, Burge still earns a police pension.

these are not uncommon, as many cases are brokered without a trial.

In court, at James's trial, Duane said he was coherent the night of the fire, despite having taken cocaine. His ex-girlfriend Dawn also said they had been taking animal tranquilizers called "tic"—angel dust. "And I asked him what he did, and the only thing he did was smile at me," Duane told the court about seeing James the night of the fire. "You can see the whole yard from the window."

James was angry. "I just sat there in amazement and awe that he had such a vivid imagination."

The trial lasted about eight hours over two days. Dawn also provided shaky testimony that mostly supported James but contradicted her earlier accounts to the grand jury, where she claimed James had admitted to the fires. James did not testify. The defense rested, calling no witnesses. Then: *Guilty.* James was stunned.

"It doesn't take much to convict a person," he says. "It does not take anything more than what somebody says."

Even more shocking to James: the state wanted the death penalty.

"I was never told," James says. "It freaked me out."

As he awaited sentencing in the fall of 1989, with nothing to lose, James escaped from jail. His easy exit was made on a drug bribe. A correctional officer altered records and allowed James to post bond and walk out of the building without immediate consequence. Chicago newspapers reported the escape and subsequent capture, in Macon, Georgia, in October 1989. He was on his way to Florida to stay with his sister for a while, James says, but he called the Cook County State's Attorney when he learned of the pursuit.

"Hey, don't worry—I'll be back in time for my court date."

He was told to stay put. Officers in tactical gear showed up to his hotel room.

It would be another twenty-three years until he would walk without chains.

III.

"It's because of kids like that people like me are free."

They called it the M&M shop, like the chocolate candy. It was Menard Correctional Center's maintenance department, the one responsible for doing repairs throughout the maximum-security prison. For James, during his first stint at Menard, it meant something to do, time away from his cell, where he would otherwise spend twenty-three hours a day, every day.

He had always been a good handyman, so he fixed everything from plumbing to carpentry. It took his mind off his fate of being told when to shower and when to eat for the rest of his life—six times over, if that were possible. Six life sentences.

After entering the prison system in 1990, James was transferred from one Illinois prison to another. He spent about eight years at Menard in the nineties, moving on to Joliet and Stateville until 2011, when he returned to Menard. The final move back devastated him because he was to lose his sole support, thirty dollars a month from his job as a print-shop mechanic at Stateville. At Menard, he'd be stuck.

Menard had changed. In the early nineties, the gangs controlled the prison, and it was a wild place. Unrepresented, James was vulnerable until a family member's husband, a Latin King, wrote to some of his brothers in prison to protect James.

But everything changed in 1996 when a national scandal hit the Illinois Department of Corrections, resulting in an extended lockdown in state prisons. Richard Speck, a mass murderer who had slain eight nurses in Chicago in 1966, appeared on a videotape anonymously recorded by an attorney that showed him "snorting cocaine, engaging in sex and bragging about living the good life at Stateville prison," reported the *New York Times* in May 1996. Illinois lawmakers watched the video, now infamously known as the "Speck Tapes," which depicted other outrageous prison conditions. (Speck died in 1991, before the release of the tapes.)

"When those came out, all hell broke loose," James remembers. "It gave enough of a public outcry that they had to make these sweeping changes. The pendulum swung the other way. It got abusive. It got real bad."

During a shakedown in 1996, the prison confiscated some Christmas ornaments James had saved up to purchase as gifts for his kids. More devastatingly, James spent months in solitary confinement after correctional officers found homemade knives belonging to his cellie, who James says turned him in.

Fifteen years later, when James returned to Menard after his transfers elsewhere in the state, the rules, written and unwritten, were different. James was in the shower when a gang of men started closing in on him. But he was spared when an old buddy intervened. "This is a friend of mine. You don't mess with him," he told them. From then on, James was protected again.

Over the years, almost all of his relationships outside of prison faded away. His marriage to Bonnie lasted until 2000, when she wanted a divorce. From prison, James reunited with Donna. Then that ended, too.

Contact with his son, James Jr., had tapered off. As a kid, James Jr. had visited the prison with Bonnie; he moved in with her when he was eight after spending a year in a homeless shelter with his mom, Dawn. Bonnie was close to Dawn throughout her addiction. "Bonnie was with her until the day she died," James says of his exes' friendship. "She was in the room."

On prison visits when Bonnie brought his son, the two James Kluppelbergs sat together at one of many tables and chairs in a big open room. They ate potato chips with ketchup—the closest thing to French fries in the Department of Corrections. The potato chips had ridges, James Jr. remembers.

"It had to be ridges because it supports the ketchup," he says.

Prison staff would take two Polaroid pictures during the visits. One photo to stay. One to go.

When James Jr. was in junior high, the visits stopped after James and Bonnie divorced. James kept writing to his son, but the letters went unanswered. He mailed elaborate drawings as gifts he had purchased from other inmates who were artists. No response. Disappointed, James persisted. "You have to do it and try your best."

He also lost touch with his mother leading up to her death. His mom hadn't written him in years, for which James had only one explanation. "Time," he says, averting his glance. "It's that sad and simple. Out of sight, out of mind."

In 2004, his sister called him with bad news. "Cancer?" James asked. "This don't happen overnight."

They had forgotten about him, his sister apologized. After this initial call, the prison called his sister back and his mother was put on the line from her deathbed. "She cried," James remembers. "She knew that it was me. She cried a lot. She said how sorry she was for everything."

He told her he loved her. "Not to worry," he said. "It was going to be OK."

Letters with strangers kept him going. He would handwrite notes to his pen pal, Rena'. He also corresponded with his daughter Sarah, whom he had never met but who had found him in prison.

He also found fulfillment in education. Carrying six life sentences meant the prison didn't care to enroll him in anything. So James took free correspondence courses from a program called Family Radio School of the Bible. He also became an ordained minister through the Universal Life Church, known to freely offer ordination to all.

But in 2008, on a gray, dank day, he had a life-changing meeting with three visitors, including Chicago attorney Gayle Horn, now a partner at Loevy & Loevy, who ran a new clinic called the Exoneration Project at the University of Chicago Law School. With her were two students. Horn had been handed his case by Jane Raley at the Center on Wrongful Convictions, who had been in touch with James by mail. "I want to help you," Jane told James. Her hands already full with Kristine Bunch's arson science case, Jane asked, "Can I talk to some lawyers for you?"

James had written "in excess of a thousand letters" to law schools and lawyers over the years, asking for help. When he finally received a letter from the Exoneration Project, James broke down. "I cried like a baby on the floor of my cell by the bars where it was delivered," he remembers. "Somebody was listening. Finally."

Gayle remembers their first meeting. "From the beginning you get a sense he's an incredibly candid and compelling person," she says. After taking on the case, she assigned two third-year law students, Cadence and Ashley, to undertake the research. They seldom used the small annex off the law school designated for the new clinic in 2008. Instead, they were out in the field, investigating—what lawyers call the fact-finding stage, which takes hundreds of hours. They divided the investigation into tasks and set out about their work. With a full class load, Cadence and Ashley would spend about three hours in the field after their classes and put in extra time on the weekends.

"It took up a lot of time," Cadence remembers. "It was because that's what I wanted to do."

Their diligence paid off. Uncovering new evidence, the student sleuths put forth their findings in a new appeal that was filed in federal court in June 2008. The federal case was later frozen to allow a separate state appeal to run its course, with a rare nudge from Judge Amy St. Eve, who wrote that, due to new evidence, there was "good cause" that James's claims of "actual innocence," in her court and in state court, had merit.

The appeals discredited the state's evidence that had prevailed for almost twenty years. On top of the students' findings, other new evidence had been uncovered by fire and accident expert Russell Ogle. Ogle had investigated hundreds of fires and explosions, and, hired by James's legal team to review this case, found serious flaws in the trial testimony of Commander Francis Burns, the state's expert witness. Ogle analyzed the dozen post-blaze photos of the collapsed home that killed the Lupercio family in 1984. One photo shows firefighters digging through debris to determine burn patterns; two other photos focus on the burn patterns. In another, Commander Burns wears a white coat, and most of the floor to the wood-framed home is missing.

At trial, Burns testified that the "large, shiny alligatoring" pattern from the debris meant the fire had spread fast, as in an arson. But Ogle's report showed it was quite the opposite. The pattern results from wood burning a long time—a prolonged, intense fire. The photos also show the burn pattern on a structural piece of wood that would have been protected from the fire's place of origin. Ogle reported that the commander had misinterpreted the V-shaped pattern. And he pointed to testimony about a space heater's being hauled out of the debris, even though Burns told the court that no accident could have caused the fire.

Cadence and Ashley found another suspect who could have started the fire—if it wasn't an accidental blaze. They discovered that within hours of the fatal fire, police had arrested a suspect in connection to the incident. Evidence of the arrest was never turned over to James's defense.

Police reports indicate that the suspect, a thirty-seven-year-old neighborhood woman, confessed within hours of the fire that she might have started it after setting fire to her own apartment building, not far from the Lupercio home. The tenant told police she was angry at her landlord, and, after a few beers, took a sheet of paper to her stove burners and set the kitchen curtains on fire. She picked up a six-pack of Old Style and left, visited some bars on Ashland, and returned home hours later to find a collapsed building, reports say. Because she was drunk, she didn't remember what happened next or where she went. But as she spoke to police that same morning, she walked on the tips of her toes because her feet were tired from her trek the night before. She was later convicted of starting the fire in her apartment building.

"I never liked Jim."

The words were inked into an affidavit less than three weeks before James's new legal team filed his appeal. The author of the affidavit—Duane Glassco, by then forty-three years old. Gayle and the students had visited him in a Michigan prison several times to interview him.

"I only gave the testimony that I did so I could get a deal on my cases. I got a deal on my charges," Duane wrote in his recantation. He admitted he was high at the time of the fire and didn't see anything.

At the time, those charges included burglary. Two decades later, Duane's criminal record had become more and more checkered. Correctional records show Duane had been convicted of sexual assault, sentenced to eight to fifteen years when he signed the affidavit in 2008. Four years later, he pleaded guilty to manufacturing meth, among other charges, and could spend as many as thirty years in a Michigan prison.

"Before I gave my testimony, I met with the police and prosecutors," Duane wrote. "They told me what I needed to say."

And there was another revelation: Duane confessed that he had actually overheard a prosecutor discussing aerial photos that showed the view from the attic window where he had claimed to see James walking near the site of the fire—but another building would have blocked Duane's perspective from the attic. In addition, the attic window would have been boarded up for winter,[13] preventing him from seeing anyone enter the building.

University of Chicago Law graduate Karl Leonard joined the Exoneration Project as a summer volunteer during a period of downtime after graduating and passing the bar in 2009. James's case was one of a handful he was assigned.

Having worked on the case for a year, picking up where Ashley and Cadence left off, he met James for the first time in lockup behind a judge's courtroom at 26th and California at the Cook County Courthouse in 2010. James was about to have a hearing that would deny the state's attempt to shut down his appeal. With Gayle, Karl walked over to James's cell, one of several in a line, a noisy area where prisoners await hearings and lawyers stop by to check in with their clients.

The appeal moved forward, and the lawyers spent another two years preparing to prove James's innocence at a hearing. But what absolutely no one expected was that the state would tell the judge that they would not be moving forward after all in 2012. All charges would be dropped. This news blindsided James's lawyers as they met in the judge's chambers to schedule the hearing.

Shocked at this sudden unexpected turn in the case, Karl started planning for James's release the next day. This was a new task for him. There was no playbook for helping an exoneree set up his life after nearly a quarter of century behind bars. But Karl wanted to make sure James was secure, and, after investing in the case, he wanted to see it through. "I cared about what happened to him personally," Karl says.

On the list was accommodation. For starters, he booked a hotel where James could stay for about a week. Beyond that, Karl was at a loss. He looked into halfway houses, the best they could have found for him, without any luck.

---

13. At James's motion for a new trial, Dawn Gramont testified the landlord kept the attic window boarded up to retain heat in the winter.

And there were more immediate concerns: How would they get James on a plane? Did he even have an ID anymore?

James had prepared. Having tucked away his birth certificate, Social Security card, and other documents for this moment, he sought help from prison officials to expedite a temporary ID.

IV.

"You know, I may have been deprived of my life for twenty-five years, but my children were deprived the privilege of a father. That's something that a lot of people overlook. There's a lot of victims in this. It isn't just the people who perished in the fire. It isn't just me. It spider-webs and laterals out to my children, my grandchildren, my wife, my sisters, my brother, my mother."

"Your aunt just posted something saying your dad's getting out," Felicia Kluppelberg told her husband, James Kluppelberg Jr., by phone.

Felicia had been cruising Facebook at their home in Merrillville, Indiana, where they were raising two young daughters, when she saw the news clip. She called her husband immediately. A journeyman electrician, he was out working at the Springfield Avenue pumping station in Chicago.

That night when he came home, they watched the news together. His dad was on TV. This strange yet familiar man was back in the world.

A few years earlier, Gayle and one of the law students had come to James Jr.'s door. He and Felicia were preoccupied with their newborn, Rylie, who was suffering from seizures.

As they asked questions, James Jr. considered for the first time that his dad might have been wrongly convicted. "I thought he was guilty," he admits. "There was no one that said he was innocent"—except at times his mother, Dawn, when she was on drugs.

Two weeks before James's release, Dawn died. Cancer and drug addiction took her. Some of her final days were spent at a nursing home next to Cook County Jail, where James had disappeared into the Department of Corrections almost twenty-five years before, presumably forever.

In the hospice, Dawn ripped out her oxygen tube and took her final breaths. James Jr. and his half-brothers—Duane's sons—pooled their money for her cremation and memorial service at a Baptist church in Tinley Park, southwest of Chicago.

As James Jr. lost his mother, he wondered, having spent much of his formative years without her: Did he ever have her?

Then it seemed, as James's face flashed across the TV screen, he might be gaining a father.

"Do you know who this is?"

James Jr. was on the job when his dad returned his call. He had reached out to the lawyers after seeing the story about James's release on the news. "Yeah," James Jr. answered, laughing slightly. You know. Of course.

James Jr. told him he was at work and couldn't talk too long. A supervisor overheard and urged him to take the call. Taking a break, he asked how his dad's first night had been and when he could see him. James's schedule was pretty open.

That evening, at the WGN News studio in Chicago, James Jr. arrived in his work clothes where his dad was to be interviewed.

"There's someone here who looks just like you," someone on the news crew told James.

It was an emotional reunion, though neither man remembers there being any tears or much spoken. They embraced, silently bringing to a halt the years that had long kept them apart.

After James's TV interview, he met his son back at the lawyers' office, driving separately. Another interview was on deck. As James Jr. waited for him, he began to wonder how his father was going to make it with only fourteen dollars and some change in his pocket. Once it was a wrap, James Jr. thought it best to take his dad to Kmart for the basics: jeans, shirts, belt, watch, wallet, and sunglasses. Things a man needs to get by. Next on the list: a steak dinner. "Give me a rare piece of meat and I'm a happy man," James said.

As they talked, to James, it felt as though they had never been robbed of twenty-three years. As though it were just a father and son grabbing a bite. At the time, James thought his son had always believed in his innocence. "We just connected back that quickly," James remembers. "It really was awesome to have that happen without all the awkwardness that you would think would come with something like that."

But for James Jr., reconnecting with his dad was strange. James's unfamiliarity with the world around him shifted their roles, whatever they had been in the first place. "I never had a father figure, so I don't look to him like he's my father. It's just weird."

James Jr. dropped him off at the Holiday Inn in the early morning hours after a long night of catching up. The next day, he planned to pick up James to meet his two granddaughters for the first time.

"He's not going to be able to stay at that hotel," James Jr. told his wife, Felicia, when he got home.

The young couple had met as fifteen-year-olds on Chicago's southwest side. When Felicia became pregnant with their first daughter, James Jr. decided to forego his college wrestling scholarship and find a job to support his new family. After his own tumultuous childhood, he wanted to work hard and create some stability.

Two years after their first daughter was born, he and Felicia married and moved to Indiana, ready to leave the city and its risks behind them. Felicia remembers not being able to walk around her neighborhood without being whistled at, starting around age twelve. "The gangs started getting really bad," she says. "The schools aren't good."

Their three-bedroom house in Merrillville, Indiana, was small and cozy, yet big enough for their family of four—two girls, ten-year-old Melanie and four-year-old Rylie. When Felicia asked what her husband thought about asking James to come live with them, she knew he might be against it. The couple had once opened their home to James Jr.'s mother, Dawn, and the relationship went sour.

"She robbed us, she was doing drugs," James Jr. says. "Told her she'd only be able to stay if she was clean." They asked her to leave. The subsequent estrangement had added to the pain of her passing just before James was let out.

Felicia thought they should at least give the guy a chance. "Family to us is a lot. It's everything to us."

The home had only two dedicated bedrooms, a tight squeeze. But a lone computer room could be converted if they could find a trundle bed. James Jr. was mulling it over when he picked up his dad the next day to meet his kids.

When they walked in the door, James's two big-eyed granddaughters ran up to him and hugged him. James was stunned at the welcome, Felicia remembers. She could see his heart melt a little.

The expanded family headed to a birthday party for a friend's baby. James wasn't feeling too comfortable around new people. "Here I am being introduced to my granddaughters for the first time, and then on top of that, I'm being sent to a birthday party with total strangers. A bunch of them," James remembers. Reeling at times, he toughed out the nerves and ended up staying the weekend with James Jr. and Felicia.

When James Jr. dropped him off on his way into work Monday, he had given it enough thought. "So I know you're not going to have a place to stay after the hotel," James Jr. started, backing into the question. "Do you want to come stay with us?"

"That would be great," he said. James was humbled. "Very, very, very humbled."

A few days later, James Jr. pulled up to the Holiday Inn for the last time. James didn't have much to his name except about a half dozen heavy file boxes full of case documents that he'd accumulated in prison. They got a cart from the front desk and loaded them into the car.

Back in Merrillville, James Jr. and Felicia had prepared for his arrival, moving their daughters to an air mattress in the family room until the small front computer space could be turned into a bedroom for James. James stayed in his granddaughters' bedroom. "Definitely a girly-girl room," he recalls.

With a roof over his head and his family nearby, James slept in his granddaughters' bunk bed. Pink Tinkerbell sheets covered his stocky frame.

V.

"Felicia basically took me around town and showed me and taught me things. She was an extraordinary help to me. She was very patient, and I'm very grateful for all she's done."

James hadn't slept much since his release. His internal clock was still on prison time. Somehow, he managed to squeeze in a few hours at his new home. The next morning, he peeled off the Tinkerbell sheets and got up to see who was up and around.

James Jr. had already left for work. Felicia sat in the kitchen. James didn't sit down next to her. He stood—that was his habit. He was quiet, but Felicia got him chatting. The young mom was approachable. She brimmed with sweetness. Only in her late twenties, she seemed like an old soul, with kind, half-moon eyes that smiled all on their own. "I felt as if I knew him for a long time," she says.

It would be Felicia's task to show James how the new world worked, and she relished the opportunity. Everything was at your fingertips now, she explained to him, pulling up Pandora Internet Radio, typing in different songs and artists. After a few computer demonstrations, she hopped up. "Let's go shopping," Felicia suggested. "Let's go look around."

They drove around Merrillville, stopping by Meijer and Kmart. James was fascinated, halting in his tracks to examine unfamiliar objects for sale. Felicia didn't mind taking her time in the stores. It was nice having someone to walk with her at the mall for a change, given that her husband wasn't a big fan of browsing or window-shopping.

Inside his son's car, the doors automatically locked around James. He was startled. "They trap you in your car now?" he asked, bewildered. But in little time he felt more comfortable out on the roads.

Soon, James got behind the wheel himself, practicing in the parking lot of Merrillville High School. It was a veritable *Freaky Friday* moment as James Jr. taught his father how to drive again.

"It was so weird," James Jr. says, shaking his head. As a teen, James Jr. had gone through this rite of passage without his father, learning the basics from a driving school and his stepmother, Bonnie, who was raising him at the time. "He seemed to pick it up right away."

James needed a little more practice before trying for his driver's permit, so Felicia let him take the car for a spin after a Saturday breakfast at the Cracker Barrel. His granddaughters sat strapped in behind them.

Then there was email. James Jr. helped him set up a Google mail account. But James Jr. quickly discovered his dad had no interest in social media. "He still don't have a Facebook to this day," James Jr. noted in 2013. In two years' time, though, James would finally cave and create a profile, shirtless photos and all.

Months after his release from prison, James began to expand his circle, attending church with James Jr. and Felicia. It was an older congregation at Merrillville Wesleyan. Many parishioners had already heard about James. They turned to him as their handyman for odd jobs, which suited James. He needed the money.

First, though, he offered his earnings to James Jr. and Felicia. "Don't worry about it," James Jr. said. "I don't need it. You need it. We're here to support you until you can get started on your own."

Instead, James contributed where he could around the house, watching his granddaughters and cooking meals for the whole family. "I want to make my sauce," James announced one day. "I need my pressure cooker." With his new Internet skills, he found a deal online, bought one, and made his special spaghetti sauce flavored with pork neck bones.

When James Jr. and Felicia tasted the sauce, they looked at each other in surprise. "Wow, this is really good!" Felicia managed between bites.

James would make large batches so they could bag it up for weeknight freezer meals. On other nights, he cooked straightforward, meat-and-potatoes meals. Simple meals, like chicken soup, beef stew, chop suey, and roasts.

For James Jr. and Felicia's ninth anniversary, James took their girls for the weekend, treating them to Santa's Village, a theme park an hour and a half away in Illinois. Later, they met up with James Jr. and Felicia in Michigan City, Indiana, at an outlet mall. James treated his granddaughters to some new shoes for school—black Mary Janes for Mel, who was entering fifth grade, and a pair of brown Mary Janes by Keds for Rylie, who was starting kindergarten.

The days out in the world with his new family were full of discovery. But sometimes, in the middle of the night, James would go sit outside and look at the quiet Indiana sky, alone. "For a long time, I never saw stars, because in a maximum-security penitentiary, you're not allowed out after dark."

James's pen pal Rena' cleared it with her bosses to take off for a few days and visit about a week after James's release. She arrived at O'Hare from New Mexico on an American Airlines flight. James was waiting. She appeared down-to-earth—long blonde hair, T-shirt, jeans, raspy voice, and a wide smile.

"He was extremely nervous," Rena' remembers. "He didn't know where to sit or stand."

She was nervous too. They knew each other, but not in person. And their relationship was laden with ambiguity, as friends-turned-romantic-interests.

James and Felicia welcomed Rena' to stay in their home, but Rena' found it awkward staying in another woman's house, she says. After politely accepting for the first night, she used her employee discount to stay at a nearby hotel for the rest of the trip.

Rena' watched as James's granddaughters clamored for him. He would pick them up and carry them around like precious cargo. He was a grandfather, but he had a certain adolescence about him as well. The family dog, Thor, a rottweiler–shar-pei mix that James Jr. and Felicia had found on Craigslist a few years back, also favored James, following him about the house. Rena' quickly found James to be gentle, kind, and considerate. And perhaps, at times, a little too doting.

"You need a fork? I'll get you a fork," James would say, leaping into action. Rena' had long been a self-sufficient woman, highly educated and hardworking. She was used to getting her own forks.

"When he went to prison, relationships were different. Women were more dependent on men," she notes of the culture clash.

Despite their compatibility and friendship, after their short visit of a few days, Rena' realized she had her own life back home. And James had no way to support himself, let alone contribute to a relationship. But when Rena' returned to New Mexico and to work, she added to her routine a daily phone call with James. It was a start.

VI.

"What do you say to children you haven't seen in years? Or haven't ever met? 'Hi.' The rest comes naturally."

James's daughter Sarah was checking Facebook on May 31, 2012, the day of his release, while sitting through an introductory college business class in Richmond, Virginia. James's sister, whom she didn't really know, had sent her a message: "Your dad is out."

She walked straight out of class and started to cry, calling her other aunt, Laura, to verify. "I need you to check this out," Sarah told her. "I don't have time. I'm in class. Find out what's going on."

"It's true," her aunt Laura texted back. She had seen the news stories about James's release that day.

Within hours, they tracked down his attorneys and got ahold of James at the airport. Ironically, that call—from the daughter he had never seen—was the first call from family he received upon his release.

Although Sarah was the only one of his three children without his last name, she had been the only one to keep in touch with him in prison in recent years. They had "met" through letters when Sarah was fifteen years old.

James had briefly dated her mother in the eighties. When Sarah was a few months old, her grandparents and aunt Laura, who raised her, took her to Virginia. By her teen years, Sarah yearned to know who her father was, though she was afraid to discover that another parent didn't want her, she says.

"Look, you need to find him," a counselor had told Sarah's aunt. "She needs the closure. If he doesn't want to have anything to do with her, then so be it. She needs to know."

Laura called an information number in Chicago and was connected to a listing. "Can I please speak with James Kluppelberg?" she asked.

"Hold on one second—this is his ex-wife, how can I help you?"

"I have his daughter, and I'm trying to find him."

Donna gave her James's address in prison. Later that evening, Laura talked to Sarah. "Your father is in prison," she told her, handing her the address. "You can write him. You can not write him. This is your choice."

Soon, Sarah wrote: "Dear James, You may not believe this, but I'm your daughter."

James did not know that he had fathered a child with Sarah's mother, which added to the shock of hearing from her. "I was stunned," he says. "It was all just very insane." But when James opened her letter in prison, a nearly thirteen-year correspondence was born. With the letter, Sarah attached a bundle of photos chronicling her childhood. "I wrote her back and told her, 'Wonderful to get to you know you,'" James says. "I was full of questions."

That first year, their letters consisted of one big get-to-know-you session. What they liked, what they disliked. Family history. "Things that you miss with a child growing up," James says. Then, when the fatherly instincts kicked in, he began to get on to her about her smoking. "Women on the maternal side of my family that smoke don't live to see sixty," he warned her.

A teenage girl, Sarah liked dragons, he learned. James paid an artist, a fellow inmate, about forty dollars for a drawing of a dragon. Others went for as little as five dollars. "It was a real nice one," James says. "Guy did it in pencil for me."

Sarah sent him pictures as well, ultrasound images when she became pregnant with her daughter, Tori. James commissioned some more artwork, sending her a package of barnyard animal drawings—about $160 in the prison marketplace—after Sarah told him she planned on an animal theme for the nursery. "I had twenty or thirty of them water-painted," James remembers.

For the first six to eight years into their letter writing, Sarah wasn't sure if her dad was innocent. She lived with the mindset that if he didn't do it, he would eventually get out. *And if he did do it, then he's where he ought to be*, she reasoned. "And God saw fit that he got out," Sarah says.

When James took her call at the airport, it marked their second phone call in thirteen years. She had never visited. Living in Virginia, his Illinois prison was too far away from her responsibilities. But now it was time to meet.

The soonest they could arrange a visit was the Fourth of July weekend, in Fort Wayne, Indiana, where Sarah had some family. She piled in a

Chevy Blazer with her aunt and daughter, Tori, headed northwest for the ten-hour trip. Sarah was excited and worried. *Will he like me?* Her mind wandered as they drove along the interstate. They had only made it half-way before they ran out of gas. A storm had blown through several states, knocking out power. Her aunt's brother brought them some gas, and they made it to a service station in West Virginia, where they slept in the car. Finally, at the La Quinta Inn in Fort Wayne, she met James. He and James Jr., Felicia, and the kids—whom Sarah had also never met—came up to their hotel room.

"It was emotional, surreal, breathtaking," James says, struggling to remember the details. "I just remember us all walking in, and I might have given her a hug. It was one of those things as it was happening, you don't see it happening. It's a blur."

Sarah remembers the moment as more tense, meeting both her half-brother, James Jr., and her father. "I mean, it's the first time I met the man. I was twenty-seven years old," she says. "He had only been out a couple months. We were all adjusting."

James spent the whole next day with his kids and grandkids at an arcade and bowling alley. He tried to bowl, but his arm gave out. Instead, he just watched his granddaughters play with Sarah's daughter, Tori. "Melanie and Rylie just took to her instantly. It's the types of things you hope to have someday when you're locked up, and then to realize that, finally have that happen, is priceless."

With the ice long broken, the family finished the night at a fast-food joint, Dog 'n' Suds, a drive-in. There they broke bread together, chowing down on hot dogs, fries, and onion rings. James washed it down with a root beer as his granddaughter Rylie dipped her plain hot dog in ketchup. Sarah took photos of the family between bites. "Rylie fell asleep in my lap," James says, looking at one picture.

After breakfast the next day, the short visit came to an end. James Jr. had to work the next day. "Time was short," Sarah remembers. "We were upset about having to go."

But they all pledged to see each other again. "It was easy then to stay in touch, cell phones and everything," James says. "And I was out. Staying in touch wasn't going to be a problem."

Within months, James would keep a photo of his granddaughter Tori in his cell phone and chuckle at the image of the red-headed toddler tasting her first lemon.

VII.

"You type my name into Google and it lights up like a Christmas tree."

James spent his days looking for jobs and his nights on the computer filling out applications. The handyman pay wasn't going to be enough to get his own place, and even though his lawyers were seeking state compensation, there was no guarantee of funds.

He turned to the likes of Monster.com and other job-search sites, where he created alerts and applied for hundreds of positions—sometimes as many as ten in one evening. Most of the time his inquiries were ignored. He also collected dozens of rejection notices. "It just goes on and on and on and on," James said, scrolling through his inbox of job submissions.

As he scoured the web, the Internet had already indexed him. News stories about his case and his wrongful conviction abounded. With employers Googling prospective hires, the label of "convicted murderer"— even one whose conviction was tossed out—was damaging.

James hoped to find a job in maintenance, what had been his trade back in the eighties. In prison he had held many jobs, from entering data for vehicle registrations to manufacturing mattresses and other materials, operating printing machines, maintaining the prison's plumbing, and doing electrical repairs. "My dream would be an apartment-complex maintenance man," James said. "That would be really nice. That's what I'm good at."

He didn't conceal his wrongful conviction on his resume. In fact, he put it up top:

> Highly motivated and dedicated worker seeking a maintenance position with opportunities for advancement and long-term success. After having his wrongful conviction overturned at the request of the State

and spending over 24 years in prison unjustly, skilled and ambitious worker seeks the opportunity to join a company and contribute his skills. Adept at multi-tasking, managing a varied workload, and finishing projects on schedule.

His lawyer, Karl Leonard, wrote him a letter of recommendation to help address concerns about James's background. "I am an attorney and friend of James Kluppelberg," the letter began. "Mr. Kluppelberg is working to rebuild his life after spending over 24 years in prison for a crime that he did not commit. I believe that hiring him would be a great decision." Karl went on to describe the circumstances of the wrongful conviction—"junk science" behind the alleged arson and a so-called witness who cut a deal in exchange for his statement. He explained how the University of Chicago's Exoneration Project investigated the case decades later, leading to a judge vacating the conviction and ordering James's release in May 2012. "Mr. Kluppelberg can never get back the time he spent in prison for a crime that he did not commit," Karl wrote. "However, from that terrible experience, he comes out a dedicated and skilled worker looking for a chance to make something out of himself. I, and everyone who has worked with Mr. Kluppelberg, can vouch for his desire to be a great employee."

Finally, a recruiter from human resources for a Kmart distribution center in Manteno, Illinois, called James to arrange an interview based on his maintenance experience. James was excited to make the hour drive. When he arrived, he promptly began filling out paperwork.

"What's up with the twenty-five-year gap in your work history?" the HR lady asked him, looking over the forms.

"Well, didn't you read my resume?" James asked.

She hadn't.

"Then why did you call me?" He handed her a copy of his resume. She read it over and looked up at him. "I'll be right back."

When she returned, her words deflated James. "I'm really sorry to have wasted your time, but we don't hire convicted murderers."

He offered to show her articles about his case, detailing his wrongful conviction. The case was overturned, he explained.

"It doesn't matter." If he couldn't clear the background check, he couldn't work there. The ambiguity of having a conviction overturned and the inconsistency of the exoneration process, in Illinois and across the United States, not only hindered exonerees like James from finding work but also publicly kept them behind a wall of suspicion.

"If I was a murderer, I wouldn't be standing in front of you right now," James persisted. "They dropped the charges. They let me go."

When he realized the conversation wasn't going anywhere, James left and headed back home, driving the 2005 Dodge Caravan his son had lent him for the job hunt.

James decided to sell his white-gold wedding ring for some extra cash. He received about $160 for it at the Southlake Mall in Hobart, Indiana. Married and divorced twice, he was used to having some weight on his finger. "It's my fidget tool," James says. "Some people smoke. I just don't feel right without out it."

In prison, the ring had provided comfort and a sense of connection, even when he felt he had long been forgotten. After selling the wedding band, James bought a new ring for forty dollars. It signified nothing other than it took the place of something that was missing.

Also missing on James's right hand was a pinky finger. He had a habit of telling people he lost it in a piece of machinery—which was true, in a way. As a boy, he and his friends liked to ride on a rolling parking gate. James was hanging on the top when the gate cut his finger. After a few corrective surgeries, they took his finger for good. The knob at his pinky knuckle is still tender but not as bad as it used to be, when the slightest brush felt like a hammer was hitting it.

Besides his wedding band, the other item he always carried with him, tucked away in his Velcro hunter's camouflage wallet, was a laminated card documenting his 1985 high school equivalency certificate from the Illinois Community College Board. He had obtained a copy of the card after his release and went to have it laminated at an office store.

But what he lacked in possessions, he made up for in newly created memories, such as spending Thanksgiving dinner with his family. His granddaughter Rylie had clocked a kid who outweighed her by twenty-five pounds. The schmuck had pinched her, which she found unacceptable, returning his gesture with a closed fist. "She don't take no shit from nobody," James laughed. "I bet he won't do that again."

James needed new work experience for his resume. To help him, Rena' cleared a visit with her boss for James to come down and work at the Econo Lodge that she managed in Silver City, New Mexico. He would stay about a week, fixing drywall, plumbing, and doing electrical repairs or anything that was needed.

"If you want to prove your work ethic, you're going to have to show me," Rena' told James. And he did. In an August 2012 letter of recommendation, she praised him, detailing his skill and patient demeanor when doing repairs: "Always cordial and respectful of the hotel's guests he never failed to address each person he met with a smile and kind remark," Rena' wrote.

Silver City, a copper mining town, was losing its industry, causing a dip in business for Rena'. When James told her, early on, that he wanted her to move up north, Rena' had her reservations. "I refuse to support or take care of another man," Rena' said, noting previous boyfriends who had taken advantage of her financially. "They were always codependent and saw me as more of a meal ticket than partner."

A job and a place to live, she told James. That's what it would take for her to pack up her life. So James made it his goal to save every dime from every odd job he could to put down money on a place and pay for it three months in advance. He wanted to prove to Rena' he could make it. James continued to be grateful for his son's help, but he couldn't help feeling like a burden at times, though he enjoyed getting to know his grandchildren.

Rena' and James talked every day, and James got a Bluetooth device so that he could talk hands free as he drove around to apply for jobs or help out the church folks. He had outfitted his son's '05 Dodge Caravan with a power inverter to convert the van's power to household current, which allowed him to hook up a printer. From the van, he printed extra copies of his resume, recommendation letters, and articles about his case. Or he could print directions, as he traversed Indiana and Illinois while looking for jobs.

"Somebody would ask me for something and instead of having to come back or mail it, I'd say, 'Give me a minute,' and I'd go out to the van and print out what they wanted," James says.

James was motivated to create a life for himself, for Rena', but he became frustrated when it wasn't materializing as fast as he hoped. "She wanted proof that I could stand on my own," he says.

While the logistics of their future together were uncertain, James managed to visit Rena' again. The two of them drove from Silver City to Tombstone, Arizona, for a weekend trip. Living up to its name, Tombstone's Boothill Graveyard captured James's interest. The historic site featured the graves of "outlaws, victims, suicides, and hangings, legal and otherwise, along with the hardy citizens and refined element of Tombstone's first days," according to a tourism website.

One tombstone sat amid those of the outlaws and hardy citizens, among rubble and rocks, with a cross in the background:

HERE LIES
GEORGE JOHNSON
HANGED BY MISTAKE
1882
HE WAS RIGHT
WE WAS WRONG
BUT WE STRUNG
HIM UP
AND NOW HE'S
GONE.

James stopped and pulled out his cell phone to snap a picture. He thought, "They've been getting it wrong for a long time."

VIII.

"The days in front of me are a lot shorter than the ones behind me. I ain't got time for nothing but moving forward."

Karl Leonard wasted no time filing for a certificate of innocence for

James. This would allow James to show official proof of his innocence beyond having his conviction overturned, which only meant the trial evidence could no longer stand.

The petition landed on the clerk's desk less than two months after James's release. Under Illinois law, the certificate would entitle James to about $200,000 in compensation and allow him to expunge the murder convictions. Tasked with proving James's innocence, Karl diligently attached twelve exhibits to the petition. Meanwhile, James wasn't counting on a check anytime soon.

"These things can drag on for a long time," Karl warned.

The State of Illinois met Karl's dispatch with a response nearly seven months later. Prosecutors asked the court to deny James's request. Prosecutors were still positioned to "steadfastly maintain" his guilt and "vehemently contest" his innocence, they wrote in their responsive filing. Further, the state argued James was responsible for his own demise because he "set in motion the investigation in 1988 that led to his conviction" by reporting car fires in 1987, which had brought him to the attention of police.

Within weeks, James's legal team responded that the state was "flat-out wrong."

"Petitioner can dispatch of the absurd contention made by the State in its Response that Mr. Kluppelberg somehow contributed to his own conviction by virtue of having 'been a suspect,'" James's lawyers wrote.

It would take a hearing, a year after the petition was filed, to set forth the evidence of innocence once more. And without his name cleared and without compensation to help him survive, James would keep bunking at his son's house and driving his son's van, crisscrossing Indiana and Illinois in search of employment and independence.

"Ten bucks an hour is better than no bucks an hour," James said, clipping his fingernails at Kuma's Corner, a popular Chicago burger restaurant. He was there to celebrate his new temporary job, at a steel-tubing manufacturer, right after his interview and factory tour. James ordered an RC Cola and kicked back.

The ninety-day job carried the possibility of permanent employment. He had to buy steel-toed boots for the occasion. "Overrated," he said of the work shoes. "Cold in the winter, and hot in the summer." He had first bought a pair of boots at Payless that he didn't like, and Kmart didn't have the size he needed. He checked back again, and a pair in his size had surfaced, but not without some dried mud in the threading. When James pointed out the flaw to the cashier, she swiftly gave him a discount. "Sold!" James said. He loved a bargain.

The employment agency that had found the job for him would take a cut of his earnings. Under the agency's terms, he would also have to pay for health insurance every week. But with what was left over, James could make good on his goal of finding his own place and moving Rena' from New Mexico to Indiana. "Your turn," he planned to tell her.

Two days later, and almost a year shy of his release from prison, James went in for his first day of work. It was Easter Sunday.

When his shift began at 11 p.m., James showed up with a deep cut on his forehead. He had been tearing apart a playhouse for a lady at his church when his foot slipped and landed on a pry bar, which jumped up and smacked him between the eyes. His safety glasses deflected the bulk of the damage. "Cost me seven stitches and one hell of a headache," he said, pulling out his phone and producing a grisly picture of the injury: "Lanced it because it was pulsating."

The headache persisted as he got out of bed at 6 a.m. that Sunday to volunteer as a cook for the church breakfast. He prepared a feast of scrambled eggs, sausage links, hash browns, biscuits with sausage gravy, donuts, coffee, and juice. After the meal, he went home to recover, missing the service.

James found the first days on the job at the steel plant physically exhausting. He stood on his feet the entire shift, except for a forty-minute lunch break, moving heavy tubing. "You're just constantly moving," James said. "No standing, no stopping. You do that, it's over with."

His steel-toed boots got covered in oil, turning several shades darker due to the oil saturation. There was oil everywhere at the plant, it seemed. "I could probably walk in a river right now, my feet would stay dry," James noted.

James had other paying gigs. On occasion, he spoke on panels about his wrongful conviction, a commitment he would undertake even if the organization could not pay. Concordia University in River Forest, Illinois, invited him to come talk to students attending a criminal justice class. The topic was women, gender, and prison. James was to introduce a male exoneree's perspective. On a damp Wednesday night, he arrived with the gash on his forehead still healing.

Bundled up in a gray hoodie and blue polo shirt, a flashlight strapped to his hip and his Bluetooth earpiece in place, James had to head to his steel-tube manufacturing job after the talk. Glasses sliding down his nose, James looked at his watch, remarking that he had made good time, having come from a hotel an hour away, where he had crashed after his graveyard shift. "It was more economical to pay forty dollars for a room," James said. "Didn't make sense to drive an hour home, just to turn around."

At Concordia's weathered student center, James went to grab a bottle of water before the panel. College students scrambled to get the microphones to work in the small space as the professor huddled with the panel members, all women except for James: an assistant district attorney from DuPage County, Illinois, an associate judge, and a former Illinois Department of Corrections employee.

"I guess I'm the odd one out in this little panel," James told the students. "I can answer any questions. I've got no rules. You can't embarrass me, shock me, or offend me. Trust me on that. You're here to learn."

A student launched the panel discussion by asking about plea deals. The assistant district attorney, Jennifer Lindt, jumped in, giving a few examples of petty crimes, one involving theft of beef jerky. "Why is it always beef jerky?" Lindt laughed. "Doofuses!"

James smiled graciously. The next question for the panel: perjury. James took that one. He had lived it. "In my case, a multiple convicted drug felon decided he didn't want to go to prison for crimes he committed, and he told authorities he saw me enter and leave the building in question, and that's all it took," he answered. "Twenty years later, he came forward and said he made it all up because he was afraid to go to jail for his crimes."

A student shifted the discussion, asking about James's release from prison. "Did you feel the need to reestablish your masculinity?" she probed.

"No, that wasn't really the issue," James said. "The issue for me was reintegrating myself into society as a whole." He paused and looked at the student and then around the room at the dozen and a half other young adults listening attentively. "Imagine what the world was like twenty-five years ago. Cell phones were this big!" James mimed holding a comically large phone, as if it were a brick. "Computer screens were black. Floppy disks flopped."

In the eyes of the Department of Corrections, he was a throwaway, James told the class. A lifer, entitled to nothing to prepare him for reentry into the world, he said—no programming, no schooling, no nothing. "They're not going to waste resources on keeping me up to speed. They gave me the fourteen dollars I had in my account and said, 'There's the door.'"

Another student wanted to know about the safety of women correctional officers in male prisons. "Off limits, as far as violence goes," James explained. "That was something you just don't do. When riots would break out, women would be snatched up and thrown in a cell and the door would be shut. They were off limits."

Over the years, he had heard of three incidents over the years where female guards were harmed. But on the flip side, any sign of civility from a woman in prison was interpreted by his peers in prison as a come-on. "First thought in their mind is, 'Oh, she wants me,'" he said.

The professor closed the panel by asking about the worst injustices they had seen.

> Poor mental healthcare.
> Sexual abuse.
> Institutionalization.
> Juveniles entering the system and never leaving.

The list went on.

James sometimes enjoyed giving these talks, finding it cathartic, even though it could be hard to remember the trauma. "It hurts," he says. But he also looked at it as a mission. "If people like me don't put ourselves out there, the public will never know."

IX.

"I have no doubt that my life would be totally different. I would have a very successful business by now. I'd be looking towards retirement with great anticipation. Now, it's extreme horror because I haven't been able to pay social security taxes for the last twenty-five years. I haven't been able to plan a retirement plan. I haven't been able to do all those things that you're supposed to do when you're young so that you can relax when you get to be my age."

Every month, dating back to his time at Menard, the Illinois Department of Healthcare and Family Services sent James a bill. It always said the same thing: "You are required to pay the terms of the child support order listed below."

The bills didn't stop once James had left prison. Instead, they continued to mount. The back payments were for one of his daughters, Samantha, who was now an adult. He and her mother, Donna, had had a bumpy marriage in the eighties, which ended in divorce. They got back together for a stint in 2000, while he was in prison, fresh off his divorce from Bonnie.

Even though James had been locked up for most of his daughter's life, most child support agencies in the country consider imprisonment a form of "voluntary impoverishment" and do not put the debt on hold. As a result, James had racked up close to $18,000 of back child support payments. The bills also stated that 9 percent interest a year "may or may not be included." In prison, he couldn't have supported a child because he wasn't earning a real wage, apart from the pittance the Illinois Department of Corrections gave him for various prison jobs.

Released from prison and faced with this debt, he couldn't pay it, and he couldn't pay to fight it. So the bills kept coming.

James was hired full time at the steel-tube manufacturing plant where he had been temping. His pay increased from $10 an hour to $14.69 an hour. He had saved as much as he could, and he was ready to deliver on his promise to Rena' that he would rent his own place so that she could move up north.

Because James had no credit history, they put almost everything in her name and found a cozy two-bedroom in Crown Point, Indiana, where James Jr. and Felicia had since moved. It was quiet, and the neighbors were nice.

But by the time James hopped on a plane to Albuquerque to move Rena' up to Indiana, he found out he was losing his job. The factory required that he be able to operate an overhead crane to lift heavy objects on a trolley along a rail. "I couldn't feel safe doing it," James said. "I couldn't feel comfortable. Three buttons that control six functions. You are flying a load over people's heads."

The hefty, U-shaped piece of machinery didn't seem to have any brakes. The harder James tried, the worse he operated the crane.

After months of an aching back and legs, extreme punctuality, and a willingness to work overtime, James left without so much as a letter of recommendation.

On the Fourth of July, James flew to Albuquerque, rented a sixteen-foot Budget truck, and drove to Silver City. Three of Rena's staff members at the hotel helped her load up an entire lifetime's worth of boxes and furniture. It was going to be a tight fit in the new home waiting for them on the other side of the country.

Rena' had the usual household items—couches and chairs. She also favored the unusual—swords, knives, Asian axes, katanas (Japanese swords), and two guns for self-defense. "It's not just a collection," she explained. "Many people, when they have a bad day, they have something to relieve their stress. Some people like ice cream. Other people, like me, like swords. It's how I clear the cobwebs of the day."

All packed up, they caravanned to Indiana. Rena' started out in the lead in her F-150 truck while James drove the sixteen-footer. Only about 1,500 miles and they would be home.

A few days later, James was back in the Midwest—and back in Cook County for his innocence hearing. He nervously parked his son's minivan on the street near the courthouse. "I was finally getting to tell my side of it. That I didn't have anything to do with it. That I was innocent."

Rena' attended the hearing, the first time since James's trial that he had any family or friend to support him in court.

A judge held not only James's future in his hands but also his past. "He held the difference of me being able to say I was not convicted of a crime. That I was innocent of what you read about on the Internet."

The hearing was the culmination of a year's worth of back-and-forth court filings and evidence exhibits for his certificate of innocence, which would not only clear his name for good but also enable him to receive compensation from the state. Filling the seats around James and Karl were Gayle Horn, from the Exoneration Project and Chicago law firm Loevy & Loevy, and Tara Thompson, who also represented James and had worked on his case before his release in 2012.

But another legal matter was brewing. Weeks before the court hearing, James's attorneys at Loevy had filed a separate civil lawsuit on his behalf, suing the notorious, disgraced former Chicago police commander Jon Burge, as well as more than a dozen other police officers and members from the Chicago Fire Department and the City of Chicago. At the time, Burge was incarcerated on a 2011 conviction for lying about police torture (the statute of limitations for the torture charges themselves had run out), in which he and others had suffocated suspects with plastic bags and shocked them with electrical devices, among other brutal tactics.

In James's case, the Loevy group argued, his police beating and coerced confession, in spite of its having been tossed out by a judge before his 1989 trial, had set in motion the prosecution that cost him almost twenty-five years of his life. Their new lawsuit was one of several filed in recent years against the City of Chicago, which had already paid tens of millions of dollars to compensate torture victims and formerly incarcerated people who were wrongly convicted due to police misconduct.

Even if James won the lawsuit, potentially worth millions of dollars, it would take years for him to see a single penny. This made the bid for compensation at the state level through the innocence hearing all the more important to his survival.

The first hearing passed quickly, but it wasn't over yet. The judge scheduled another for a few weeks later. He really seemed to be listening to both sides, which was hopeful, James thought.

When James left the courthouse and returned to his son's van, he stopped to see a slip of paper tucked under the windshield wiper. It was a ticket for expired license plates. Having recently registered the vehicle, James headed to the back of the van to check what had happened to the temporary plate he had secured over the old one. It was still there. Puzzled, he drove back home.

The photo documentation of his ticket later arrived in the mail. In the picture, his temporary tags had been pulled away for the camera, exposing the expired license plate and making it appear as though James was driving outside of the law. James was furious at this injustice. He decided he wasn't going to be pushed around while officials covered up the truth—even if it was just a sixteen-dollar motor vehicle ticket. He was going to fight it and clear his name.

There was good news ahead, however. An employment agency called and asked if he would want to work as a maintenance man at a five-story nursing home in Chicago. It was a nine-to-five gig, starting at fifteen dollars an hour. He'd get a bump in pay if the facility decided to keep him after the temporary hire. The only downside would be commuting from Indiana every day and wading through heavy Chicago traffic to get back home.

James took the job. The first day of work, he removed a refrigerator, repaired another, installed an air conditioner, started repairs on a John Deere lawn mower, and worked on a weed whacker that had a spark plug with too much gas in it.

X.

"There's no real common denominator to say this is what makes an exoneree. Because we're all different. We all have different cases. We all come from different parts of the city. Different parts of the state. The only thing that we have in common is that we were all wrongfully accused and convicted."

James was en route to a small celebration for a fellow exoneree. Throwing the party was Loyola University professor Laura Caldwell, who ran the Life After Innocence program, a fledgling experiential-learning program at Loyola University School of Law. He arrived at the nearly empty Lincoln Park four-lane bowling alley, Eminem playing in the background. The exoneree being celebrated was another survivor of Burge's campaign of torture, Eric Caine, who had just received a $10 million settlement from a civil lawsuit against the Chicago Police Department the week before, making headlines.

Caine was among the more than one hundred Black men tortured under Burge. In 1986, the torture Caine suffered through led him to falsely confess to participating in the stabbing mutilation of an elderly couple in their South Side home. Also tried and convicted along with him was former death row inmate Aaron Patterson. Chained to a hoop on the wall of an interrogation room, Patterson had etched a message onto a metal bench with a paperclip: "Police threaten me with violence. Slapped and suffocated me with plastic. No lawyer or dad."[14]

Patterson was sent to death row. In 2003, then Illinois governor George Ryan freed him and fourteen other men who had been sent to death row based on confessions forcibly obtained by Burge's rogue crew. After becoming a symbol for those who survived the Chicago police's reign of terror, Patterson experienced a staggering fall from public grace after reuniting with his gang. In 2007, he was sent back to prison for thirty years on gun and drug charges. "I'm not scared of no time," said Patterson, during what the *Chicago Tribune* described as a forty-minute, profanity-laced statement to prosecutors. "What can you do to me? . . . I've seen twelve people walk to their deaths."

Meanwhile, for twenty-five years, Caine languished behind bars. In 2011, the State of Illinois dismissed all charges against him, and a judge ordered his release.

"I got this card for Eric!" Laura said, waving it about at the bowling alley party, as she and her students prepared for his arrival. "What should we say?"

"I think something about closing this chapter of your case," offered Emily DeYoe, an adjunct professor for the Life After Innocence class and assistant public defender for Cook County.

---

14. Aaron Patterson's father was a Chicago police officer.

Laura wrote out the card as a small group of law students waited for guests to show up. Algie Crivens was the first exoneree to arrive at the party, before James. A bald man with light wispy eyebrows, he showed up in a shirt and tie, ready to bowl. With scarcely a word, Crivens walked up to the lane and hurled the bowling ball down, each frame ending with a big crash. Crivens spun around after his turn, put his hands on his hips, and took a deep breath. He untucked his shirt.

"There we go!" Crivens shouted with a big smile after bowling a strike.

Crivens was released in 2000. It took years for him to find decent work, picking up jobs here and there, living with his parents. He finally moved out and bought his own two-unit building in Calumet City, Illinois, where he lived in one unit and rented out the other.

An hour later, Caine had not yet arrived. Crivens told Laura and her students that he had talked to Caine the previous week, after he had won his settlement. "He's riding on cloud nine," he said.

James, fresh off the clock, walked through the door with Rena' and snuck up behind Laura. Rena', in a T-shirt as usual, had slipped on a ring-to-bracelet hand chain for the occasion.

"Ahh! How are you?" Laura exclaimed, hugging James.

Rena' piped up and flashed a friendly grin: "I'm Rena', Jim's girlfriend."

"She just moved to Chicago!" Laura announced to the party.

"Yeah, I lost my mind!" Rena' joked. As she told the story of how she and James met, James checked to see if she needed anything to drink.

A law student asked Rena' if she was a good bowler. Not since bowling for a physical education class in college, she said.

"I haven't bowled in a quarter of a century," James added, forgetting the time he'd bowled with his family just after his release, until his arm started to hurt.

Laura grabbed her phone to capture the moment on video. James positioned himself, then pushed the ball down the lane. It hit the gutter about a third of the way down. "Shit!" he said under his breath, turning red. Rena' cringed and smiled at the people watching. On his second try, the ball stayed straight, hitting two pins. Everyone cheered.

Looking down at the black, scuffed-up bowling ball, James smiled. Engraved on the top were the words "Brunswick Black Beauty" and in three thin, spaced-out letters, "J-I-M." He showed the others, oddly proud of the coincidence.

But Caine was still a no-show, even after they'd finished their game and snacks. Disappointed and puzzled, the group finally left.

As it turned out, Caine couldn't attend because he'd been arrested out where he lived in River Forest, Illinois. For months, he had felt targeted and harassed by police. This time, the officer apprehended Caine for playing music too loudly in his car. Dashboard camera footage later revealed the music was coming from the squad car. But Caine's troubles with the law were far from over. Soon he would land back in jail for eight months on drinking and driving charges. Back on the outside, he bounced back again, opening a chicken-wing restaurant in downtown Chicago.

"It's been rough and good. As you know, I'm in a perpetual state of celebration, so even my bad is good to me," Caine told TV hosts on Chicago's *Windy City Live* program in 2015. "I'm on-the-job-training when it comes to life."

XI.

"I don't want to be remembered as the guy who lost a quarter of a century of his life. I want to be remembered for what I do now."

In August 2013, tears streamed down James's cheeks in a Cook County courtroom when a judge deemed his case "an injustice," declaring him innocent and granting him an official certificate.

"It was like tons of weight being lifted off me," James told the *Chicago Tribune* after the judge's ruling. "My life was restored."

To celebrate his court victory, Laura Caldwell and a third-year law student, Abigail, organized a barbecue dinner for James and his family, selecting some of his favorite eats and inviting other exonerees.

James arrived at the Lincoln Park barbecue joint a little late. Stepping out of the pouring rain, he rolled his navy-blue sleeves up to his elbows. James had been delayed because about an hour and a half before quitting time, he'd gotten worried he had lost the master keys at his new handyman job at the nursing home. "I thought I was toast," he said. "They were going to have to rekey the whole building."

Fellow exoneree Antione Day nudged James and told him he had just lost his keys the other day when he went to McDonald's to buy a double cheeseburger meal for his granddaughter.

James's daughter Sarah was visiting with her three-year-old daughter, Tori. The tot danced around with her young cousins, Melanie and Rylie, as James held up his cell phone to take a video of the spirited bunch. "Oh, just to have a fraction of that energy," Rena' said, looking on.

James's family was surprised Rena' had joined in the party. Since her move, she had kept her distance, even though she and James lived a few blocks away from their family in Crown Point, Indiana. When the family went out to the zoo or to the beach, Rena' would hang back.

"We've invited both of them to Indiana Motor Speedway," Felicia mentioned. "He'll go. She won't."

Rena' wasn't very comfortable around kids. "My history makes it difficult for me to be around small children," Rena' explained. "I didn't have children because I don't feel like I handle them well. I don't babysit. So, I don't know what to do with a child. It's becoming more of an issue."

James didn't push too much because he knew Rena' was adjusting to life in Indiana. She was working nights as a dispatcher for a trucking company, while he worked long days at the nursing home, so their time together was limited. Rena' had her health problems, too—diabetes, high blood pressure, and asthma. Working opposite schedules, James would crawl out of bed in the early morning hours when Rena' returned, and they would catch up. It was their time to reconnect.

At the head of a long bar table, James took his seat and started digging into a full plate of meat. Abigail perched on the cross-bar of a stool to get everyone's attention before the party began. "James is my individual client for Life After Innocence, but I don't even use that name anymore because he's become one of my closest friends," she said. Turning to James Jr. and Felicia, she added, "I can't thank you all enough for being that strong support system."

Then Abigail turned back to James, who was smiling slightly, a decided departure from his usual deadpan demeanor. "I can't tell you how much I admire and look up to you. Everything you've been through. If I can have half as much perseverance as you, I'd be very lucky."

James's grandchildren piled up on his lap, clambering onto him on the stool. "One, two, three!" Laura said, snapping a photo of his family. "And one more," she added, as they all held their smiles.

On the way out, Rena' slipped Laura some cash for the party. "For the next guy," she said with an assuring wink. With scores of exonerees in Illinois, someone else would need it.

A few weeks later, James had to take a Thursday off work. His son's van had died a few times, and he needed to replace it. When the engine light came on, James spent $700 to replace the plugs, wires, and ignition coil. But the next day, the engine light came back on, and, after holding the van for another three days, the mechanic finally gave up: "We don't know what's wrong with it."

James tried to get a loan, but he was turned down. "I have a shitty credit history," he remarked. He had to borrow money. After looking around, he settled on the same make and model as before, just two years newer—a 2007 Dodge Caravan for $6,500, greenish-blue in color. The engine was clean, and by buying the same kind of van, he could easily trade parts between them. The old van had a radiator with a lifetime warranty and new tires, brakes, plug wires, and ignition coil.

With his wheels back in place, James felt he was back on a roll. The following February, he took a ten-day trip to visit his daughter Sarah and her family on the outer banks of North Carolina. They saw alligators, went bowling, visited an aquarium, swam at a clubhouse pool, tried on silly hats at a souvenir shop, and celebrated his granddaughter Tori's fourth birthday. Tori's striking red hair had grown thicker and longer, forming a stronger halo-swirl above her head.

On the trip, James cooked every night, treating his family to ribs, fries, grilled steaks, and chicken. He baked potatoes and served up corn on the cob. He made his special pasta sauce with pork neck bones, layered and baked with cheese ravioli and mozzarella.

By the following June, when James headed back east for Sarah's college graduation, his job was in jeopardy again, due to work injuries. He had hurt his knee pushing a dumpster, and he suffered from debilitating carpel tunnel in both arms and wrists—unresolved medical issues from his incarceration, James says. He needed three surgeries and was relegated to desk duty at the nursing home while his bosses figured out what to do with him. His return to handyman duties was looking less promising.

That summer Rena' also slowly started moving out of their house. Everything belonged to her, remnants of her life back in New Mexico, except the bedroom furniture. When James asked her why furniture was disappearing, at first he accepted the answer that she was just freeing up some space. But by the time she dropped James off at the surgical center, she said she'd be gone by the time he got back.

"She wasn't vindictive or vicious or anything like that," James remembers.

During his incarceration, sometimes she had been the only one to write to him, his only contact in the outside world. James could come to accept that he was losing a girlfriend, but he didn't want to lose his friend and pen pal of more than twenty years.

They kept talking, although it wasn't the same. But months later, when Rena' needed a tooth pulled, James drove her there and back and looked after her while she recovered.

James found himself back in court again in July. This time it was to determine if he still owed child support for his estranged daughter—now an adult—for the nearly twenty-five years he was in prison, during which he wasn't earning a livable wage.

By then, he had received a compensation check for his wrongful conviction. But the state had snatched back $20,000 of it, holding it for his back child support payments.

From the second row of the courtroom, James wiped his tired eyes, lifting his glasses and propping them on his bald head. He sat behind the other fathers, all of whom were being brought to task for not paying their exes. The first guy up was trying to avoid paying his wife's lawyer fees. The judge ordered him to pay $1,500 a month for three months.

"Fifteen hundred!?" he bellowed.

The judge looked at him blankly. "Yeah."

The next guy approached the bench. No lawyer, he represented himself, shirt untucked and backpack in tow. He interrupted his wife's attorney several times. It had been a long court fight, and he had filed a lot of motions himself.

"I haven't received any notice," he told the judge.

"What notice do you want?"

"Could I get an answer on my motion?"

"Today?"

"Oh, no? That's cool."

"This is not my average child support case," the judge reminded him.

James whispered to himself as he waited: *If she doesn't think this is average, wait 'til she hears mine.* He was next up. The motion: to reduce or eliminate child support.

"If you may recall, Mr. Kluppelberg was wrongfully incarcerated for about twenty-five years serving a life sentence," his lawyer told the judge. "The state subsequently held that money for support. He applied for a 'clean slate' and was denied."

She asked the court to waive all the years owed. The judge said she would enter the order to direct the money back to James. With more cases on deck, the judge paused. She took a moment to look at James. She shook her head, and her all-business tone softened to empathy.

"I'm sorry about this phase of your life story."

Then she wished him the best.

Her kindness left James dazed. He let out a big sigh and answered her: "I'm walking free. Just moving forward. Thank you, ma'am."

PART FOUR

ANTIONE

Convicted in 1992
Exonerated in 2002

Courtesy WBEZ/Andrew Gill

I.

"You don't know which way to go, what to do or how to get it done."

On May 8, 2002, Antione Day was wearing another man's clothes. Heavy spring rain was falling on the razor-wire fence and security gate sequestering the Cook County Jail in Chicago. Beat-up sedans and noisy industrial trucks rumbled past on California Avenue.

He had emerged from the jail minutes earlier, walking free for the first time in almost a decade at age forty. Inside, he had been stripped of his uniform stamped with CCDOC—Cook County Department of Corrections—and led into a room where used garments were piled up to the ceiling. He selected the least offensive sweatshirt and sweatpants he could find from the stinking heap and put them on.

"People sweating and farting in those clothes," Antione remembers with disgust.

Outside, the dreary weather greeted him. His hometown appeared foreign as he stood in the rain, "smelling like a mule."

He had nowhere to go and no way to get there.

Earlier that day, Antione (pronounced "An-twon") had been sitting with his lawyer in the perpetually old-school criminal court building at 26th and California. The columned building had seen the likes of infamous mob boss Al Capone, whose homicidal smirk was memorialized in an undated photograph hanging in one judge's chambers.

No media took Antione's picture the day he was released, nor on the day in 1993 that a judge sentenced him to sixty years for murder, twenty-five years for attempted murder, and five years for unlawful use of a firearm by a felon. He was to serve the sentences concurrently. Now, sitting at a hearing leading up to a new trial that could grant his freedom, Antione found himself daydreaming. He wondered how long the proceedings would take before he could go back next door to the jail and lift some weights.

"The case is over," said Judge James B. Linn. His words fell flat, almost unnoticed in the courtroom. The prosecutor, assistant state's attorney Rimas Cernius, proceeded with a legal housekeeping matter—a request to reimpound the evidence, locking it away.

Judge Linn interrupted Antione's daze with an unusual question.[15]

"How are you feeling, Mr. Day?" Antione heard the judge ask from the bench.

"I'm good," Antione answered, tentatively.

"Are you ready to go home?"

Struck, Antione darted his head toward his attorney, Howard Joseph—"Mr. Joseph," as he called him. Mr. Joseph, a sharp-minded, sloppily dressed, silver-haired man in his seventies, was smiling wide. The two had a long-standing joke, a back-and-forth during Antione's incarceration, where Mr. Joseph would pester him to prepare for his ultimate release, so confident was he in Antione's appeal.

"Are you ready to go home? Do you have your clothes packed? Got some clothes ready to go home? It's going to happen when you least expect it," Mr. Joseph would warn him during his legal visits to the prison, which had stretched over more than nine years.

"Mr. Joseph, I will go home butt-naked," Antione would reply. "I don't need no clothes to go home."

Their banter often played out over *Time* magazines and Good Humor ice cream bars. Mr. Joseph would purchase two of the same ice-cream flavor from the visitation room snack bar—sometimes he would buy two strawberry shortcake bars, sometimes two toasted almond.

"You should get your mom to bring you some clothes because you're going to walk out of here," Mr. Joseph would tell him.

In the courtroom, the judge looked at Antione for a response. Antione turned around, scanning for faces. He couldn't find his mother. She wasn't there. No one was.

Then he heard Judge Linn tell him he was free to go home.

Antione turned to Rimas Cernius, the assistant state's attorney who had argued against him at his late 1992 trial. He hollered at him: "You knew I didn't do this! You knew I was innocent!"

Minutes earlier, Cernius had informed the judge that after talking it over with his supervisors, they decided they could no longer meet the burden of proof in the case. As Antione berated Cernius, he heard Judge Linn repeat: "Go home."

---

15. The court reporter did not capture this aside in her transcription of the hearing.

Escorted back to the jail, in the bullpen behind the courtroom, he came across another ghost from his past, defense attorney Steven Decker. In 1990, Antione's family had paid Decker to accompany him to the police station, amid rumors about Antione's involvement in a weekend shooting on the West Side. Antione recalls Decker leaving him alone with police for the interrogation and questionable lineup.

Decker, who doesn't remember Antione or the amount he was paid, describes his process like this: "You would surrender him to the detective, try to get the detective's name, then I would give him my card. I would write my number on his hand or underwear." This would ensure the client would still have his lawyer's number if his personal items were taken away after an arrest. "Plus, it's just a good reminder also for them not to speak to the police. I only wish my name was Calvin Klein. That way they would could have my name and number on his underwear."

Today, Decker's website advertises his defense services:

EVERYONE DESERVES A FAIR DAY IN COURT, LET US HELP YOU!
AVAILABLE 24 HOURS A DAY, 7 DAYS A WEEK
WE ACCEPT CREDIT CARDS!

Confronted with the familiar face at 26th and Cal, Antione snarled at Decker: "My case just got overturned. No thanks to you, you punk!"

The deputies kept Antione moving. It would be a long day being processed out of county jail. Mr. Joseph couldn't stay. His wife's failing health meant he was needed back home.

A sealed bag of Antione's personal property, containing a watch, some cash, and an ID, had gone missing. Whenever a prisoner is moved—for transfers or court hearings—the bag is meant to follow. But Antione didn't want to argue about the loss. "OK, where's the door? That's all I'm looking for. Nothing else but the door," he said, trying to speed up the process.

On their way out they passed through the underground tunnels that connect the jail's units, lined with bullpens with four caged sides. As he walked inmates spread the word: *Hey, he's getting out!*

Outside the jail, Antione was alone. The world in front of him appeared strange, yet once familiar. He felt joy to be free, but the emotion was laced with fear.

"I was very much afraid of the unexpected. Everything was so new. Transitioning from one world to another one. It's two different worlds." Antione waited and watched the rain collide with the street traffic. It was close to dusk. His mother's house was more than five miles away, and he had no money for the bus. After what felt like two or three hours, a man pulled up to the corner in a black sedan. Coincidentally, Antione knew him. It was Anthony, an old buddy from the neighborhood.

"What are you doing out of jail, Twon?"

"I just broke out!" Antione laughed.

He hopped in his friend's ride, and they drove about four miles to Roosevelt Road, where a string of men's clothing shops appeared untouched by time, still selling three-piece suits, alligator shoes, and fedoras. To this day, it remains one of the few spots in the city with same-day tailoring services. With white cursive lettering on black awnings, the shops stand near what used to be Maxwell Street, the birthplace of Chicago Blues and home to the Maxwell Street Market, once considered the "Ellis Island of the Midwest." The market, an immigrant gateway by the railroad tracks, was displaced by the interstate in the 1950s and was pushed out again during Antione's incarceration by an expanding university campus.

Antione's friend bought him some new threads and took him to his apartment to shower and change. Once Antione shed the stinking jail clothes, he was ready to go see his mother. He hitched another ride and rolled up to his mother's house, almost a decade since the last time he had seen it.

One of nine children, Antione grew up in Austin, a neighborhood about seven miles west of Chicago's downtown Loop. Antione's mother, a retired postal worker, lived with his stepfather on Quincy Street, just west of the tree-lined Moore Park, named after an Austin resident of Irish descent, a longtime police captain, in 1929. Today, the main attraction is a full basketball court where neighborhood kids shoot hoops.

He walked up the seven concrete steps at the double-staircase side entrance to his mother's shotgun-style brick home. The lawn had been kept up nicely, and the white aluminum awnings maintained their brightness. The house ran deep into a backyard, where they used to have Hawaiian luau-type cookouts. His mother would roast a pig big enough to feed a crowd.

The door was unlocked. Antione opened it and crept into his mother's bedroom. Littie Daye—she spelled their shared last name with an extra "e," though Antione never knew why—was lying in her bed. She screamed when she saw him in the doorframe. It was the scare, and the surprise, of her life.

When the shock wore off, he joined her in the bed, where they talked, side by side. There was so much to say, even though letters and visits to the prison had filled those missing years. Littie cried herself to sleep. Antione wept in unison, departing the bed for his mother's couch when his stepdad came home.

II.

"I did run with some unruly people because of the community I came from. I wasn't no angel."

Born in 1962 as Lee Antione Day, he was a self-proclaimed "Momma's boy." He enjoyed a happy childhood on Quincy Street, where his mother provided for the family as a postal worker. His dad, the son of a Baptist preacher from Mississippi, worked in a steel mill. He left home when Antione was a boy, but they maintained a good relationship, an "open-door policy."

Antione says he learned how to ride motorbikes in the birth canal. In reality, his love began around age eight or nine. Antione also sang and played the drums, taking private lessons and working as a musician as early as age eleven. A neighbor, Mr. Hicks, who had a drum set, taught him into his teens. In his twenties, Antione turned the basement of a house his family kept up into a recording studio, a few blocks away from the Quincy Street house. Later, at Malcolm X College, Antione took a music course but didn't complete it.

Growing up, Antione was an active kid, involved in sports and band in grammar school and middle school. He played after class and on weekends with friends from his community. They swam together, played baseball, and hung out at Moore Park. At the same time, a neighborhood outreach group, Conservative Vice Lord, Inc., provided programs for the local kids, and the Rockefeller Foundation granted the organization $275,000 for its activities, according to the Chicago Crime Commission's *Gang Book*. The only problem, according to law enforcement, was that the outreach group was actually part of one of Chicago's street gangs, now one of the oldest and largest in the city, with tens of thousands of members across the United States, with mostly African American members. While Conservative Vice Lord, Inc., gained positive repute from community leaders and politicians, police considered it to be a polished faction of the Vice Lords gang. Law enforcement now believes this group is the foundation for the entire conglomerate of the Vice Lord Nation. As narcotics were introduced to the West Side, gang activities centered on the drug trade. Today, the Vice Lords are primarily known for drug trafficking and protecting territory at all costs.

Before Antione knew it, the community activities with his friends morphed into race wars. As the once predominantly Irish white neighborhood changed, Antione remembers fighting over integration. "If we wanted to go to the swimming pool, they would not want us there," he says. "They would get out of the swimming pool and urinate in it."

Antione and his friends fought with bricks and bottles—whatever they could find. "You could have called it a gang fight."

And that is what it became. They grew more organized in their later teens. Smaller neighborhood gangs consolidated into the Vice Lord Nation. Antione became a "chief" of the Mafia Insane Vice Lords, part of the Vice Lord Nation. "I was the leader. I ran it," says Antione, who had a tattoo that read "100% Mafia Insane" on his right arm. "I did what I wanted to do. I made the laws."

As a young adult, the gang life for Antione meant selling drugs, gambling, and sponsoring games—not killing or hurting people or picking fights, he says. He did not use drugs and rarely had a drink. In 1978, he became a father at age sixteen, naming his baby boy Antione and employing the same uncommon spelling. The boy would be the first of three sons with the name Antione. Today, in his fifties, Antione has proudly fathered seventeen children—ten boys, seven girls. His kids have "several mothers," and he doesn't care to count them.

As a new father, he dropped out of high school to work, holding down good jobs at a manufacturing company, where he worked his way up to drill press operator, and afterwards, at a printing company. He subsequently worked at Mario's Butcher Shop until 1989, earning $7.80 an hour.

But he also found trouble with the law—or it found him. In 1987, at age twenty-five, he was arrested near a Chicago music venue, Park West, for possession of suspected cocaine—a charge he disputes, saying the drugs were planted on him and that he has never done any drugs. The reporting officer wrote he had witnessed Antione and another guy snorting a white substance, then found thirteen plastic bags in his pants pocket.

"Before you know it, the tow truck is there, and then I went to jail," Antione says. "Then you get to the police station and it's all, they got the power in the pen."

Antione initially pleaded not guilty, then changed his plea to guilty, encouraged by a public defender. "It was one of those things where if you let this go, this will just go away," he says. "The cops knew they lied." He was sentenced to two years of probation. After that, he became a marked man, known to local law enforcement. "I was kind of just 'wanted.' They wanted to bring me down," Antione explains.

Three months after the drug arrest, Antione was charged with unlawful possession of ammunition. "They put bullets on me one day," he says.

Antione was in front of his house and jogged across the street to his car to get a "Gatorade or juice or something" from the store. Police pulled him over, saying they heard he had a gun. "A gun? I don't got no gun." Antione remembers the officer looking in the car and coming out with a bag of bullets. The court later dismissed the charge.

Despite these skirmishes with the law, Antione was enjoying life, earning money by playing gigs with a band in and outside the city, practicing three days a week and recording music at night. During the day, he was a house husband, taking care of his nearly two-year-old son, Krishon, cooking dinner for his family, and cleaning the house while his live-in girlfriend Renita, Krishon's mother, worked. The baby slept between them in their bed. Antione would take his family to restaurants and on other outings. He took the baby to the Enchanted Castle, then a ten-thousand-square-foot family fun center at the nearby suburban Lombard Pines Shopping Center. Besides caring for Krishon, Antione lavished attention on his other babies—his motorcycles. He had a classic 1976 Kawasaki KZ900 and a Suzuki GSX-R 1100, a sport bike introduced in 1986. He loved the freedom of the open road.

On September 3, 1990, Antione was hanging out at his mother's house when a family friend, Hargrove, came and told him about a shooting murder in the neighborhood he had witnessed two days earlier. Antione hadn't heard anything about it; shootings like these were not so rare. But what was concerning was that rumors had started swirling around the neighborhood about the shooters' identities—and that Antione was one of them.

"People were shocked that it was me that they were asking about," he remembers about the community's reaction. "It was surprising."

The origin of this rumor is a rumor itself, a back story that later surfaced in an affidavit on Antione's appeal: a guy named Wood, who had been going around saying that "Twon" was one of the gunmen, had it out for Antione because he mistakenly believed Antione and a neighborhood woman, with whom Wood had conceived a daughter, were romantically involved.

Unbeknownst to Antione, the shooting had taken place less than a mile away from his mother's house at Belmonte Cut Rate Liquors. Today, the liquor store on Austin's North Laramie Street looks like a time capsule on a changing block. Its original signs are still intact, one tucked under a dingy yellow awning, declaring "The Party Store" and, as if in one breath, "Small in Size Big on Bargains." A forty-two-bulb, red-chipped arrow sign flags the liquor store from the street, its single-door entrance presenting two key locks, a deadbolt, and two padlocks; gates and bars guard the windows. Inside, there is one cash register behind glass, along with all the store's liquor stock.

Back on September 1, 1990, Belmonte Cut Rate Liquors was the place to buy cheap booze. Sometime after midnight, an Austin neighborhood man and his nephew—Thomas Peters and Darrell Gurley—stopped at Belmonte for some beer. A group of guys were playing dice outside the store, near the Twin Pigs restaurant. Peters decided to try his luck at the game.

"You go into the liquor store and buy some beer, and I'm going to be here playing some dice at this dice game," Peters told his twenty-year-old nephew—too young to legally purchase anything inside Belmonte, which didn't hinder him.

"Come on. Let's go home," Gurley urged.

"No, I just want to play one more game. Hold on one minute."

James Coleman, another guy from the neighborhood, stood and watched. He went inside Belmonte to buy a six-pack for his auntie, then opened a can of beer and set the rest on the ground. He was about to place a bet when he says he saw three men,[16] two of whom he recognized as Poncho and Punchy, approach the game and start shooting. The bullets struck Coleman's right shoulder blade and Peters's left side, traveling slightly upward, a strange movement that fractured a rib and caused hemorrhage of an upper lobe of his lung and his throat. Under Peters's left collarbone, an assistant medical examiner would later find a small, disfigured bullet fragment and put it in a special envelope to give to police—the only physical evidence from the chaotic night.

Coleman felt what he thought was sweat running down his back; it was humid outside. But when he ran his hand up his flesh, he realized he was bleeding. He was able to make it home to ask his aunt and her boyfriend to take him to the nearby Loretto Hospital. He was treated and released that day.

Thomas Peters did not survive. At first, he stumbled in the middle of the street and collapsed. Hearing gunshots seconds before, a man driving by North Laramie and Lake stopped his car just under the El track. He and his passenger got out.

"Would you take me to the hospital, please?" Peters moaned.

The men put him in the front, propping up the seat because blood had started coming out of Peters's mouth. He was bleeding from the chest and making strange sounds. Blood continued to pour from him.

---

16. Witness accounts differ on the number of men.

The car-seat upholstery absorbed the liquid. They took him to Loretto Hospital, where he was too far gone for police to interview him; investigators were already on the trail. He was transferred to Cook County Hospital and died later that morning.

Gurley, Peters's nephew, had escaped the path of the bullets entirely and ran to his cousin's girlfriend's house, then went home.

When Antione first heard about the murder, and that people thought he was responsible, his friend Hargrove also told him a guy named Vic— Victor Peters, at the time believed to be Thomas Peters's brother—wanted to ask him about the shooting. Antione didn't know him or Thomas Peters, but Vic had heard from family members that Antione was responsible for the murder. Antione went to see him.

The interaction that transpired is in dispute. Antione later testified that when Vic first saw him, he said: "Oh, you ain't the one." It is unclear how Vic would have known what the shooter looked like. Antione says Vic knew who the shooter was and knew it wasn't him.

"Not the one what?"

According to Antione, Vic replied: "Not the one that shot my brother. Well, you better leave because my mother thinks you are the one." But at trial, Vic denied saying this, also testifying that Thomas Peters was his uncle, not his brother. Vic Peters's grandmother, Janie, said at trial that she came outside and talked to Antione, though her grandson Vic contradicted her account at trial, testifying that no one else came out to talk to Antione. Antione says he never spoke to Janie and didn't see her until trial.

But on this much the stories align: Vic handed Antione a card with Chicago police detective Hugh Conwell's phone number on it. Antione called it. He wanted to lay the rumors to rest.

Conwell asked him to come in to the station. Together with his mother, brother, sister, girlfriend, and a lawyer his family had called, Steven Decker, Antione went to the police station in North Austin known as Area Five Violent Crimes, a few miles from home.

When they arrived at the police station, Conwell met them and asked them to wait at the bottom of a stairway. Two men, strangers, looked down at them, according to Littie Daye's affidavit on appeal. They later realized the strange men were lineup witnesses.

Conwell escorted Antione to an interrogation room on the second floor. Antione remembers Decker's leaving because he had to get to his daughter's birthday party. Today, Decker doesn't recall this exactly—"Maybe I surrendered him for some reason?"—but confirms his daughter would have had a birthday that time of year.

Antione says he was handcuffed (police deny this), and he refused to talk, as Decker had instructed before leaving. Conwell left and returned with some McDonald's and a pop, removed the handcuffs, and then departed again, Antione later said in court. He remembers waiting in the room; the door was wide open, and he could see across to an interview room where Darrell Gurley and James Coleman were sitting—another detail police denied at trial.

"I remember the name," says Conwell today. He retired in 1998 and now lives in Las Vegas. "You wouldn't leave a door open—I mean, just logic would show that that's not what happened."

Antione says he asked Gurley, "What are you here for?"

The two men didn't know each other.

"Man, they just brought me down here. Told me to look at something," Antione says Gurley told him. Antione did not realize why Gurley was there: to view a lineup and identify Peters's shooter.

Minutes later, Antione was standing in that lineup. Gurley, who had told police that there was a third shooter, a bowlegged man a little shorter than Antione, identified him in the fourth and final position. Then Coleman, who from the emergency room had given police a description of a six foot, 225-pound man, also picked Antione out of the lineup.

Antione, at the time, stood five foot eleven and weighed about 165 pounds. He was, in fact, bowlegged.

Police arrested him on the spot. Shocked, Antione had no idea what was to come.

III.

"It's amazing how quick they can destroy your life with a lie."

Antione was unrepresented and incarcerated for months as the state looked for his codefendant, accused shooter George Garrett, aka "Poncho."[17] His mother, Littie, posted bond for him in April 1991, seven months after his arrest, paying $27,500, or 10 percent of $275,000.

Antione describes the long stretch of time in Cook County Jail, as he waited to post bond, as "very rough" and "very violent." But after returning home to Renita and the kids, who were very worried about the murder charge, he was confident his name would be cleared.

"I knew it was bad. I knew it was serious," he says. "But I just couldn't believe that I would be convicted of that, something I didn't do."

In May 1991, novice lawyer Joan Hill-McClain took Antione's case but represented him for only four months before she removed herself, as she was also representing Garrett. With such a serious case, she didn't want to take a chance on any allegations of impropriety by representing them both. Now, almost thirty years into her career as a defense attorney, she has represented her fair share of gangbangers. When asked about Antione, she replies, circumspectly, "I remember him well."

Garrett was ultimately sentenced to sixty years for murder and twenty-five years for attempted murder, and is currently held at Shawnee Correctional Center. During a prison phone call, he maintains his innocence: "How is it that Lee Day is exonerated, and I'm still incarcerated?" Without hesitation, Hill-McClain backs up Garrett's claims. "This case has been eating at my heart for years," she says. "I don't think there's a day that I don't think about George Garrett in that case."

Hill-McClain referred Antione to another attorney, Gay-Lloyd Lott, whom Antione's family retained. Lott was a promising trial lawyer. He later became a circuit court judge and presided over the late-nineties high-profile "Baby Richard" case, an adoption custody battle that enraptured the nation. As a judge, he received a Distinguished Service Award from the Illinois Judicial Council in 2002. But later that fall, the *Chicago Tribune* reported he was "not recommended" to stay on the bench, and

---

17. The other alleged gunman, Punchy, had been murdered by the time of trial.

the *Chicago Sun-Times* cited the Chicago Council of Lawyers as saying he was "often unprepared" and issued "legally deficient rulings." But toward the end of his life Lott was inducted into the Cook County Bar Association's Hall of Fame as a "Legal Eagle," among twenty-six other prominent African American judges. He died in 2013.

In Antione's case, Lott took many missteps. According to appeal records, he was unaware that it took thirteen months before Antione was arraigned, when a defendant formally faces his charges and is expected to enter a plea. He also never spoke to any of Antione's defense witnesses until they arrived for trial, in part because the prosecution kept them from him, according to one of Antione's appeals. One crime scene witness—Antione's friend Hargrove, who first told him about the murder—had even called Lott on the phone, offering to testify, but Hargrove claimed Lott refused to interview him. Lott also confused key dates at trial, rendering some testimony useless.

"Mr. Lott," the judge said at the beginning of the October 1992 trial, more than two years after the double shooting. "Would you like your client to sit closer to you? I don't want him to look like he is an orphan."

Judge Thomas Dwyer was a novice judge, appointed to the bench the year before. A former police detective, the judge also had sixteen years of prosecutorial experience under his belt when he assumed control of courtroom 301 in Cook County's criminal courthouse. Known to be hard-nosed and brusque, Dwyer was advised by the Chicago Bar Association to "work on dispelling the perception of poor temperament," the *Chicago Reader* reported in 1993. As with exonerees Jacques and James, Antione was advised to take a bench trial, waiving his right to a jury of peers. Antione did not understand the implications of this decision, and Lott confused matters by failing to make it clear that Garrett's jury was not also Antione's jury, as the two men were tried together.

The prosecution's first witness was Janie Peters, the mother of the deceased, Thomas Peters. Now in her eighties, Janie says she doesn't want to speak about the case. But at trial she gave vivid testimony, though key details were contradicted by her grandson Vic's account in court. "They were intubating my son and blood were going everywhere," Janie said at trial, describing the scene at Loretto Hospital, where her son was first taken. He was still alive when she saw him there.

Janie identified Antione in court as a man she had seen sitting outside her house when he came to talk to her grandson Vic. "I can't recall exactly which of my relatives—one of my sons or whatever came in the house, and they said the man that is supposed to have killed Thomas is outside," she told the court. "So as I approached the yard, Mr. Day says to me—he stated that he were going to the police department and his lawyer and tell everything, because he wasn't going to jail alone."

"Had you ever heard that voice before?" the prosecutor, Rimas Cernius, prompted.

"I had heard it like on that—it were on the Tuesday, about 2:30 in the morning."

Janie testified that a man who sounded like Antione had called her before the shooting, threatening to shoot Thomas. She hadn't told police about this phone call in the aftermath of the crime. And she didn't tell anyone except her daughter and son about the phone call until June 1992, a few months before trial.

"'Tell him I'm gonna shoot him in his butt,'" she said the caller said.

Darrell Gurley, Peters's young nephew and a crime scene witness, took the stand next. At trial, he was serving time for drugs. He had an armed robbery conviction the previous year. When his uncle was shot, Gurley was about a year into a four-year probation for drugs, with one of the charges pending. In court, Gurley described the crime scene, and then he identified Antione as one of the shooters.

James Coleman, the shooting victim who survived, was called by Cernius to testify for the prosecution. But in a stunning departure from his lineup identification, he admitted on the witness stand that he had intentionally identified Antione as having been present at the shooting, knowing it wasn't true. Cernius quickly shut down the questioning: "No further questions, Judge."

After gathering herself, Hill-McClain, Garrett's lawyer, cross-examined Coleman.

"Why have you come here and changed your mind here today?"

"Because I was under oath today, and because I'm under oath, I'm going to tell the truth about what exactly happened that night."

"You're under oath today?"

"Yes."

"You lied, and you affected a man's life for almost two years. Now you come to court and say, 'I'm under oath today'?"

"Yes."

"Why did you frame him then?" Hill-McClain asked, over Cernius's objections.

"When I viewed the lineup with Twon Day in it, I was told by friends of the deceased to make sure that I picked Twon Day out of that lineup," Coleman said. "I had my reason for doing it."

"When were you told this by their friends?"

"Several days."

"After the shooting?"

"Yes."

In court Coleman described himself as a twenty-year member of the New Missionary Baptist Church. But he was no choirboy, having been convicted of attempted murder and aggravated battery in another case leading up to Antione's trial, weakening his credibility.

Testifying for the defense was Kim Lee, a neighborhood guy who had witnessed the double shooting. Lee knew all the key players in the case: he had come up with Peters in grade school; Gurley used to play with his little brother; and he'd known Antione for about a year or two, from his music. Antione's band rehearsed on Lee's mother's block, and he liked to watch the guys play. To prove he knew Antione, Lee pointed him out in court as wearing a rust-colored suit.

On September 1, 1990, after midnight, Lee was walking toward Laramie Avenue when he saw a black Buick with three men inside, Garrett at the wheel, he testified. He stopped to call his girlfriend on a pay phone outside Belmonte Cut Rate Liquors. That's when he saw Garrett arguing with Peters. "'Motherfucker, come on out your pocket and leave the money on the ground,'" Lee testified he had heard Garrett shout while brandishing a big silver gun from his waistband. Garrett was the only shooter Lee observed. When Peters started running, Lee heard a shot. Lee dropped to the ground and covered his head. Missing from the scene, Lee testified, was Antione.

Lee said in court that, a little more than a week after the shooting, he told one of the investigating officers, Detective Richard Curley, that Antione wasn't involved in the crime. At that time, Garrett was still at large, so Lee, who knew Garrett, or "Poncho," was helping Curley find him, stopping by two of Garrett's girlfriends' homes and later driving with Curley to look for him in Waukegan. On the road, having learned of the arrest, Lee mentioned Antione wasn't the right guy. "I told him that Twon was not part of the shooting," he said in court. Curley, on rebuttal testimony, denied this.

At the time of trial, Curley had almost twenty-five years on the force, having joined in his early twenties. In 1969, he was injured in a shootout with the Black Panthers, describing it as "wartime" to the Associated Press. The Panthers were firing in self-defense, neighbors told the AP, but Curley later received a Blue Star Award for the wounds he sustained, and he was commended for his heroism.

Littie, Antione's mother, didn't testify at trial, which is not unusual as the testimony doesn't carry much weight in court. (Most mothers will do anything to protect their sons, guilty or not.) But Littie wrote in a 1996 affidavit that Curley had told her near the end of the trial that the police knew Antione wasn't one of the shooters, yet felt he knew something about it. "There's no way they're going to convict your son," Littie wrote Curley had assured her. "Everything will be okay."

Littie also overheard Shawn Peters, another nephew of the shooting victim, talking to Antione and his girlfriend Renita on the first floor of the courthouse, where they had run into him outside the elevator: "I'm sorry, man—my family knows you didn't do this. I don't know why my grandmother is doing this to you."

Renita's own affidavit in 1996 corroborated the story, adding that Shawn said his family threatened to kill someone and blame it on him if he spoke out. When Antione and Renita later urged Lott to put Shawn on the stand, Lott refused, saying Shawn would probably lie.

After closing arguments, Judge Dwyer made his ruling in November 1992. Citing the "clear and convincing" police testimony about the lineup procedures, he perfunctorily found Antione guilty.

Antione shook his head as his family—mother, siblings, Renita, the kids, and others—screamed and cried.

"I was like, 'Wow. Did he really just say that?'" Antione says.

"Judge Dwyer was very unfair," Hill-McClain remembers. "I think he had problems with Black men. I think he had problems with Black lawyers as well."

Two months later, in January 1993, it was a new year. Antione had just turned thirty-one when he faced sentencing. "I had not a clue what kind of time I was looking at," he says. "Didn't have a clue."

Lott was given some time to lay out his client's attributes, which he did, albeit clumsily. "While he is not married, he is the father—he is a father, and has been supporting his children," Lott said. "So I submit to your honor that the events that the state has so meticulously recited to the court are completely inconsistent with the life this man has led."

The judge turned to Antione. "Sir, is there anything you wish to say before sentencing?"

Antione addressed the court. "I'd like to say I'm sorry for the family. I'm sorry for my family, and the things that I have been through for something I didn't have nothing to do with, knew nothing about."

He took a beat, then kept going.

Your Honor, I'd like to say that even though I may have to go to the penitentiary and spend years and years of time down there, whatever that may be, I just hope that I make a stepping-stone for my kids so they will never have to go through the same thing I'm going through. And I hope I can paint a picture for anybody else that can look at this and see that this is not what they want to be into. And I have been through this for some time now, and I have learned that the wheels of justice have been turning, hopefully, to help the family, and I still say now that I'm being wrongfully accused of something that I didn't do, and I would like to always have another chance to be a father to my kids.

"Anything else?"

"No, Your Honor."

Dwyer sentenced him, packaging all the convictions together into sixty years; Garrett received the same concurrent sentence. He detailed the next steps for post-trial motions and then asked: "Do you understand what I have said, sir?"

"Yes, sir," Antione answered.

"I wish you luck."

IV.

"I was mad at the world. I was mad at the birds that flew in the sky."

Antione was sent to Pontiac Correctional Center, a mostly maximum-security prison in Pontiac, Illinois, about a hundred miles southwest of Chicago, after being processed in Joliet. The largest employer in Pontiac, it is the site of one of the worst prison riots in Illinois history. In 1978, gang members armed with shanks charged the guards. Prisoners set fire to several buildings. Three workers died. In the next several years, little changed despite the state's spending $43.5 million to improve the prison. During a one-year span in the eighties, 256 inmate attacks on employees were reported, with injured employees receiving more than $1 million in workers' compensation. Weapons at Pontiac were stockpiled and sold as scrap. Over a twenty-two-month period in 1984 and 1985, Pontiac guards seized 1,366 homemade knives inside the prison. "Your chances of getting by two years [as an employee] at Pontiac without a fairly serious injury are fairly small," attorney David M. Goldberg, who was representing dozens of Pontiac guards, told the *Chicago Tribune* in 1988.

The prison was also dominated by gangs, mostly extensions of the street gangs in Chicago, like the Vice Lords and Latin Kings. A 1988 *Chicago Tribune* investigation described how both inmates and guards perished at the hands of powerful gang leaders, who would enslave weaker inmates, selling them to other inmates for sex. In a federal civil trial, an inmate testified that $250 was the price for a man's body inside Pontiac.

"Wasn't no room for no nice guys at Pontiac," Antione remembers, haunted by the memories. He knew some of the guys accused of killing guards. The prison did not seem to have improved since the riots. "You never get rid of hearing people cry at night or watching people get murdered right in front of you or having the guards shoot at you. . . . living in a cage like an animal, you never forget it."

Living among some of the state's most violent inmates, Antione lifted weights, boxed, and started fights. As a gang member, he had a certain level of protection. "I acted a fool for a while," he remembers. Angry about his conviction, he got into it with the correctional officers, and he was accused of assaulting a guard, staging a riot, and disobeying direct orders. Antione spent a lot of time in "the hole"—segregation. "I wanted to be the asshole they said I was," he says.

He thought about how to break out. He thought more about his case. To pass the time in segregation, he did jumping jacks and push-ups. The exercise interrupted prison's monotony, occasional chaos, and constant danger. He took his meals in his cell—special meals he cooked for himself with grocery items purchased from the prison commissary or, more often, secured through an inside hookup. "I really never went to the kitchen and ate that because I always thought they was trying to poison us. The food was very unsanitary. It was cooked very poorly."

He didn't trust the water either. He was convinced it was full of lead—a reasonable concern, as Pontiac, like many prisons, was built when lead pipes or rods were still used for water systems. The other inmates would avoid the prison water by drinking soda, but Antione stayed away from sugar for fear of diabetes. Before gallon jugs of drinking water became available in the prison commissary, he would boil his own water before drinking it.

When he was in segregation—"the hole"—Antione spent his time reading, as there was no TV. His favorite authors included Marcus Garvey, Malcolm X, and Nation of Islam leader Elijah Muhammad, who wrote the 1965 book *Message to the Blackman in America*. He read *The Spook Who Sat by the Door*, by Sam Greenlee, who told the story of Dan Freeman, the first Black CIA officer. Antione also studied auto mechanics books and drew pictures of the highway, dreaming of leaving prison and going on a long road trip. "Always said that I want to get on this highway and when I get on it, I'm going to ride, ride."

Sometimes a letter or card came in from his mother, Littie, to keep his spirits up. As a joke, she once sent him a postcard of Alcatraz Island, the famous federal prison in San Francisco Bay known as "The Rock," which closed in 1963. It could be worse, she seemed to say. When people questioned Antione's innocence, she never doubted it, encouraging him to take ahold of his situation. "You can't quit. You just can't quit because you can't quit," Littie would tell him. "No one knows your case like you do."

His mother visited a few times a year. She would always cry.

"She just couldn't believe it," Antione says. "She just couldn't believe that a lie could carry so much weight."

His siblings visited him frequently, he remembers. They never lost touch.

A few years into his sentence, in the mid-nineties, Antione's son Krishon, no longer a baby, came to visit, one of about a dozen trips. They sat together in the visitation room, supervised by guards. It was an innocent question Krishon posed, boyish and sincere: "Dad, when are you coming home?"

These words from his son brought Antione to tears. It was at that moment that he decided to stop fighting against himself and start fighting for himself. "That was my wake-up," Antione recalls. He decided to leave the Vice Lords gang. As a high-ranking member, it was a smooth enough transition. "No repercussions," he says.

Antione started spending time in the law library at Pontiac, reading about other people's cases in dim lighting, line by line, hunched over for hours. When he wasn't studying, he worked in the tailor shop, served in the chow hall, and helped out in the general storeroom. He also was selected to work in the "Hot Room," where inmates weren't usually allowed because the products stored there could be used to make hooch.

"Mr. Day works in a highly positive way, is not judgmental and conducts his work and himself in a way that makes it difficult for me to conceive of his shooting a human being or firing a weapon on a public street," a former Pontiac employee, Helen Mays, wrote about Antione in an affidavit for his later appeal. "Mr. Day talked to me about his children, his mother, how he helped her in the kitchen and liked to cook, and he would turn his life around if he got out of prison."

One day, while living at Pontiac's East House, he took it upon himself to write to the superintendent and request musical instruments. He wanted to form a band, to be back in the drummer's seat.

Antione's request was granted after thirty days of lockdown, the security aftermath of an inmate's fatal stabbing. During a lockdown, prisoners are usually confined to their cells, and most activities outside the cell—often including eating—are restricted. The notice came to him, typed out, official. Antione would get some instruments and a practice space in the chapel with time to rehearse.

The drums the prison gave him were so old and saggy they sounded like coffee cans. Antione took a lighter and held it under the plastic, warming it, pulling it taut again. It was an old neighborhood trick he had used back when he couldn't afford new drumheads. Tightened and transformed, the tones sounded more like he remembered, back when he played with his band into the night.

At Pontiac, he decided to host a talent show and held auditions of sorts to scope out the good players. Despite some mocking from other prisoners, Antione created a band, and soon more guys wanted to join. It felt good to be playing again; it was the smallest taste of freedom.

The first time Howard Joseph—"Mr. Joseph"—came to visit Antione in prison, he didn't call. There was no message. Antione had never seen his face.

A Chicago real estate attorney, Mr. Joseph lacked experience in criminal appeals, but he had taken an interest in the case because his son Rick had worked with Antione's sister at a video duplication company. Antione's family retained him, and in a February 24, 1993, typewritten letter to Antione's mother, sixty-six-year-old Mr. Joseph notified her that he had filed a notice of appeal five days earlier. This came a month after a judge had rejected Lott's post-trial motions for a new trial or a mistrial.

Antione was in the gym at Pontiac when he was told he had an attorney visit. "I ain't got no attorney visit," he said. He went over to the visitation room. There, a gray-haired white man faced him. He looked like a mix of the TV detective Columbo and the more contemporary Dos Equis silver fox, the "Most Interesting Man in the World," but rougher and more tousled. He wore corduroy moccasin slippers as shoes and let his necktie fall askew. He shuffled when he walked.

"Sit down," he said.

Antione sat.

"You're Lee, right?" Mr. Joseph said, calling him by his proper first name.

He nodded.

"I'm going to get you out of here, but I want you to be patient. I see what they did to you."

Antione felt hopeful, and for the first time, excitement that he could earn his freedom. He trusted Mr. Joseph. "I knew he was very smart," he says. "Very smart."

Their visits over the next nine years were frequent but almost always unannounced. At other times Mr. Joseph would call the prison and the duty warden would put Antione on the phone. The calls were short and to the point.

Sometimes, during face-to-face visits, Mr. Joseph leaned forward, his briefcase in the center of his chest, and whispered, "Did you do it? Did you do it?"

Antione always told him no.

Mr. Joseph tried, without success, to pull several legal levers for Antione's appeal. But for Antione's post-conviction petition, a state appeal that allows new evidence to be introduced, he meticulously gathered affidavits from witnesses. Christopher Brown, a police officer from Maywood, a township near the Austin neighborhood, had grown up with Antione. As a character witness, he provided a statement: "He was a gentlemen [sic] at all times and never carried a weapon," Brown wrote.

Mr. Joseph also collected affidavits from crime scene witnesses—Kim Lee and Hargrove, the friend of Antione's whom Lott had not called upon—presenting evidence that Judge Dwyer hadn't heard when he made his ruling. Antione's mother signed an affidavit as well. Littie's account was compelling, as she described meeting James Coleman, the shooting victim who survived.

> Shortly after the shooting, James Coleman, who was wounded by the shooters, came to my house with a friend and told me the police and others were setting Lee up. He stayed for over an hour, telling me that Lee was not one of the shooters, that he was a good guy, that he was

not at the scene of the shooting and that he did not gamble; that Poncho Garrett and "Punchy" (who resembled Lee, both also being bow-legged) were the shooters and Thomas Peters (the deceased) and two others had beat up "Punchy" in a fight over a child; that police detectives had threatened him with twenty years in prison if he told; that he was just out of jail and didn't want to go back.

In April 1996, Mr. Joseph submitted the appeal—a tome that argued Antione's due process rights and other constitutional rights, such as to effective assistance of counsel and to a jury trial, had been violated. The petition landed on the desk of Judge Thomas Dwyer, the same judge who had found Antione guilty. Dwyer promptly denied the appeal less than two weeks later. Mr. Joseph filed a motion to reconsider, which Dwyer also denied a few weeks later. Mr. Joseph appealed further, and, in 1997, the state appellate court ordered a reversal of the decision and sent the case back for an evidentiary hearing. Again, Antione's petition was denied in 2000 by a different judge, and Mr. Joseph appealed the decision.

But in 2001, the state appellate court, agreeing that Lott had not properly represented Antione, ordered a new trial. When Antione found out Mr. Joseph had won him a new day in court, he was working out in the prison yard at Stateville Correctional Center in Joliet, where he had been transferred in the late nineties. A fellow inmate was reading a *Chicago Tribune* article dated September 1, 2001—exactly eleven years since the shooting at Belmonte Cut Rate Liquors.

"Hey, ain't your name Lee?" asked a fellow inmate called Big Smooth.

"Yeah," Antione answered.

"And ain't your name Day?"

"Yeah!" Antione said, snatching the newspaper from his hands.

A state appeals court Friday ordered a new trial for a man convicted of a 1990 Chicago murder, ruling that the man's defense attorney did a poor job during the trial. . . . Lee Antoine [*sic*] Day's lawyer rendered ineffective assistance because "his performance fell below an objective standard of reasonableness," the court wrote in an order reversing the conviction. . . . If not for lawyer Gay-Lloyd Lott's errors, the court said, the result of the defendant's trial might have been different. Day was convicted of first-degree murder for the shooting death of Thomas

Peters and sentenced to 60 years in prison. . . . Lott erred by refusing to present testimony that might have helped his client, including that from a witness to the shooting who would have said Day was not present at the crime scene, the court said.

Antione raced inside to phone Mr. Joseph, who hadn't yet heard the news. "Mr. Joe, you're my angel."

"Don't call me your angel," he replied.

Antione had long put faith in Mr. Joseph, despite his inexperience in criminal appeals and less than professional attire. Once at a hearing for his case, Mr. Joseph shuffled over to the defense table, his corduroy moccasins—lounge slippers—sliding noisily on the courtroom floor. "People thought he was a joke because of the way he dressed," Antione says. He remembers that a prosecutor once whispered to him, upon seeing Mr. Joseph slither into court, "You're in trouble."

"No, you're in trouble," Antione shot back.

V.

"I don't think they should stack the deck and put people in dangerous situations so that you wouldn't get out."

Antione's new trial never came. Nine months after the court ordered a new trial, as Antione waited in Cook County Jail, the prosecution dropped the charges in 2002, without any notice to Antione or his family.

Before the case ended, as he languished at Cook County Jail, an even more destitute environment than prison, Antione's perseverance was put to the test. In 2001, Antione was housed in Division XI, now a medium-security facility for men at Cook County Jail. In the early morning hours, while most inmates were sleeping, Antione was perplexed when he was moved to Division I, the jail's oldest building, opened in 1929. Today, the maximum-security, four-story building is divided into eight blocks, holding up to 1,250 inmates.

In the unfamiliar cell, Antione's new bunkie was asleep. A few hours later, breakfast was served, and the cellmate sat up on the bunk. Antione froze, registering the face staring back at him. It was the man accused of killing his oldest son, one of his namesakes, Antione.

Antione had found out about his son's murder three years earlier while at Stateville. He had just returned from working at the tailor shop, making prison uniforms, when one of the chaplains came to his dorm. "Priest told me he had some bad news," Antione remembers, rubbing his eyes, conjuring the terrible memory. "He said there's been a death in the family. He made it so drawn out, he made me mad. I was worried it was my mom."

He learned it was his nineteen-year-old son, a new father himself, who had been shot in the head and groin, lying in a wintry grave for nearly a week before he was found, a plastic grocery bag fluttering next to his body. His orange-trimmed coat was pulled up to partially cover his face. An acceptance letter to ITT Technical Institute was waiting for him in the mailbox at home when a neighbor discovered the scene alongside an outside stairwell of an abandoned house.

Antione grieved, crying when he was alone. He put in a request to attend the funeral and was denied. "You hurt," he says. "In prison, that's how people become so hard because you don't let things affect you anymore. Because you know there's nothing you can possibly do."

On February 8, 1998, the younger Antione found himself cornered and caught in a web of family ties and lies, armed robberies, arrests, and revenge. Accused of snitching, he was lured to the South Side of Chicago, where 9 mm bullets claimed him—but not before being tortured, Antione had heard.

In 2001, at Cook County Jail, Antione sat a few feet away from a man he knew, a man who would later be convicted of his son's murder—the same man who had served as a pallbearer at his son's funeral.[18]

From prison, the man convicted of the murder of Antione's son and sentenced to sixty years maintains his innocence. In a case overflowing with rumors and unreliable accounts, one of the state's key witnesses against him recanted in 2010, saying he was promised a deal if he gave certain information about the murder.

---

18. Today, Antione doesn't want the man's name published, though a mountain of court documents and appeals reveals his identity.

But faced with his son's accused murderer in 2001, Antione was not convinced by his story of being framed—and he remains assured of his guilt today. "I wanted to kill him right there," Antione says. "I could have been killed, or he could have been killed."

As the man spoke, Antione wouldn't let his words affect him. "You know how you just look through people like they aren't even there? That's what I did as I decided whether to kill him or not."

It was a setup, he thought. With his freedom so close he could almost reach out between the jail's bars and touch it, Antione wasn't going to give in to his instincts. Collecting himself, he told a passing guard, "Hey man, I refuse housing," a safety measure that allows inmates to request protective custody.

Hours later, Antione remembers being taken to segregation until the next day. Within months, he was walking out of Cook County Jail a free man.

VI.

"Finally got something done. Made my challenge worthwhile. Felt like I accomplished something because everyone said I couldn't do it."

The Quincy Street house had shrunk. At least that's what it seemed like to Antione when he woke up the first morning after his release. He had slept on his mother's couch, and, in the daylight, he was able to properly see the place, his childhood home. Everything appeared so small to him, a miniature shadow of what was.

His kids, in contrast, were much bigger than he remembered. He had seen some of them over the years as he tried to parent from prison, offering advice and looking over their homework, even if it had already been completed. Upon his return from prison, they trickled in for visits, sharing tearful reunions. But the accumulated pain from all those lost years outweighed the joy, as Antione tried to reconnect with his children and reenter their lives.

His son, Krishon, had just graduated from eighth grade when Antione came back. Antione was closest to him out of all his kids during his incarceration. At thirteen, Krishon was old enough to understand that his father had gone away to prison, but he never quite knew why, though Antione explained he was innocent. It wasn't until Antione was released that Krishon's mom gave him some more details. But when he mustered up the courage to ask his dad himself, Antione told him, "Don't worry about it. You just don't get yourself into any situations."

Back under his own mother's wing, Antione spent his first few days chatting away with her and reassuring her that everything was OK now—her baby was back. Littie kept him fed, cooking up feasts of baked chicken, sweet potatoes, greens, and cornbread. Antione couldn't eat enough seafood. "Food I wanted when I got out was shrimps," he says. "I love shrimp, and there was having no shrimp in prison—absolutely not."

During the day, Antione felt excited to be out, welcoming some visitors, mainly family. But late at night, his belly full of his mom's cooking, Antione would be wide awake. The car horns and streetlights disturbed him, signaling a scary world beyond the bricks on Quincy Street. Soon he ventured out into the neighborhood, discovering through rumors and sideways glances that his conviction still haunted him. People either figured he beat his case or had earned an early release. That Antione's case was dropped, that he had been wrongly convicted, was not well understood in his community. Doubt emanated from passersby, even after he had covered up his "100% Mafia Insane" gang tattoo with a black panther biting a snake—because he had shed that other life.

One friendly face that greeted him across the fence was his next-door neighbor and former music instructor, Mr. Hicks. He had seen Antione's talent from an early age. "Come over and play," Mr. Hicks said. "Let's play a little bit."

Antione was on the drums, Mr. Hicks on the xylophone. He could tell Antione had kept up his skills in prison. It was no matter that he had been practicing on a dilapidated prison drum set all those years. Mr. Hicks was proud of his student.

"First thing we did, we got me my license," Antione remembers. His friend Darnell took him to the DMV for the driving test. Antione found it real easy, as though no time had passed. Then it was time to find himself a car. At first he drove a family car, a Chevy Cavalier, and he took it just about anywhere he could go in a day's time—Michigan, Ohio, Wisconsin, Minnesota. On weekdays, he shuttled his mother to and from their family doctor's office as her health deteriorated. Kidney problems, the doctor told him.

Racking up miles on the Chevy, Antione got to thinking he'd like to build something of his own. He was pining for his old motorbikes, which his brother had sold while he was in prison. Antione tinkered around with the Internet on his mom and stepdad's desktop computer, teaching himself how to surf the web, and he ordered parts for a Suzuki Hayabusa motorcycle. The sport bike's 1999 frame came from Texas. The engine, too. The plastic parts came from California. Slowly, piece by storied piece, Antione created something strong and solid out of the parts. When he put the motorcycle to pavement, the world still seemed brand-new. He crossed through the neighborhood, got on the highway, and rode.

Soon he wanted another ride, but he needed money. Antione went to one of his best friends, Doc, whom he had long entrusted with a big secret—a three-by-two-foot, black-and-gray safe. Before he went to prison, Antione had asked Doc to keep it for him, and Doc hid the safe in his closet. "Couldn't trust him with your woman, but you can give him anything," Antione laughs. The safe held about $18,000 of savings, money set aside from work and his band earnings. Nobody knew what was inside but Antione. With a fat wallet, he bought a racing car, a 1979 Pontiac Grand Prix. He called it "The Breadwinner."

After living with his mother for a few months, Antione moved in with a girlfriend for about a year and a half. The relationship didn't last, and Antione's residence continued to bounce around town.

Mr. Joseph wasn't finished with Antione's case. "When I get him out, we're going to sue the city for millions of dollars," he had told his son Rick.

Thirty-four days after Antione walked out of Cook County Jail, Mr. Joseph filed a federal lawsuit against the City of Chicago and detectives Hugh Conwell and Richard Curley, alleging that they conspired to have

Antione picked out of a lineup by coaching an eyewitness to identify him. Mr. Joseph also tried to hold them responsible for allegedly preventing another eyewitness from testifying at the trial—Antione's family friend Hargrove, who could have established that Antione was not present at the shooting. And a third claim: under Illinois law, police had falsely arrested Antione because they lacked a warrant and probable cause.

Mr. Joseph was a few months shy of seventy-seven when he filed the civil suit for Antione. He had moved his law practice from its Lakeview neighborhood office on Broadway in Chicago to a spot on Lincoln, further north. In his later years, he had stopped practicing real estate law in favor of criminal defense work. His office was stuffed with antiques, furniture he had brought back to life over the years, having spent many weekends refinishing the pieces in the family garage.

With time on his hands, Antione helped Mr. Joseph clean and organize his new office space. Mr. Joseph, who insisted on using a typewriter, maintained a haphazard filing system with folders stacked everywhere that only he could locate.

Despite his dedication to Antione's case, Mr. Joseph was up against several statutes of limitation that had run out on Antione's legal claims, expiring while he was incarcerated: a two-year limit for conspiracy and personal injury, and a one-year limit for false arrest. "Time-barred," the court replied in February 2003, and it would not reset the clock to Antione's release, even though his time in prison had disadvantaged him from pursuing these claims.

Mr. Joseph filed another lawsuit in Cook County in May 2003, one year after Antione's release, but the city's lawyers shot back, saying that in light of the federal lawsuit, the claims should be dismissed because they had already been denied. Mr. Joseph appealed the case further, and one court gave him a shot, considering the case even though it didn't contain the proper format and citations. But in January 2005, three judges ruled in favor of the defendants—the City of Chicago and the detectives. The judges offered no opinion on whether or not the police had indeed conspired against Antione. They explained they couldn't grant the appeal because the facts of the case had already been argued before a different court, where Antione had lost. With no other options in sight, Mr. Joseph could go no further.

Even though the big payout never came, Antione's family and friends hinted at money, calling him for their share. People would pester Antione when they saw some guy on the news receiving millions for a wrongful conviction. "Man, he's lucky," Antione would tell them.

A friend told him about a building management company that was looking to hire. Antione put in his application. He figured it was best to be honest, so he told one of the hiring managers about his wrongful conviction, his court documents in tow. Within a few days, Antione found out the job was his, and he got fitted for a uniform. It was a Friday. It was a good day.

But by Monday, he was called back into the office. Turns out, the company couldn't hire him after all. He couldn't clear a background check. His rap sheet turned up murder and attempted murder. At the time, Illinois lacked a law to help exonerees clear their convictions from their records. "That was one of the first serious cuts I took, you know?" Antione says. There were no training programs, no reentry services or resources for people like him.

Some of Antione's buddies around town had been working on big construction projects around Chicago. Their boss was Steven Garth, who owned a general contracting company. Antione decided he needed to meet Garth and convince him to give him a job. He put on his work boots and belt and waited around a project site for his chance.

"Why are you standing there?" Garth asked when he first saw him.

"Man, 'cuz I need a job, you know, and I'm going to stand here until somebody hire me because I know there is something here I can do."

Unmoved, Garth left. Antione stood and waited while it rained. When Garth came back, he told Antione he would give him a shot. "Come in Monday," he said.

On Antione's first day, a supervisor let him know this would be his one shot. "If you don't work out, you don't work out," he said.

It worked out. Antione learned how to build a scaffold on the job and how to safety-check it. He learned how to stack bricks. He became an asset, he says. He worked on Chicago's Millennium Park, the $475 million project that had started in 1997 while he was incarcerated. The park sits on four feet of topsoil. Beneath, Styrofoam and other materials form a manmade foundation that keeps the park from collapsing. Antione helped lay the concrete, framing the ground. He worked on the concrete steps, slathering and smoothing until it held, working upward.

In construction, the days moved so fast. Antione was amazed by how days, weeks, and months would disappear. As the calendar escaped him, Antione would think about how time used to crawl in prison. "Tick-tick-tick," he remembers. "You know, one hour took a whole month, it seems like." His kids were getting older, and so was he. And he added two new young ones to his brood with his girlfriend, eventually his wife, with whom he later had a third child. They moved from one suburb to another, establishing a life together.

He never saw the completion of Millennium Park in 2004. First he was moved to another site, and then he quit his job in construction. There was a great task at hand. His mom needed a kidney. Kidney disease, Antione says.

Touting himself as a nondrinker and nonsmoker, Antione considered himself the healthiest of his nine siblings. Except for some knots that had sprung up on his arms and legs, and troubled eyesight, he had kept himself fairly healthy in prison. He was filled with gratitude at the opportunity to prolong his mother's life. The way he saw it, she had always kept him going. Now it was his turn.

When medical staff offered him living-donor counseling before the surgery, he scoffed. "Man, I don't need no counseling," he told them. "Whatever my momma need, she going to get it." All he needed was a date and a time.

A few days later, he was in the prep room. His last big meal before the donation surgery was a feast of shrimp and king crab legs.

The doctors cut through his abdominal muscles to remove his kidney. The transplant was a success. Antione's recovery took several months, and he struggled to walk. "I felt like a pregnant woman, however that feels," Antione says with a laugh. Laid up, he spent much more time at his mom's house, unable to work. Together, they watched old films like *Gunsmoke* on the Turner Classic Movies channel. "We watched all the Westerns, and all the old movies [*sic*] like *Dark Shadows*."

The extended recovery didn't bother him once he saw his mother becoming stronger again. "That was the most uplifting part for me, saving her life," he recalls.

Antione knew Mr. Joseph's wife, Lois, was sick. She had warded off several bouts of cancer over many years, but she was unable to recover from this last and final bout, in early 2007.

Antione wanted to pay his respects, but when he stopped by the law office, it was empty. Mr. Joseph had fallen ill, too. Following the death of his wife, Mr. Joseph had moved into a care facility in Rogers Park, a northern neighborhood of Chicago. It was there that he fell and broke his hip. He never left the hospital. His sons came to visit him at the hospital and found him on a respirator, unable to speak. They briefly left to get some lunch, and when they returned, he was gone.

The *Chicago Tribune* ran his obituary on July 4, 2007:

> Howard G. Joseph, 82, beloved husband of the late Lois Joseph; loving father and grandfather. Funeral Service 10 a.m. Friday at Piser Funeral Services, 9200 N. Skokie Blvd., Skokie, IL. Interment will be private. In lieu of flowers, memorials may be made to the American Cancer Society. . . .

Antione didn't learn Mr. Joseph had died for months. "I was trying to find him," he says with remorse. "I just lost him." He had been so busy—working, paying bills, trying to salvage a new family and raise his kids, keeping them close this time around.

Three days after Mr. Joseph's death, Antione married his live-in girlfriend and mother to his young kids in a small ceremony at their home. "Having the kids, you feel you want to do the right thing," Antione says.

VII.
"When they see your record, you going to jail."

In 2006, after a long day of working construction, Antione went to pick up his kids from daycare. Police pulled him over. Antione's rap sheet did not put the patrol officers at ease. His criminal record was compounded by murder and attempted murder charges, with no way to expunge them, even as a wrongly convicted person.

Terrified, his kids watched from the back seat as police pointed a gun in his face, Antione says. The car—The Breadwinner—had been reported as stolen. Antione had his suspicions about who could have called in this false report: an ex-girlfriend. "This is some nonsense," he told them. "This is my vehicle. My name." He remembers a sergeant, or some superior, being called to the scene. They didn't arrest him.

Later, in 2008, he faced domestic battery charges in Roselle, Illinois. He had faced related charges a couple of years after his release when an ex-girlfriend called the police, saying that he had thrown a shoe at her. In that instance Antione had been immediately handcuffed and was charged. He pleaded not guilty, and the case was dropped. In this later instance, a school nurse and social worker had flagged that one of the children had called in sick without a parent's follow-up call. A house check discovered that his young children and stepchildren were home alone, supervised by Antione's sixteen-year-old stepdaughter. The reporting officer observed a wedding photo hanging over the stairway to the basement, and he asked the children about Antione. One of the stepchildren reported getting a "whoopin" with a belt for not doing her chores, which Antione denied. Her arm appeared bruised and reddening, according to the police report, and the girl seemed terrified about what would happen if her mother found out police had been to the home. When Antione came home from work, his wife had not yet arrived. The police were waiting for him, a signed warrant for his arrest in hand, and $5,000 bail already set by a judge. He answered their questions, explaining that his stepdaughter had frequently refused to go to school. But seeing his criminal record, and with the evidence of the bruise, they took him in.

At the police station, he bonded out after nine o'clock that night. The kids were sent to stay with their grandmother.

"Discipline is one thing, but the bottom line is you can't strike children with a belt," the caseworker told Antione at the police department. In her report, she wrote: "He stated he understood and the stress of trying to provide a good home for five children, only two of which are his natural children along with other children he has that are older and not living with him was difficult."

The case, like the others against him after his release, was dropped—nolle pros—no prosecution.

VIII.

"My life was broken. I had to restart myself to get myself to grow again."

Antione had been out of prison for eight years when he learned there was a word for someone who was wrongly convicted and whose case had been overturned: exoneree.

Married, Antione was working hard to piece his life back together. Preoccupied, he hadn't heard that there was a new law in Illinois to compensate exonerees like him. He didn't know there was a time limit to file for this so-called certificate of innocence, and he didn't know he would have to petition a judge, mostly likely through a lawyer, for this certificate.

The new law, passed in 2008, wasn't the strongest in the country, only offering up to $200,000, depending on the length of incarceration. It required the defendant to prove his own innocence to the court. This was a different burden of proof than the prosecution assumed at trial—working against the passage of time, as witnesses may have died or evidence may have been destroyed.

Antione had already fought past some of the stigma of being a convicted murderer, salvaging his reputation by working in the community. After taking time off to recuperate from his mother's kidney donation, he needed a job again. But unlike the last time he had found work, standing around a construction site until someone hired him, this time the job came to him.

An old prison buddy, Charles, was working with a reentry program for male parolees—the Community Support Advisory Council, a faith-based program within the Illinois Department of Corrections—and turned to Antione for help. He seized the opportunity, starting on the West Side and then moving north to work at the Howard Area Community Center in Rogers Park. The new job came with a title: Antione Day, Outreach Coordinator.

Antione discovered that he was effective at counseling parolees because he knew them. He was one of them. Guilty or not, he figured they were the same, his brothers. They were the same when law enforcement forced them out of their cars in front of their children. They were the same when they were denied jobs based on background checks. They were the same when they slept on their mother's couches. They were the same when they needed food.

"You gotta ask for help," Antione would say to his guys. "Ain't nobody know how your stomach touching your back but you."

His office, the Howard Area Community Center, was located across the street from Food Mart & Tobacco, Bargain Paradise and Currency Exchange. It was a little rough-hewn but professional, with studded blue chairs and simple office furniture, partitions, and a few computers. On nearly every wall, bulletin boards featured inspirational posters and cut-out letters.

E-M-P-L-O-Y-M-E-N-T R-E-S-O-U-R-C-E C-E-N-T-E-R.
Want to start a new life after prison? We can help.
Go confidently in the direction of your dreams.

Potted plants lined the front windows, popping out of every corner, all the way to Antione's back office, where there were more of them, clustered on top of file cabinets, peeping out between a collaged picture of Martin Luther King and Barack Obama, amid cut-out quotes from Booker T. Washington, Harriet Tubman, Malcolm X, and Frederick Douglass.

It turns out these plants had been previously thrown out, broken, dried up in dumpsters, or left on the side of the road. Antione would save them and nurse them back to life, taping the leaves, filling the pots with warm water, and spraying the leaves with a dish-soap solution to kill the bugs. Underneath his desk, Antione kept a bucket with a cup to ladle the water. The plants became so lush and vibrant that his office couldn't contain them. He would give them away. "I was broken. I was left to just die. I think the same spirit in me is what keeps the plants growing," he says.

The job required Antione to go back into the prisons, which was emotionally taxing. It made him reflect on who he once was.

"It's hard when you get ready to leave," he says. "I can leave. I don't have to stay here."

On visits he was treated like a guest speaker, rather than a former inmate or offender. One of his responsibilities was to make connections with incarcerated people before they were released, letting them know where to find him on the outside. He promised to help them when the time came.

Sometimes weeks later, sometimes years later, the guys would come find Antione.

"You said you'd help me if I came here," said a haggard man, fresh out of prison, one day at the center. He wore a red hat, jean shorts, black sneakers, and white socks pulled up just below his chunky calves. He carried a bright blue duffle bag. His thick black-framed glasses looked like an extension of his face, as though he hadn't removed them in years. From prison, he had written to Antione for help.

"You got back to me in two days!" he said, dumbfounded. "You dated the letter on top like they taught us in school. I just want to say thanks."

"Gotta be a man of my word," Antione assured him. "Whatcha need?"

"I need housing," the man said, explaining he had hepatitis C. "I took care of my Social Security on my own."

He had a place to stay for a few nights, so Antione set up a meeting to talk in a couple days about his options. Antione would help him, he promised.

In 2010, Antione was coming from a meeting when he heard a familiar voice. "I know that voice," he said to himself. He turned the corner to see Marvin Reeves, a heavy-set man whom he had done some time with in prison. He didn't know Marvin was out of prison. Marvin, too, had been wrongfully convicted, accused of a quintuple murder on the South Side. His conviction hinged on another suspect's confession, that of former Illinois death row inmate Ronald Kitchen—obtained through torture by an underling of disgraced former Chicago police commander Jon Burge. Later, in 2013, Reeves and Kitchen received a $12.3 million settlement from the City of Chicago.

"Marvin!"

"Twon!"

The two men embraced, shook hands. Marvin was accompanied by a bright-eyed woman with red, swirly hair, Laura Caldwell. She was a lawyer who ran a program called Life After Innocence. She had brought Marvin to the Howard Area Community Center for some job counseling. "The universe totally arranged a bunch of things so that Antione and I could meet," Laura remembers.

The three got to talking, and Antione mentioned that his case, like Marvin's, had also been overturned.

"Wait a sec," Laura chimed in. "How did your case get overturned?"

Antione told her how Mr. Joseph, his real estate attorney friend, had worked on his appeal and how the state had dropped the charges against him in 2002.

"If what you're telling me is true, and you were convicted, and you did nine years and then your case is overturned, then you'd be an exoneree," Laura told him. She paused. "Do you know you're an exoneree?"

"A what?"

"You went to prison for something that you didn't do—I mean, did you do it?" Laura asked.

"No, nowhere near it."

"Then you're an exoneree."

Not only was Antione an exoneree, Laura explained, but since his case was overturned before an Illinois law for compensation was enacted, time was running out to file his petition for a certificate of innocence. She figured out they had about a month to make their case declaring his innocence and seeking compensation for the near-decade of which he had been robbed.

Without delay, Laura deployed a team of law students and got to work.

Antione found some of his old legal documents at his place in Villa Park, Illinois, where he had moved, but most records were carefully stowed away at his mother's house. Littie's health was beginning to disintegrate again. Although Antione's kidney sustained her for a few years, she was on dialysis, getting worse.

He wanted his mother to live to see his name cleared, so he rounded up ten legal envelopes and manila folders packed with documents and dropped them off at Loyola University School of Law for Laura and her students. Laura had been unsure if he would actually do the legwork to dig up the old files. "She just wanted to see if it was what I said it was," Antione remembers.

And it was. Laura quickly examined the records, assigned some law students to the case, then told Antione, "Well, I'm just going to slap something together with the basic facts. I'll file this if you want." It was the first certificate of innocence petition Laura had handled on her own, and she was nervous—but she appeared confident to Antione.

"Trust me on this," she assured him. "I don't know exactly what's going to happen, but this is what you want to do."

"I trust you, Laura."

Third-year law student Stephen Donnelly had enrolled in the Life After Innocence class that term. He had some friends who had become involved in the program and reported great things about it. Life After Innocence quickly became known as the only Innocence Network member organization that focused solely on helping exonerees after release from prison. The class operated like a small firm as student lawyers-in-training reported billable hours and stayed on top of their casework.

"This is the first real assignment that was given to me," said Donnelly in 2013, then an attorney at a small litigation firm.

The task before them rolled into class one day as a law student pushed a cart with bankers' boxes full of court transcripts and records. The documents were an utter mess.

Donnelly and a classmate, who needed some work hours, eyeballed the reams of papers and divvied them up. In a law library conference room, they opened up their laptops, put on music and earphones, and pounded out case summaries in a Word document to report back to Laura.

"It was very, very confusing because of the characters' names throughout the trial. There was Punchy, Poncho. . ." Donnelly remembers. "It just seemed there were definite credibility issues with each witness."

Reading through the transcripts, Donnelly tried to envision Antione. One day, Laura introduced the man himself to the class. He was the first exoneree Donnelly had ever met, and his case read like a storybook. The law students could barely believe that it all could have gone so wrong.

Later, at a burger-and-wings joint near the law school, Antione joined the class with some other exonerees. "I remember being floored by his personality and the head that he has on his shoulders despite everything that he had been through," Donnelly says. "I can't even imagine how I would handle being placed behind bars for a crime I didn't commit."

The students and Laura worked hard, and with one day to spare before the deadline set by the new compensation law, two years after its enactment, Laura filed Antione's petition.

Then they waited for a response from the judge.

Almost a year later, in 2011, Antione was back at 26th and Cal. He sat with Laura in court for a hearing on his petition. Cook County Judge Paul Biebel didn't prolong the inevitable. It was good news. Judge Biebel quickly granted Antione his certificate of innocence and issued a written order, which perfunctorily outlined his case history and the certificate of innocence requirements.

> As such, this Court concludes that Petitioner did not, by his own conduct, voluntarily bring about his conviction, and he has met his statutory burden of showing that he is innocent of all offenses charged in the indictment.

After the hearing, Judge Biebel called Antione into his chambers. They took some photos together, Antione recalls, and talked over corn chips and soda. "He was proud of the work I was doing then in the community," Antione says. "He was real welcoming. He told me any time you want to stop by, stop by."

Antione felt vindicated. More than twenty years had passed since the shooting at Belmonte Cut Rate Liquors. When his innocence petition was granted, Antione had been out of prison almost as long as he had been in prison. Earning this certificate of innocence was a bittersweet victory—he had already discovered that freedom was an illusion. There was no escaping his past.

"It took so long for me to be considered innocent," he says. "The only burden I'm really free of is the jail cell," Antione says.

After the hearing, a more upbeat Antione gave Laura a ride on the motorcycle he built, his 1999 Suzuki Hayabusa. He dropped her off for afternoon lunch and cocktails with some girlfriends. The women invited Antione to join. "If this is what innocence is like, I like it!" he told the group of women, inviting a chorus of laughter.

But there was only one woman whose recognition mattered to him, and she was lying in a hospital bed at the time. Littie had hoped she would be alive to see her son's name cleared. She was happy for him, "but it was kind of too late," Antione says.

IX.

"As long as I have the know-how of who she is, she always there."

In his community, the words *dying* and *death* are taboo. Antione favors the word *passing*, instead. He doesn't like the word *dying*. He won't use it.

He had spent a hot summer night in a chair by his mother's hospital bed. His stepdad, Littie's spouse of about forty years, was there for a while, but then he left.

Antione sat in the room with only his thoughts and his mother, who was unresponsive. Despite the legal victory, his life had upended yet again. He was separating from his wife. His young children had moved out of their home. And now his mother was slipping away from him, too.

The medical staff insisted Littie could not hear Antione when he spoke to her—but she would open her eyes when he called her name. "Mom, you gotta get better," Antione would tell her. "You gotta get outta here. Let's go home."

She would look at him, blankly. She couldn't speak. She couldn't answer him.

Antione left for work on his motorcycle the next morning. When he got to the Howard Area Community Center across town, the hospital called and told him to come back. He knew it was serious.

Outside the hospital, Antione parked his bike and saw his brothers and sisters waiting for him near the entrance. Antione went in.

She was gone.

Antione cried and held her in his arms. "Just wanted to wake her up," he remembers. "The most important thing in my life had just left me."

His siblings planned the homegoing service at a neighborhood church. Littie had made a single yet somewhat difficult post-mortem request of her family: she didn't want to be laid on her back. She had hated the idea of people looking down at her in a casket. Instead, her children managed to prop her body upright for the funeral service. Antione can't recall exactly how they pulled it off.

At the service, Antione pulled himself through a Donny Hathaway song that he and his mother used to sing together, "A Song for You."

> *I've been so many places in my life and time.*
> *I've sung a lot of songs.*
> *I've made some bad rhymes*
>
> *I've acted out my life in stages*
> *With ten thousand people watching,*
> *But we're alone now,*
> *And I'm singing this song to you.*
>
> *I love you in a place where there's no space or time*
> *I love you for my life, you're a friend of mine*

And when my life is over, remember when we were together
We were alone and I was singing this song to you.

As Antione sang, his son Krishon walked into the church and sat toward the back. He watched as his dad sang to his grandmother, upright in the coffin, facing the crowd. "That was too much for me," Krishon says. After the homegoing service, a soul food reception followed at Christ the King, a Jesuit high school across from Littie's house on Quincy Street.

Down the street at the corner was a cousin's house that Antione had started fixing up about a month before. The project had given him a new purpose and focus, putting his construction skills back to work.

For a while, Antione had pondered an idea. He thought about creating a transitional home for newly released exonerees, a place where they could ease back into life without the pressures of finding a job and their next meal. He had talked about it with his mother, when she was still lucid. Littie gave the project a big OK.

In 2011, Antione kept running into Jarrett Adams, a young Wisconsin exoneree who was originally from Chicago. They saw each other at events coordinated by the Life After Innocence program that Laura ran. About twenty years Antione's junior, Jarrett had only been out of prison for a handful of years.

Like Antione, a wrongful conviction had robbed him of his youth. In September 1998, Jarrett was two months shy of eighteen when he and two friends traveled from Chicago to Wisconsin to attend a party. The three kids returned with a false accusation of rape. The racially charged case resulted in Jarrett's conviction in 2000, which carried a twenty-eight-year prison sentence. With the help of the University of Wisconsin's Innocence Project, Jarrett was exonerated seven years later on evidence that his state-appointed attorney had failed to investigate and secure witnesses who could have cleared him.

"You sit, hope, and wish for the day to come and when it finally gets here, you're so exhausted that you really want to just move on," Jarrett remembers. Like Antione, he walked back into the world without any living, medical, or financial assistance from the State of Wisconsin. He wore a jogging suit purchased from the commissary and orange shoes provided by the jail. He had thirty dollars left on his account—and was later charged sixteen dollars for the rubber-soled canvas shoes.

Also like Antione, Jarrett slept on a couch at his mother and step-father's place. They were seniors living on fixed incomes. With a nearly ten-year gap in his resume and his last known address a supermax, Jarrett couldn't find work. "The news of my conviction and it being overturned was a click of a button away on Google," he recalls.

Jarrett turned to academics, attending junior college and later enrolling at Roosevelt University, where he graduated with honors. He landed a job working as a full-time federal defense investigator. Next came law school at Loyola, where Jarrett quickly became the face of the program—his story played to the school's mission. As he garnered praise for being in law school, people didn't fully understand that Jarrett was still paying debts incurred as a result of being locked up, wrongfully convicted, and fighting his case. Even more unluckily, he couldn't seek much compensation. In Wisconsin, where Jarrett was convicted, the compensation statute for exonerees was one of the weakest in the country, only offering up to $25,000 to those who could prove that they didn't bring about their own wrongful conviction.[19] Jarrett received nothing.

"All the charges were dismissed, and so now you're asking me to come back around and prove that I was absolutely innocent? That was a standard that it didn't even take for me to be found guilty!" Jarrett says.

After their initial introduction, it wasn't until Jarrett and Antione met again at an Innocence Network conference in 2011, in the company of two other exonerees, that they learned of each other's near carbon-copy stories of being released from prison. They both knew of other exonerees who didn't even have that much—guys who were sleeping in drug houses or signing contracts with family members to give up some of their future compensation (if any) for a roof over their head.

Antione told Jarrett about his idea, the one he had shared with his mother before she passed, to create a place for exonerees where they

19. In March 2016, Wisconsin legislators killed a bill that would have increased exoneree compensation to $50,000 a year, up to $1 million.

could escape such uncertainty and find some stability. Jarrett thought they could also provide resources and training to help these exonerees reenter society, as no such state-funded programs exist in Illinois for exonerees upon release.

They left their meeting inspired, giving genesis to their hope of starting a nonprofit organization together. Antione already knew the spot and the name.

He wanted to call it Life After Justice.

X.

"Building a base to create an atmosphere of safety for everybody, and we have a housing facility that we can incorporate where guys can come and feel safe and have an environment that's productive for themselves—it'd be great."

"Antione can be a little bit of a dreamer," says Brad Lorden, a Loyola University law and business graduate. "That's one of the things I love most about him."

In 2012, Lorden was a student when he put together a small business plan for the organization Antione and Jarrett wanted to start. Laura suggested they connect with a business class at Loyola that could help solidify their plans.

The pair wanted to help other exonerees become self-sufficient, first by giving them a place to lay their heads at night, what they envisioned as the Life After Justice house. Job training would come later, when the exonerees were ready, they thought.

But how the organization would become self-sustaining was another question, especially in a house that would incur expenses like property taxes and supplies and repairs. So Brad and some business classmates took on the project. At the end of the semester, they presented their business plan to Antione and Jarrett at Loyola's Water Tower campus in Chicago. Antione and Jarrett were deeply touched that the business students had put so much time into a real plan, with the potential to improve the lives of real exonerees.

The students proposed that Life After Justice provide a grace period to exonerees first entering the house, during which time they could live there rent free. Then, after a set period of time, the house would expect them to contribute back through a particular job. The exoneree could supply a small amount of rent to help pay the monthly expenses of the house. They also figured that there might not always be a steady stream of exonerees coming into the house, so Life After Justice could then open up the place to parolees.

After the students finished their presentation, the entire class rose to its feet upon learning Jarrett would be entering Loyola's law school in the fall. "It was one of them things that made me realize just how far I had came," Jarrett says.

About eight months later, the organization was given 501(c)3 tax-exempt status approval, and Jarrett had the first semester of law school under his belt. Antione kept fixing up his cousin's house on Quincy Street while he set his sights on another potential property for the Life After Justice house, right around the corner on Adams Street.

"Is this Mr. Day?" Jarrett asked into the speakerphone, pretending to be a telemarketer. Laura stood next to him, fiddling around with the conference call setup as Brad walked in the room to join her Spring 2013 law clinic.

"Yes, it is."

"How are you doing today, sir?"

"Doing well," Antione said, tentatively.

Jarrett burst out laughing. "I'm just messing! C'mon man, you know my voice." Unlike the other law students, Jarrett had just come from work, dressed in a purple-and-white checkered shirt topped with a black sweater. His more casually clad classmates settled in around a conference table. Among other responsibilities, Laura's weekly, workshop-style class was to provide initial support to Life After Justice.

Laura showed Jarrett a picture of himself for a story about finishing his first year of law school. All eyes were on him, a vision of overcoming adversity. At times, Jarrett just wanted to be known as Jarrett, law student. He had grown tired of being known as the exoneree-turned-law-student.

"My teeth are white?" he suggested to Laura, laughing, looking for a positive.

On the class agenda was a planning call with Antione to discuss next steps for Life After Justice. On the conference line, Antione could be heard at the Howard Area Community Center, preparing for his Wednesday night support group for ex-offenders.

"Let the man in the wheelchair sign in first," the class could hear Antione say to the support-group attendees. "Everyone sign in."

"He's the king of multitasking," Laura chuckled.

When Antione returned to the conference call, they talked through what logo to pick for the new Life After Justice organization. Should they go with the one showing prison bars? Or should they pick something more forward-thinking, like a bird crossing over? Then there was the status of the house. Antione was juggling two properties in Austin. One of them might become the house, at least temporarily. "We got to start somewhere. We can start downtown in Trump Towers for all I care." The students loaded Antione with questions: How long should exonerees stay before paying rent? How many units will be in the house? How many beds?

Laura could sense Antione's uneasiness. "We've got a roomful of lawyers here, so we're just making sure we're dotting the I's and crossing the T's," she assured him.

"I'm definitely not frustrated," Antione said. "I'm excited!"

The class went through potential zoning issues and real estate questions. The meeting spiraled. Jarrett interrupted the discussion and reminded everyone of the mission. "My goal is to pull other people through the window I came through," he said. "We win if we have one Antione Day."

The group fell quiet, then resumed working.

Less than two weeks later, on a windy April day, Jarrett, Antione, and Laura (and her dog Shaffer) posed for a photo in front of a boarded-up brick bungalow in Chicago's Austin neighborhood. Jarrett captioned the photo in big cursive letters, time-stamping it and sharing it on social media: "Life After Justice House."

Drug deals don't happen on the corner by his mother's house, Antione insisted during a walk around the neighborhood in March 2013, because the people in the community respect him. "It just ain't going to happen," he said. "Sometimes you have to put your foot down. I ain't the damn police neither."

Antione planned to name the block he grew up on after his mom. Brick bungalows and long shotgun-style rectangular homes lined the streets. Some had big red "X" signs in the windows, marking the empty homes as a warning to firefighters that the structures could collapse.

In Austin, Antione couldn't take two steps without getting stopped by acquaintances to chat. He had been spending most of his time there, fixing up old properties in the year since his wife and kids moved out of their family home in Villa Park, about a half hour away, to Arkansas. He went from seeing them every day to only a few times a year. "One of the most difficult times I've ever had," he says.

So he buried himself in work and his community.

"How you doing? You all right?" Antione called over to a neighbor walking down the street. His voice was still a little hoarse from a stubborn head cold, made worse by singing at the Illinois Bar Foundation's annual Battle of the Bands fundraiser on a chilly February night a few weeks before. He had bundled himself in a navy-blue pullover for the $100-a-ticket event at Buddy Guy's Legends, a famous Chicago blues club.

With his band of fellow exonerees, Antione had performed favorites like "Mustang Sally," "Stormy Monday," and "Sittin' on the Dock of the Bay" for the after-work crowd, who feasted on barbecue and an open bar. The other dueling bands on the roster consisted of ensembles with bad legal pun names, like The Objections and DisBard. But Antione's band had a simple name and premise: Exoneree Band.

His buddy, Raymond Towler, played with him. Raymond lived in Ohio, where he had spent almost thirty years of a life sentence behind bars for a rape and kidnapping that he did not commit. Raymond was twenty-four when he was wrongfully convicted and fifty-two when he won his freedom. At Buddy Guy's, a thick gray beard covering his face, Raymond tuned up his guitar while his girlfriend shot video with a handheld camera, standing mid-crowd. Later in the night, Exoneree

Band played a song Raymond had written for a friend still on the inside. "For a guy who didn't get out of jail," Antione said into the microphone. He had some of those friends, too.

Walking around Austin, Antione came across an old buddy at an intersection. He halted in his tracks and smiled as Johnny stopped his car in the middle of the road. He jumped out to greet Antione.

Johnny was a short, weathered man. His blue pearlescent studded boots clicked on the pavement. He and Antione exchanged pleasantries. Another friend, with whom Antione had gone to kindergarten more than forty years before, drove past. He waved. Chicago Public Schools had recently announced the closure of four neighborhood schools, impacting thousands of families, and the Chicago Teachers Union had been rallying all week to save the schools. Antione feared that the neighborhood kids, relocated to other schools, would be put at risk by having to cross gang areas as they traveled farther from home.

As Antione caught up with his old friend, mid-road, Johnny's face turned somber. "When I decide to change, I mean it," he told him, peering out from under his ball cap. "I don't wanna be like I used to. You know, man? It's scary."

Johnny had spent the last two months living in a halfway "sober-living" house among bad influences. He struggled to stay clean. "I became a criminal in the house," he said, shaking his head.

Antione, averse to substances, couldn't relate. Instead, he told Johnny about the Life After Justice house, still in progress. "One of the reasons I'm wanting to do that house is guys like yourself that are trying to change and better themselves," he said.

Johnny had been on disability since 1989, he said, and it wasn't enough for him to live on. "I mean disability is only nothing," he said. "I need more than that! C'mon, you can't make it! I want to get off disability and work!"

"And you can," Antione said. "But can you work? What kind of work would you do?"

"That's a good question," Johnny shook his head. "I don't know."

"So you need to think about that."

A kid emerged from around Johnny's parked car and asked Antione for a light.

"No." The kid walked away.

"He wants a light so he can light a joint. These kids is crazy," Antoine said, turning back to Johnny.

They talked about rising up and changing the neighborhood. "Take it one block at a time," Antoine said. "You and me, we walk together."

"All right, bra', take care of yourself, man!"

Johnny got back in his car and drove off. Antione lapped the corner and walked to one of the prospective Life After Justice properties, a house on Adams Street he had purchased. He'd hired a few guys to help him out. Inside the house, patches of hardwood peeped through construction scraps, and a tarp covered the kitchen and common area. "We have beautiful wood floors," he explained. "I just left this down so they don't scuff them all up."

He planned to sand and varnish the floors and doors, then paint the walls. Antione had a friend who worked for a paint company and brought him some free cans. "A bed there, a bed there, a bed there," Antione pointed to different corners of the same small bedroom. It would be a tight squeeze. People sleeping in close quarters.

The kitchen would be a popular spot, Antione mused, as many guys coming out of prison have learned how to cook for the masses. But he would assign somebody to cook meals for the exonerees in the house. He didn't believe in having everybody cooking and using the kitchen at once. "It's dangerous and unclean," he said.

In the basement, music blared, and a pot full of wet dog food sat on the ground—for Hannibal, Antione's dog, who had one blue eye and liked to tear holes in the wall when he wasn't chained in the backyard.

"They've had to repair the same spot twice," Antione said.

Hannibal, a smart security guard, had been successful at keeping most vandals out of the building after someone had stolen all the wiring in the house. Antione knew who had done it, and he confronted the guy. "Told him I didn't have it," Antione said. "He brought it back."

When Hannibal died unexpectedly a year later, Antione wrapped him in plastic, placed him in a cardboard box, and buried him in his mom's backyard.

Upstairs in the prospective Life After Justice house, bedrooms connected to more bedrooms. Antione envisioned that one day the exonerees would move to his other property, and he would take on the Adams Street house as his residence. "I'm by myself now," he said, pointing out where the Jacuzzi would go in the dark and dusty space. "I don't need no three-bedroom house no more." Antione continued to live in Villa Park, where his home was mostly empty. But in the remodeled space in Austin, he envisioned his young kids, when they visited from Arkansas, staying in the connecting rooms, formerly the house's boiler room. One side for the little girl, one side for the two boys.

"Daddy, where am I going to sleep?" Antione's daughter asked him during a visit to the property. She was ready for her own room. Antione assured her she would get a place to sleep before the boys.

The crew was working slowly, but Antione hoped the space would be ready before the eleventh anniversary of his release from prison, in May 2013. He had wanted to prove to Laura that he could make it happen in thirty days. Then, thirty days became sixty days. Then, more time.

Two years later, the building was inching closer to completion, while his cousin's house around the block on Quincy Street couldn't make it past a city inspection. Jarrett, who had finished law school, had wanted to consider other properties elsewhere in the city. But Antione couldn't give on up Austin and his dream to transform it, block by block, starting with his mother's. Like his vintage motorcycle that he labored over, piece by piece, building from scratch—he knew he could do it.

XI.

"It was a secret from me that he even got in trouble. If they had told me from the beginning, I would have told him don't talk to no police and make no statement. 'Cuz they'll use it against him."

One of Antione's sons needed a lawyer.

Krishon, a twenty-four-year-old senior football player at Southeastern

Oklahoma State University in Durant, Oklahoma, had just finished his finals and was weeks away from graduating in 2013 when he and four other teammates faced serious criminal charges. They had faked armed robberies as an April Fool's Day prank on their friends and found themselves arrested, fingerprinted. The case blew up with national media coverage.

Krishon was incredulous—*How did I get here?*

"I don't know what would possess five black college students to put on ski masks and pretend to be robbers in an age when black males are often profiled as criminals," wrote *Chicago Sun-Times* columnist Mary Mitchell, who covered the story after the NAACP sued Southeastern Oklahoma State University for its handling of the case. In her article, Mitchell quoted a local minister, Reverend Ira J. Acree of the Greater St. John Bible Church: "Maybe other people could get away with pretending to be criminals, black people can't do it. It was a big deal down here."

Antione had missed Krishon's most formative years, arriving back into his life right before high school. The memories of going to the Enchanted Castle to play, or living with Antione back when he was a house husband, had faded. The gap between them, which had begun when Antione was shuttled off to prison two decades earlier, ran deep.

Suspended and later expelled from school, Krishon faced jail time on multiple charges, including conspiracy to commit a crime, assault and battery, and "wearing a mask, hood or covering for the purpose of coercion." He turned to Antione for help. "I found out in the eleventh hour," Antione said. "I want him to learn something from this. When I talk to him, I'm the old man. But when you're in hot water, when your ass is on the line, then you call Superman."

In the early morning hours of April 2, 2013, after a series of innocuous pranks all day, Krishon and four buddies decided to scare their friends. They dressed in dark clothing and covered their faces with masks fashioned from a pillowcase. Krishon and his friends were Black in the city of Durant, which was 85 percent white. The targets of their prank: at first, other teammates. And later on, their white girlfriends.

Krishon and the other young men banged on doors, busted in, yelled, and pretended their cell phones were guns so convincingly that police reported one of the victims (a friend) as saying he actually saw two

9 mm handguns. There were no guns, and no one was physically harmed. But the girls were terrified. One of them frantically called the cops, even though she was told the staged robbery was a joke.

After a police investigation ensued, along with rumors about what had really happened, the five players turned themselves in. "You tried to scare little white girls," Krishon says an officer told them during their interview with police. The officer also memorialized the same statement in his report, albeit with a different tone: "When speaking to one of the parties above I asked if he knew that he scared a lot of young ladies with the prank. He laughed and said it wouldn't have been funny if they wouldn't have been. He said it was just a prank taken too far."

Krishon had long tried to stay out of trouble. Above all, he never wanted to do time like his father. "I feel stupid for putting myself in a situation where I had to go to jail because I told myself I never would," he says.

After their suspension from the university, the students appealed. It seemed ill-fated from the start. Krishon overheard a board member say to a professor that he would have shot them if they had knocked on his door. Meanwhile, the district attorney for the Nineteenth District of Oklahoma wanted to prosecute. Antione paid for a lawyer.

Later in 2013, the players were offered several plea deals. Krishon rejected all of them. But when his mom started talking about getting a new lawyer, he decided it was time to take the punishment and move on. Krishon plead to a misdemeanor charge of "wearing a mask," or so he thought. In late 2015, he learned his record instead shows misdemeanor assault.

He and the other students ended up with about a month of jail time, part of a ninety-day sentence, plus three years of probation and a couple thousand dollars in court fees—which Krishon was to pay himself.

"They made us stay the whole thirty days," Krishon says. "They made sure of it."

He seemed nervous about doing the time. But his dad reassured him. "No matter what, you have an out," Antione told Krishon. "Keep your head up and learn about your case."

Jail was about what Krishon had imagined, patching together memories of visiting Antione in prison over the years. Krishon felt anger, as he had imagined he would. He worked odd jobs, as he had imagined he would. And the guards were on a power trip, as he had imagined they would be.

He coped, but "it wasn't something I'd ever do again," he says.

Krishon left jail with about a semester of college to redo. Kicked out of his university for a year because of the prank, he would have to finish his business marketing degree somewhere else. His football record had given way to his criminal record.

Until he figured out where to complete his schooling, he would earn a paycheck as a counselor at a fitness center. Every month, as his court fees—which defendants must pay themselves—would come due, he would pay up and feel mad at himself all over again.

When he finally got his legal bills whittled down, he turned to Antione for some money. This time he wanted a motorcycle, not a lawyer. Antione, who in recent years had added a 2009 Harley-Davidson Sportster and yellow Honda Gold Wing 1800 to his collection, was a proud father and willing to talk.

Krishon returned to school and entered his final semester in January 2016.

XII.

"Being in prison and thinking of other people being in that same situation that don't deserve it—it's hard for me."

Office hours were over, and the weekly community meeting was soon to start. Antione sat hunched over at the front desk of the Howard Area Community Center, writing a letter to an inmate. He didn't know the guy.

Every week, about ten letters would arrive for Antione from state prisons where he had visited and given talks to reach out to soon-to-be parolees. Inside the prisons, Antione would introduce himself and encourage guys to get in touch when they needed help upon release. "I'm not a letter writer," Antione said. "No novellas." He always tried to write something back because most of the letters he had sent from prison went unanswered, and he knew that inmates only got a few stamps a month.

His former "cellie"—Dennis Mixon, a guy who lived in his four-person dorm at Stateville Correctional Center—also wrote to him. "He know that I'm not going to write no letter," Antione laughed. In prison, Antione had known his "rappies" (the other men on his case), but it wasn't until he and Dennis bunked in the same room and realized their families knew each other that they became friends. Dennis was quiet and pensive. He liked to write stories and poetry and read books on African American history.

Antione and Dennis mostly kept up by phone. Sometimes Antione would call Dennis's mom, a woman in her seventies, for updates and to pass along messages. For years she had relied on other people to drive her to the prison a few times a year. She never learned highway driving, and she wouldn't go in bad weather—not after hitting some black ice on the way to Tamms Correctional Center one year, where Dennis was in solitary confinement. The prison closed in 2013.

"I try not to be angry," Nedra Mixon said. "Their plan is for him never to come out of there."

In 2014, the word on Dennis wasn't so good. At fifty-two, he had suffered strokes and had trouble with his kidneys, no money for a transplant, and difficulty using one of his feet. Back when he was at Pontiac Correctional Center, the prison staff couldn't put shackles on his legs because they were so swollen, his mother says. Antione tried to work his relationships with the Department of Corrections to get Dennis transferred to a facility with better healthcare.

"Antione is the only one (besides my mother) who has tried to help me on the outside," Dennis wrote in a letter from Menard Correctional Center. He detailed his strokes and explained he had to do physical therapy on his own.

Dennis was accused of and confessed to a 1992 double murder on the North Side. Seven other men were also reportedly coerced into falsely confessing as well. One of the men, Daniel Taylor, confessed as a seventeen-year-old, even though it was impossible for him to have committed the crimes because he was in police custody for disorderly conduct at the time of the shooting. Taylor was exonerated in 2013.

Five of the men who falsely confessed were convicted, and eventually, over many years, all were set free—except Dennis.

"They got all these other boys found innocent after all these years. Why are they still holding Dennis?" Antione asked. "He ain't the guy who will go and slay two people."

In a 2003 prison interview with *Chicago Tribune* journalists Steve Mills and Maurice Possley, Dennis cleared Taylor and the others of the crime by telling them he was present at the crime scene. "I had never seen those guys before," Dennis told the *Tribune* of his codefendants. "I met them in jail."

Dennis told the journalists that it was not a drug debt that led to the double murder but a dispute over $300 worth of missing electronics equipment. Two other people corroborated Dennis's account, including a man who says he was outside the building where the murders occurred and saw Dennis leave the building just as the gunshots were fired.

But Dennis's own words to reporters and later, to prosecutors, may have damned him.

"We met with Mixon in prison, where he was serving a life sentence without parole after being convicted of the murders," wrote former *Tribune* journalist Possley in a 2013 story for the *Atlantic* about Taylor's release. "He told us three other men were with him at the scene of the murders, but that Daniel and the other six defendants were not among them."

By placing himself briefly at the crime scene, according to the 2003 *Tribune* story, Dennis subjected himself to Illinois's law of accountability, whereby a person is legally accountable for another's criminal conduct if he promotes or facilitates the crime.

Days after the *Tribune* story ran, a Chicago attorney, James K. Leven, wrote Dennis a letter. "I just want to say that I wrote you this letter because I am concerned about your welfare," Leven typed.

> In my opinion, you should not rush to judgment that you are legally responsible.... The key question here is whether you shared the intent of the killer to shoot and kill Lassiter and Haugabook. Did you know in advance whether the killer intended to commit a crime or engage in violence? Your actions indicate otherwise. First, you were not present at the scene of the crime. You left the apartment immediately after one of the two persons in your group threatened violence against Lassiter and Haugabook.

Antione, unaware of these legal nuances, took up his friend's cause, peddling Dennis's case around Chicago to anyone who would listen. He talked to lawyers, journalists, and innocence advocates. When he attended the Innocence Network conference every year, Antione would bend many ears about Dennis. "I truly believe that Dennis had nothing to do with this murder," Antione said. "Knowing him, I just don't see it. I was in prison with a thousand murderers and rapists and killers. You can tell just about who is who."

What Dennis was guilty of, Antione believes, is having a drug addiction and as a result, confessing to the police. The kind of addiction that would make you "say your mother killed Kennedy just to get out of a situation," he says.

Today, Dennis is cautious to divulge any more details of what happened the night of the double murder. The way he sees it, he has helped everyone else with their cases, leaving himself without a foothold to appeal his own case. In a March 2015 letter, he wrote: "Yes, I was hurt and my family has suffered as well, especially my '14' children. To date I've been gone for 22 years & all of my children are grown and I've missed out on raising all of them & being in their lives."

A few minutes before 6:30 on a Wednesday evening, Antione set his letters aside and told everyone in the computer lab to take a seat and power off the screens. Chairs lined the long room and wrapped around the corner. The room was full of parolees, kids, and parents from the community for Antione's weekly Overcomers meeting.

The younger folks piled into the Howard Area Community Center to use the computers. No Internet at home. The door was open to them. They liked to hang out.

"You smell like a stank cigarette," Antione told one guy before starting the meeting and turning to the group. "Anybody been watching the news? Nobody been watching the news? Because this news is all about y'all."

Antione talked about new policies that he thought would hurt people on parole. He shifted easily to other topics—finding jobs and taking responsibility for one's family. "It's easy to make a baby, but it's hard to be a father," he said knowingly, collecting nods from the group.

Antione had favorite sayings that he pulled out in rotation to motivate the Overcomers each week—a mixed bag of expressions, including "A closed mouth truly don't get fed" and "When you settle for less, you always get less than you settle for." And he often mentioned drugs and alcohol—life's vices that did not tempt him—as examples of what holds people back. "Y'all listening?" he hollered. "This is for the grown folk. Not the little kids. 'Cuz some of these kids got more responsibility than us grown folk."

As Antione spoke, some men looked straight down. Others never broke eye contact. Gleefully, the kids joined the grown men in their closing cheer, standard Overcomers protocol:

> *Put your hand in my hand, together we can make it.*
> *Put your hand in my hand, together we can make it.*
> *Put your hand in my hand, together we can make it.*
> *Guess what, y'all? We made it.*

After releasing hands, the men and children formed a line for free haircuts. Antione headed up to the front where a barber, who went by "Mr. Antonio," was already clipping a man's hair.

"How you want the sides?" Mr. Antonio asked. Antione nudged the man getting his hair cut. "How'd you get in the chair first, man?" The guy shrugged as clumps of his hair fell on the faded blue carpeting. House music started to fill the room.

Antione grabbed a hair clipper and started in on another man's head, going quickly in different directions, as the man winced. Antione hated baldies. He didn't like touching the skin on their heads.

"Hey there, can I get two regular haircuts? What's that, twenty dollars?" a lady busted in with her two little boys. She was joking.

"No, it's fifty cents apiece!" Antione smiled.

"Nah, y'all ain't worth it!" she laughed.

Mr. Antonio took a soft brush and swept it across the forehead of the man in the chair before him, who was perfectly still, mouth relaxed, eyes fixed on the ground.

"Do y'all do designs?" one of the little boys asked as soon as his mother left to run errands.

"Does your mom allow you to have designs in your hair?" Charles,

Antione's boss, asked. Charles was a real ball-buster, who did time with Antione. In prison, they wanted to kill each other. Today, on the outside, Antione still refers to him as "King Asshole," just because Charles hates it.

"The kids gotta go. It's late," Antione said.

A third barber emerged and started trimming the back of one of the little boys' heads. The younger one leaned forward, his eyes darting up to watch the other haircuts in action.

"Hey, call your mom and tell her to bring a bologna sandwich back!" Antione joked to the other little boy, who was patiently waiting his turn. The boy didn't understand.

Mr. Antonio propped the younger brother on a booster seat atop an office chair. The boy looked down, eyelashes full and bashful as Mr. Antonio clipped the cape around his white T-shirt.

The sky had turned dark when the boys' mother returned with some shopping bags. Mr. Antonio finished trimming around one of the boys' ears as the other brother played with coins on a side table.

"Twenty-five, fifty, seventy-five, a hundred cents!" he exclaimed, revealing a gap-toothed smile and looking up for his mother's approval.

"That's four quarters," she assured him. "Where's your jacket?" Then, turning to Antione: "I'll come up next Wednesday, and y'all give me a press 'n' curl!"

"It's a good thing," Antione remarked. "You know, not everybody can afford haircuts."

"Did you say thank you?" she said, turning to her little boys. They nodded *uh-huh*.

Mr. Antonio headed out behind them, too. Antione stopped him. "I appreciate you coming to volunteer, man," he said. "I appreciate it man, I really do."

There were a few more guys left to go before Antione could close up shop.

A few weeks later, he hosted a cookout for the neighborhood kids, putting out some hot dogs and playing games. He knew they were hungry. Hungry for food and hungry for leadership beyond the gangs.

"Because not everyone gets a second chance," Antione said, thinking of his friend Dennis. And many others.

XIII.

"The burden of having to go through that, the mental damage that it does, the physical damage that it does—it is a burden, and it continues to haunt you."

Antione overslept. It was a Saturday morning and his three-year-old daughter had been visiting from out of town, so he'd lost track of time between the ice cream cones, movies, and going to the zoo. But this morning he had an important errand, and he was already more than two hours late for it, trying the patience of Rick Joseph, the late Mr. Joseph's son.

Seven years after Mr. Joseph's death, Antione had connected with Joseph's son Rick. He had made plans to see Rick before, but Antione kept missing their appointments. He had finally lost Rick's number when his phone was stolen from his car at a hardware store in the summer of 2013.

That morning, taking sips of water to wake himself up, Antione drove to Rick's suburban home about an hour outside Chicago in Buffalo Grove, Illinois. On the passenger seat, Antione had an award to give to Rick. The Howard Joseph Award.

Inside a blue velvet case, etched on glass, it read:

Loyola University Chicago
School of Law
And
Life After Innocence
Present
The Family of Howard Joseph
With the inaugural
Howard Joseph Innocence Award
On October 25, 2012
For commitment
To serving the innocent

When Antione pulled up to Rick's home, a slim-built, graying man was waiting for him in the driveway. Antione immediately handed him the award. Rick took the case and invited Antione inside.

"I can't get you anything?" Rick offered.

"Nah, I'm good—this water is enough," Antione said. After a moment, he told Rick, "You look like your dad."

"Yeah, some people say that."

Standing in his kitchen, Rick slid the velvet case off the glass award, reading the text and smiling. "This is awesome."

"We were trying to get it together," Antione said, explaining the yearlong delay in delivering the award. He took a seat at the kitchen table. "I'm a bad timekeeper."

"It's OK. I'm glad you're finally here."

They reminisced about how Mr. Joseph came to take Antione's case—because Rick and Antione's sister knew each other.

"When I gave her my dad's name, I never thought in a million years he'd be the one to take the case!"

Rick's wife walked into the room, smiling. "Kim, this is the famous Antione Day," Rick said.

She shook his hand and asked to see her father-in-law's award. "Take it out, take it out," Kim said.

"This is the first one," Antione said of the annual award.

As the ice broke, they began to swap more stories.

"I go up, and here is this little old white man," Antione told Rick. "He said 'Sit down.' Didn't introduce himself or nothing."

"I knew he was going to get you out," Rick said.

They talked about Mr. Joseph's final years. "He died broke," Rick said, almost proudly. Mr. Joseph wasn't about the money, he seemed to say.

After a pause, he retreated to another room and returned, holding his father's law degree from Northwestern University. He handed it to Antione. Antione stared at it. He ran his hand over the seal. Then he raised it to cover his face.

He began to weep.

"It's all right," Rick said. "Want a Kleenex?"

"Oh, man," Antione sniffed, tears falling from his face.

"I didn't know you were such a sissy," Rick teased. "No long-lost brother of mine is going to be sitting here crying!"

"God, Rick," Kim chimed in. "Have some tact."

Antione took off his glasses and wiped them. "I'm always mentioning his name," Antione said, voice cracking. "In all the work that I do, I never forget about him. My mentor programs. My drug-abuse programs."

They stood up to take pictures with the Howard Joseph Award and the law degree, together in the same shot.

As Antione got ready to leave, Rick gently pushed the degree toward him. "I want you to take it," he said. "Keep it in the family."

"No, no, no. . ." Antione shook his head, tearing up again.

"It means more to you than it does to me," Rick said. "Want me to get you a hanky?"

"I probably need a bath towel!" Antione joked, as fresh tears rolled from his eyes.

"Just don't lose it."

"That'll never happen," he said, looking down and rubbing his eyes. He took a breath. "Man, I didn't cry this much when they gave me all that time. Oh wow, man."

An hour later, they eased back out to Antione's car, chatting about a nearby Harley shop, Antione's band, and the Life After Justice house.

"You have a CD?"

"I can get you one."

Outside, Antione hugged Mr. Joseph's law degree to his chest, clutching it like a life vest. "I'm gonna guard this with my life."

They hugged goodbye. Through the car window, Antione hollered that he was headed to the bike shop Rick mentioned. "Tell 'em Rick sent you," he said. "They don't know me. But tell 'em anyway!"

Antione nodded and waved.

A year later, Antione hopped in his boss's car to pick up some sub sandwiches and drinks for a staff meeting with some parole agents. He was around the corner from the Howard Area Community Center when one of his commander friends from the Department of Corrections called him.

The friend told him someone who identified himself as a police officer had stopped by the center. He had tipped them off that he had run Antione's plates, saying there was a warrant out for his arrest. For murder.

Toting sandwiches, cans of soda and bottles of water, Antione wondered, *Who is this guy?* He got back in the car, rushed back to the community center, and, from the parking lot, called a few attorney friends. After earning his certificate of innocence, Antione's record should have been cleared. "It was like déjà vu all over again," Antione said. "Somebody again has taken the time out to lie and conspire to have me locked up."

The scare would turn out to be nothing at all. No new warrant had crossed anyone's desk, he was later told. But in that moment, sitting in the parking lot of his workplace, huddled inside the car, Antione froze. He worried about being hauled back to jail. He didn't want to lose his job or his kids.

His mind was flooding with thoughts: Should he go back inside and greet all those parole agents? Should he run back to his mother's house on Quincy? When would this trial for his life ever end?

After a minute, Antione got out of the car. His heart beat fast and strong. He walked to the door. Inside, he did not think of leaving.

AFTERWORD

I would be remiss not to highlight two overlooked areas in the complex world of wrongful convictions. First, the impact on crime victims' families when a case is overturned. And second, another grim reality, whereby a person enters prison an innocent, but after the harm of incarceration, reenters the world a criminal.

Annette's Story

There are many people who experience the collateral damage of wrongful convictions. The families of crime victims, whose belief in a defendant's guilt may have provided them with some resolution, struggle to accept new evidence of innocence and shift their perspective on a conviction. Annette Cabassa is one such survivor.

In 1976, fifteen-year-old Annette watched as her father left their home on Chicago's South Side in search of her nine-year-old sister, Lisa. A hardworking steel-factory worker, he often worried about the whereabouts of his three children, taking the family car to the streets after dark to round them up before bed. But on that January night, Lisa never made it home.

The police came to the door hours later. The search was over. The family dogs, a lab and a mutt, curled up together in a huddle. "They knew that death had come upon our home," Annette tells me.

Police found a little girl, raped and strangled, in an alley dumpster. Annette's mother jumped and screamed. Her father went to the morgue to identify Lisa.

Soon Lisa's toothy class photo was plastered throughout the South Side. Neighborhood groups offered $5,000 in exchange for information leading to the arrest and conviction of the person who killed the little Puerto Rican girl. The community packed Lisa's funeral, where she lay cloaked in a green dress, her hair spiraled in "banana" curls, as her mother called them. Heavy makeup barely covered her bruises.

Within weeks, the announcement came that police had caught the guy, a neighborhood teen named Michael Evans, the brother of a girl in Annette's gym class. Police had a confession, they said, and later, they nabbed another teen, a shy guy named Paul Terry. Two trials later, the youths were sentenced to life in prison.

For the Cabassa family, the case was closed, justice served. But twenty-seven years later, Evans and Terry made history by walking out of a Chicago courthouse as free men, exonerated by DNA evidence in 2003. The case remains Illinois's oldest wrongful conviction to be overturned.

Bewildered and smiling, the vindicated men emerged from offices behind the courtroom, greeted by applause from supporters wearing matching yellow T-shirts.

Despite the new evidence, Annette couldn't believe in Evans's or Terry's innocence. Neither did the officer who arrested Evans, Dennis Banahan. He stood by the original evidence, saying DNA proved little in this case. "The right guys were arrested," Banahan, now retired, told me in 2014. "The pathologist told us at the time that there were multiple offenders. The state stipulated that. We knew that. That didn't preclude them from being the guys who abducted her off the street. Or the guys that raped her vaginally. Or strangled her to death. Or raped her orally."

Outside the courthouse, reporters turned their attention to Annette as she exited. "This is like killing her all over again," she told them. "I hope they don't live long enough to enjoy it."

Annette went home, punched the walls, and cursed God.

"I thought about killing them," Annette told me in 2014, at a McDonald's in Chicago's Logan Square neighborhood. "I don't know how to fight back. I feel very alone."

Annette is one of hundreds of surviving family members who live in the shadow of a wrongful conviction. When new evidence shatters faith in a defendant's guilt, the families of victims experience another loss: someone to blame. Research by the Innocence Project shows that in more than 40 percent of the DNA exonerations in the United States, the true criminal remains at large.

Not surprisingly, families of victims struggle to shift blame to another perpetrator, especially if that person remains unidentified. A 2003 study of the effects of wrongful convictions on victims' families, particularly in capital cases, found that family members do not tend to agree that the exonerated defendants are innocent. In only seven of the twenty-seven cases studied (slightly more than one-fourth) did the relatives indicate that they believe the exonerees are in fact innocent.[20]

"What that does for someone is throw them into fear, doubt about the system, doubt about their place in the world, absolute disbelief in the system," says Meg Garvin of the National Crime Victim Law Institute in Portland, Oregon.

Garvin seeks to address the needs of crime victims' families during the exoneration process, mitigating harm while protecting the interests of the wrongly convicted.

"The two human beings forgotten most are the exonerees and victims, because the process is kind of a conveyor belt process," Garvin says.

Often, victims' families are not notified about possible new evidence

---

20. Samuel R. Gross and Daniel J. Matheson. "What They Say at the End: Capital Victims' Families and the Press." *Cornell Law Review* 88, no. 2 (2003):486–514.

of innocence. Or if they are informed, often the call or knock at the door
by investigators causes additional trauma. "Then, if they were a witness in
the case, the guilt is astounding," Garvin says.

For Annette, she says she turned to a life of drugs and exploitative
work as a stripper to numb the pain from her sister's death. The tragedy
splintered her family. It creeps into all her relationships, making it hard
to forge bonds.

Later, her faith in God helped her overcome her anger toward Evans
and Terry. Today, she doesn't know whether they are innocent or guilty.
All she knows is this: "Without forgiveness, we cannot survive."

Andre's Story

Andre Davis was nineteen years old when he was hauled away for the
rape and murder of a three-year-old girl in Rantoul, Illinois. It was 1980.

After thirty-two years in prison, much of which was spent in solitary
confinement at the now shuttered and notoriously inhumane "supermax"
Tamms Correctional Center, Andre was released. The crime scene evidence excluding him as the perpetrator had been tested and available
for several years (the venerable Jane Raley had filed for DNA testing
in 2004). It took until 2012 before prosecutors dismissed the charges
against Andre.

When Andre left prison, he said goodbye to no one. He was to be
put on a bus or a train—to nowhere. "I had never interacted with anyone
for fourteen straight years—now you want to put me on a bus or a train?"
Andre tells me.

His father came to pick him up four or five hours later.

"Everything, my entire life fit in one box like this," he says, motion-
ing the size of the box. "When I walked out of there, I just looked at that
box. It's crazy. Thirty-two years, this is what I have. This little box."

Following his release from prison Andre worked odd jobs, gave
speeches about wrongful convictions, and volunteered to pick up trash
on a neighborhood block. He also was arrested on a few occasions—for

marijuana possession, for a DUI, for driving with a suspended license, and for violating his bail bond.

For his wrongful conviction he earned a certificate of innocence from the State of Illinois, receiving the highest amount of compensation possible. "It felt [like] cheating," Andre says. "They gave me $230,000. You call me in the courtroom and rule in my favor and that at the end of the day, you saying, 'All right, $230,000 for thirty-two years of somebody's life.' It felt like $230."

While all exonerees struggle to adjust after incarceration, for Andre, his time in solitary confinement at a place like Tamms set him so far back that rebuilding his life seemed only material in nature—clothes, shoes, apartment. These gaps could be filled. But the psychological damage was perhaps too deep a chasm.

I first met Andre in November 2013, at a fundraiser for the Center on Wrongful Convictions in Chicago. At the time, people were signing a poster card for Jane Raley, who was battling her illness, letting her know with markered messages that she was missed at the event.

A new exoneree, Andre took the stage with Indiana exoneree Kristine Bunch.

"We have to keep fighting. There's more people to go. Thank you," Kristine said at the podium. She walked over to Andre and gave him a hug. It was his turn to say a few words. Wearing a suit and tie, Andre walked over to the microphone.

"Hello, everyone. I'm Andre Davis," he said. "I am someone that was locked up for thirty-two years for something that I didn't do. Thankfully to organizations such as Northwestern and several colleges, organizations, people that are here right now as I mentioned. We know that wrongful convictions is a serious issue. OK? I was locked up for thirty-two years."

The next time I saw Andre was in June 2014, in a news headline that read: "Andre Davis, Released from Prison after a Wrongful Conviction, Is Charged with Murder Again." This time, Andre stood accused of the October 2013 death of nineteen-year-old Jamal Harmon. Authorities alleged that he stabbed Harmon, stuffed him in the trunk of his car, and then dumped his body in an alley after Andre's nephew allegedly shot at him. The grisly incident—whatever truly happened—occurred about a month before I had met Andre at the fundraiser.

When I absorbed the news of Andre's murder charge, I was shocked at this turn of fate. I attended some of his pretrial hearings and watched as an oversized jail uniform, pant legs rolled up, hung on his body.

After pulling court documents, I learned more about the accusations against him: according to an assistant state's attorney, Andre's nephew was hosting a lingerie party with strippers and "perhaps a porn star," where there was also a dice game and subsequent argument with Harmon.

Harmon was shot three times—the face, lower neck, and left side, according to prosecutors—and he was stabbed two times in the torso, with two long incised wounds along the front neck.

Prosecutors say they have witnesses, one who claims to have observed Andre carrying Harmon to the trunk and who said Andre later admitted to cutting his throat. At a pretrial hearing, Andre's defense team at Northwestern University's Bluhm Legal Clinic has challenged the credibility of these witnesses, described as "violent members of dangerous street gangs," with the state's key witness having taken a tequila shot and smoked three to four blunts at the time of the crime. This witness's videotaped interview with police, Andre's defense says, was clearly rehearsed. A critical legal issue in the case is whether Harmon was already dead when he was allegedly stuffed in a trunk with his throat cut. This detail could determine whether Andre returns to prison. But would it diminish his alleged participation in Harmon's demise?

Andre was held at Cook County Jail for almost a year before he was released on a $100,000 bond, awaiting trial. If convicted, the maximum sentence he could receive is life in prison, but even the minimum—twenty years—is a de facto life sentence for Andre, who is in his mid-fifties.

I had the opportunity to talk to him, although I had to agree not to ask questions about his current criminal case. We met in an eighth-floor conference room at the Bluhm Legal Clinic.

Andre jumped when I reached out to shake his hand.

We discussed how, during his stretch in county jail, Jane Raley had died. "That was one of my best friends," Andre said. "She fought so hard

to get me out. The only person that fought for me and stayed in my corner was now just gone."

Andre also told me about his difficulty budgeting money and his love
of shopping and clothes. For our interview, he was fashionably dressed,
having donned a maroon White Sox hat, maroon denim, and a matching
baseball tee. He wore two rings—one was a gift for his recent birthday
("My girl gave this to me") and the other he bought for himself, multiple
gold rows of little diamonds, which he wore on his left index finger.

As for how the world had changed, Andre felt people weren't as cour-
teous as they once were: "Especially the areas where I frequent, they rude.
They mean to each other. They don't look at each other. They don't speak.
It's strange. I was talking to a friend of mine on his porch, couple days
ago. This lady who lived right next door spoke to him, and he didn't say
anything. I was like 'What's up? Do you know her? Do you not know her?'"

Andre is not the only exoneree to face serious criminal charges after
an exoneration. Most famously, Steven Avery, the subject of Netflix's hit
documentary series *Making a Murderer*, who spent almost twenty years in
prison on an eyewitness misidentification, was exonerated of sexual assault
by DNA testing in 2003. In 2005, only seven months after the Wisconsin
Department of Justice developed a new protocol for eyewitness identification prompted by Avery's case, a twenty-five-year-old freelance photogra-
pher, Teresa Halbach, was attacked and murdered. Her Toyota RAV4 was
found in Avery's salvage lot, where she had come to photograph a vehicle.

The evidence against Avery appeared damning: investigators found
her bone fragments in a pit, Avery's blood in her vehicle, a bullet fragment in his garage, and Halbach's car key in his bedroom. In separate
trials, Avery and his nephew, the latter of whom experts say falsely confessed to the crime, were convicted and sentenced to life in prison.[21]

One of the many fallouts of these revelations is that they contribute
to the stigma exonerees face on the outside—the perception that they're
not really innocent or that they somehow merely "beat their cases." Indeed,
after Avery's downfall and arrest, commentator Nancy Grace decried his

---

21. *Making a Murderer*, which first streamed in December 2015, casts serious
doubt on Avery's second conviction, indicating patterns of corruption at the Man-
itowoc County sheriff's department, including signs of evidence-planting.

release on national television: "The real crime is they let him out in the first place—thanks a lot, Wisconsin Innocence Project!"

If there are any lessons to be learned from these stories, it would be to properly identify them as cautionary tales of the permanent damage inflicted by our criminal justice system. Those of us who cover these crimes in the media must also resist sensationalizing their prevalence: a few cases do not indicate a trend of criminality or violence. They do indicate, however, tragic anomalies that need attention. Less anomalous is the fact that some exonerees do self-destruct, through criminal activity, substance abuse, suicide, or other means. Some end up in mental hospitals, notes exoneration expert Samuel Gross of the National Registry of Exonerations.

As exoneree Marvin Reeves, a victim of the Burge-era torture, who spent almost two decades behind bars, put it: "You can be trapped in the wild and that doesn't make you an animal. But to survive in the wild, an animal you will become. Same thing in prison. You can be a choirboy and wrongfully accused and sent to prison. That doesn't make you the monster that society believes you to be. But in order to survive in prison, you have to become that monster. Prison only makes people smarter criminals."

Before wrapping our interview, I asked Andre whether he identified more with being a formerly incarcerated person or being an exoneree.

"Incarceration, hands down," he told me. "That's something that's going to be part of my fabric. It's also hard. It's one of the reasons that I see the world the way I do, because of that experience. That's going to stay with me forever."

ACKNOWLEDGMENTS

Writing a book is a long lesson in vulnerability. It is a lonely task, yet cannot be done alone. Without the support of family, friends, mentors, and other champions, this work would not exist.

To my parents, Lew and Colleen Flowers: Thank you for fostering my curiosity, love of writing and sense of justice from an early age. To my sister Katie: Keeping up with you has been motivating. To the Whitmore family: Thank you for always asking, listening and caring.

To Chicago Public Media, WBEZ, and especially Tim Akimoff: Thank you for believing in these stories and giving them a platform to be told. To Haymarket Books and my editors: Thank you for the life of this book and the opportunity to memorialize these accounts in an authentic way.

To all my journalism and writing comrades; the Bad Ass Lady Writers; my peers and mentors at the Medill School of Journalism, especially the late Rich Johnson: Thank you for making sure the fire in my belly didn't go out.

To all the Sierra Club folks: Your commitment to environmental justice taught me a great deal, and I am so grateful for our time together while I worked on this book.

Thank you also to the many organizations whose generous and patient people contributed sources, knowledge and inspiration to this project: my alma mater, Northwestern University; the Center on Wrongful Convictions and the MacArthur Justice Center; the Exoneration Project; the Innocence Network and the Innocence Project, especially Barry Scheck and Greg Hampikian; Life After Innocence, especially Laura Caldwell, her students, and her staff; the National Registry of Exonerations, especially Samuel Gross; Jon Eldan and After Innocence; Witness to Innocence, where the late poet and exoneree David Keaton was a member, and also Kirk Bloodsworth; the Chicago Innocence Center; Erica Nichols Cook; Michele Weldon; Jarrett Adams and Life After Justice; the Jeffrey Deskovic Foundation for Justice; Loevy & Loevy; the People's Law Office of Chicago; my colleagues at the Invisible Institute; the Illinois Humanities Council; Global Girl Media, especially Tobie Loomis and Alexis Smith; and the University of Chicago, especially the Reva and David Logan Center for the Arts. And to the Online News Association: Thank you for recognizing Chicago Public Media's "Exoneree Diaries" series as a finalist for an Online Journalism Award, which brought this important criminal justice issue further into the public eye.

To Lathan Word, the first exoneree I ever met, years ago at his grandmother's house in Alabama: Thank you for your grace and courage. You inspired me to commit years of my life to this work.

To Jennifer Del Prete, an innocent mother released from prison: I am honored to have played a small part in your life story.

To the prisoners who write to me: I hear you. Thank you for not letting me forget.

To Antione, Jacques, James, and Kristine: Thank you for sharing your stories with me. May you somehow be made whole.

Finally, to Justin: You championed this project throughout our courtship, friendship, engagement, and marriage. Thank you, my love. You are my team.

RESOURCES

Action Committee For Women in Prison
www.acwip.wordpress.com
769 Northwestern Drive
Claremont, CA 91711
This organization advocates for the humane, compassionate treatment of all incarcerated women. ACWIP works for the release of all women who are unjustly imprisoned, striving to reduce the overreliance on incarceration and shift toward restorative justice through education, programming, and legislative development.

After Innocence
www.after-innocence.org
After Innocence provides reentry assistance for America's wrongfully convicted and advocates for policy reform on their behalf.

All of Us or None

www.allofusornone.org
1540 Market Street, Suite 490
San Francisco, CA 94102
All of Us or None is a grassroots civil and human rights organization that advocates for formerly and currently incarcerated people and their families, organizing around issues like record expungement, voting rights, and opposing employment discrimination and jail expansion.

Black and Pink

www.blackandpink.org
614 Columbia Road
Dorchester, MA 02125
Black & Pink advocates for LGBTQ incarcerated and formerly incarcerated people, organizing and educating against prison and systemic violence.

Brooklyn Community Bail Fund

www.brooklynbailfund.org
81 Prospect Street
Brooklyn, NY 11201
The Brooklyn Community Bail Fund works to prevent unnecessary and unjust jailing by paying bail for low-income New Yorkers accused of misdemeanors.

The Bronx Freedom Fund

www.thebronxfreedomfund.org
360 E. 161st Street
Bronx, NY 10451
The first charitable bail organization licensed in New York State, the Bronx Freedom Fund helps poor Bronx residents who are facing misdemeanor charges avoid the devastating costs of short jail sentences. The organization works with clients and families represented by the Bronx Defenders, a holistic public defender office in the South Bronx.

Chicago Community Bond Fund
www.chicagobond.org
PO Box 479015
Chicago, IL 60647
The Chicago Community Bond Fund pays bond for people charged with crimes in Cook County, Illinois. Through a revolving fund, CCBF supports individuals whose communities cannot afford to pay the bonds themselves and who have been impacted by structural violence. CCBF also engages in public education about the role of bond in the criminal legal system and advocates for the abolition of money bond.

Chicago Innocence Center
www.chicagoinnocencecenter.org
205 West Monroe Street, Suite 315
Chicago, IL 60606
The Chicago Innocence Center investigates cases in which prisoners may have been convicted of crimes they did not commit, with priority to murder cases that resulted in sentences of death or life without parole. CIC involves college students, community residents, private investigators, and journalists in the reporting process.

The Crime Report
www.thecrimereport.org
The nation's only comprehensive news service covering the diverse challenges and issues of twenty-first century criminal justice in the United States and abroad, the *Crime Report* is published daily through the year by the Center on Media, Crime and Justice at the John Jay College of Criminal Justice in New York.

Death Penalty Information Center
www.deathpenaltyinfo.org
1015 18th Street NW, Suite 704
Washington, DC 20036
The Death Penalty Information Center is a national nonprofit organization serving the media and the public with analysis and information on issues concerning capital punishment.

Equal Justice Initiative

www.eji.org
122 Commerce Street
Montgomery, AL 36104
The Equal Justice Initiative provides legal representation to indigent defendants and prisoners who have been denied fair and just treatment in the legal system. EJI also prepares reports, newsletters, and manuals to assist advocates and policymakers in reforming the administration of criminal justice.

Ex-Prisoners and Prisoners Organizing for Community Advancement

www.exprisoners.org
This organization works to create resources and opportunities for former prisoners, pushing for sentencing reform and organizing against policies that harm people with criminal records. EPOCA runs a "Jobs NOT Jails" campaign that aims to redirect money from incarceration to addressing unemployment.

The Innocence Network

www.innocencenetwork.org
The Innocence Network is an affiliation of organizations dedicated to providing pro bono legal and investigative services to individuals seeking to prove innocence of crimes for which they have been convicted, and working to redress the causes of wrongful convictions. The network's website features a state-by-state and global directory of Innocence Projects with case-specific requirements.

The Innocence Project

www.innocenceproject.org
40 Worth Street, Suite 701
New York, NY 10013
The Innocence Project is a national litigation and public policy organization dedicated to exonerating wrongfully convicted individuals through DNA testing and reforming the criminal justice system to prevent future injustice.

Investigating Innocence
www.investigatinginnocence.org
1032 South 2nd Street
Springfield, IL 62704
Investigating Innocence is a national nonprofit wrongful-conviction advocacy organization that provides criminal defense investigations for inmates.

Invisible Institute
invisible.institute
The Invisible Institute is a journalistic production company on the South
Side of Chicago that works to enhance the capacity of civil society to hold
public institutions accountable, particularly in the area of police misconduct.

Jeffrey Deskovic Foundation for Justice
www.deskovic.org
3148 East Tremont Avenue, 2nd Floor
Bronx, NY 10461
The Jeffrey Deskovic Foundation for Justice is a nonprofit that seeks to
exonerate actually innocent prisoners, taking both DNA and non-DNA
cases. The organization also supports the reintegration of exonerees.

Life After Innocence
www.luc.edu/law/experiential/lifeafterinnocence
Loyola University School of Law
Philip H. Corboy Law Center
25 East Pearson Street
Chicago, IL 60611
Life After Innocence works with Illinois exonerees to offer legal and social
support.

Life After Justice
http://lifeafterjustice.org
25 East Pearson Street, Suite 1419
Chicago, IL 60611
This organization is working to start a reentry home for men released

from prison, with preference to exonerees. Life After Justice aims to provide a variety of services to help the men successfully reenter society, such as job training, computer skills, finance classes, and mentoring.

The Marshall Project
www.themarshallproject.org
156 West 56th Street, Suite 701
New York, NY 10019
The Marshall Project is a nonprofit news organization that focuses on the American criminal justice system. Its mission is to create and sustain a sense of urgency about criminal justice in America.

The Massachusetts Bail Fund
www.massbailfund.org
2161 Massachusetts Avenue
Cambridge, MA 02140
The Massachusetts Bail Fund pays bail so that low-income people can stay free while they work toward resolving their cases. The fund provides up to $500 bail for low-income individuals.

The National Registry of Exonerations
www.law.umich.edu/special/exoneration
The National Registry of Exonerations provides detailed information about every known exoneration in the United States since 1989. Up-to-date graphs indicate patterns in wrongful convictions and outline contributing factors, such as false confessions, official misconduct, eyewitness misidentification, perjury, and false or misleading forensic evidence.

Nation Inside
www.nationinside.org
Nation Inside is a platform that connects and supports people who are building a movement to systematically challenge mass incarceration in the United States.

The People's Law Office

www.peopleslawoffice.com
1180 North Milwaukee Avenue
Chicago, IL 60642
These civil rights lawyers tackle cases of police brutality, wrongful conviction, false arrest, and other government abuses.

Prison Legal News and Human Rights Defense Center

www.prisonlegalnews.org and www.humanrightsdefensecenter.org
P.O. Box 1151
1013 Lucerne Ave
Lake Worth, FL 33460
Prison Legal News, a project of the nonprofit Human Rights Defense Center, issues a monthly magazine that reports on criminal justice issues and prison and jail-related civil litigation, with an emphasis on prisoners' rights.

Project NIA

www.project-nia.org
Project NIA is an advocacy, organizing, popular education, research, and capacity-building center with the long-term goal of ending youth incarceration. The organization supports youth in trouble with the law as well as those victimized by violence and crime, through community-based alternatives to the criminal legal process.

Resurrection After Exoneration

www.r-a-e.org
1212 St. Bernard Avenue
New Orleans, LA 70116
Founded in 2007 by exonerees, this nonprofit organization promotes and works to sustain a network of support among formerly wrongfully incarcerated individuals in the South. RAE helps reconnect exonerees with their communities.

The Sentencing Project

www.sentencingproject.org
1705 DeSales Street NW
8th Floor
Washington, DC 20036

This sentencing advocacy organization aims to reduce reliance on incarceration. It has since become a leader in the effort to bring national attention to disturbing trends and inequities in the criminal justice system through the publication of research, aggressive media campaigns, and strategic advocacy for policy reform.

Uptown People's Law Center

www.uplcchicago.org
4413 North Sheridan Avenue
Chicago, IL 60640

Uptown People's Law Center is a nonprofit legal organization in Illinois that specializes in prisoners' rights, tenants' rights, and Social Security disability benefits. UPLC focuses on class-action lawsuits against the Illinois Department of Corrections to address unconstitutional prison conditions.